Cozy Food

128 Cozy Mystery Writers Share Their Favorite Recipes

Edited by
Nancy Lynn Jarvis
For Good Read Publishers

Good Read Publishers
301 Azalea Lane, Santa Cruz, California, 95060

Copyright © 2014 by Nancy Kille

Library of Congress Control Number: 2014938343

ISBN: 978-0-9835891-7-4

Good Read Publishers, First Edition, Third Printing, November 2014

Printed in the United States of America

www.GoodReadMysteries.com

Books are available at special quantity discounts through the website.

To all the readers out there who hunger for cozy mysteries

Acknowledgements

This Cookbook is possible thanks to the good will and contributions
of all the authors represented here.

My husband Craig is truly co-editor of this cookbook.
I wouldn't even have considered doing this if he wasn't so quick to
offer his expertise and support.

Introduction

Cozies and Food

Pick up any mystery defined as cozy or easy reading and you'll notice they have several things in common.

A body is usually discovered before the end of the second chapter. The amateur sleuth who investigates the murder may be young, old, or of a "certain age," but the detective is almost always female. She gets drawn into the mystery while she's doing her day job which may be anything other than being a professional cop or an experienced private investigator. She investigates in a small community, perhaps in a literal one like the country villages and manor houses of Miss Marple, or in an abstract one like a community of realtors, square dancers, hair dressers, bookstore owners, coffee or tea houses, quilters, fashion designers, or in the community formed on a cruise ship, to name a few possibilities. She solves the mystery and makes sure the bad guy gets his or her come-uppance before the book ends.

Introduction

While the protagonist may have some hair-raising or nail-biting encounters, she generally does so in the absence of graphic sex, gratuitous violence, or harsh language. The amateur sleuth is frequently accompanied in her crime-solving efforts by her cat or dog and by her best friend or boyfriend, who is often connected with law enforcement.

We readers love to solve the crime right along with our detective, always trying to solve the mystery before she does. We love to laugh or at least chuckle frequently as we weigh the evidence. We often get hungry as we read because there are usually frequent mentions of food in cozies; some even have recipes. And even if the books don't feature food, it's hard to find a cozy mystery writer who doesn't have a few of her own treasured recipes and who doesn't love to eat.

Thumb through the pages of this cookbook or scroll the pages on your e-reader. You are sure to find great recipes from some of your favorite cozy mystery authors. Even better, you'll meet some new-to-you authors whose books you'll want to read, possibly with a cup of tea and a cookie in hand and a cat purring on your lap.

Notes from the Editor

A compilation cookbook that centers around mystery is hardly an original idea. *The Cozy Chicks Kitchen* is a terrific cookbook with recipes from a short list of some of your favorite cozy writers. Well known and prolific writer Joanne Fluke has her own cookbook with recipes from her Hannah Swenson series. *A Taste of Murder* and *Second Helping of Murder* are cookbooks with recipes from modern crime writers. It's rumored that Mystery Writers of America is putting together a cookbook.

What makes *Cozy Food* special is how many cozy writers have contributed to it. You will find recipes from your old favorites and be enticed to try recipes and books by writers you don't know. The cookbook features writers from leading traditional publishers, medium and small presses, and indie writers. Some authors have written dozens of books and multiple series; some are just starting out and have only written the first book in what will no doubt become a fun-filled series.

Cozy Food even has a couple of muffin recipes from internationally known romance writer Leigh Michaels' cookbook; she happens to be a neighbor of one of our cozy mystery writers and said it was OK. (Read the biographies and recipes, play detective yourself, and figure out which cozy mystery writer lives next door to Leigh Michaels.)

The idea for a broad-based cozy mystery cookbook could have ended quickly. If Ellery Adams, who heads my alphabetical list, had said "No" instead of "Of Course!" when asked if I could include the easy dinner egg cups recipe she posted on Facebook, that might have been the end of *Cozy Food*.

It has been a great pleasure coordinating this cookbook. I've met so many congenial people and found some recipes I can't wait to try. The recipes and biographies have been formatted for font uniformity and to fit the size of the pages, but the words are the author's. I learned a great deal about individual author's writing style, wit, and attitude from how they introduced their recipes and what they chose to include in their biographies; and I'm sure you will, too. As a result, the list of books I want to read has grown exponentially. After meeting the authors in this cookbook, your list will grow as well because you'll find there are some wonderful cozies out there that you didn't know about just waiting to be discovered and read by you.

Introduction

While I'm amazed at the breadth of author participation in the cookbook, I'm not surprised by the individual support for it. After all, cozy mystery writers are some of the nicest people you could ever invite to your home for a meal.

Publisher's Notes ... AKA The Fine Print

Recipes are published as presented by the author contributing them. Variations in measurement descriptions and instructions between recipes and within them may occur. The publisher considers this part of the charm of collecting recipes from many sources. Good Read Publishers has not test-prepared any of the recipes. Should you, the reader, discover an error which prevents you from using a recipe, please notify the publisher at cookbook@goodreadmysteries.com. We will alert the author and make every effort to correct the error in subsequent editions and will email you a corrected version.

The individual contributors and their publishers retain all copyrights for the recipes they contributed to the cookbook and may use, print, or reprint them as they see fit. Except for contributors' use of their individual recipes, no part of this work may be reproduced in any form by any electronic or mechanical means including photocopying, recording, or information storage and retrieval by any other parties without express written permission from Good Read Publishers.

Several authors offer gluten-free recipes and healthy alternatives in their recipes. If these designations are important to you, please determine for yourself that the recipes are as suggested. Good Read Publishers, contributors' publishers, and individual contributors are not responsible for specific health or allergic reactions to the use of any recipe by you or anyone consuming the dishes prepared by you or for any adverse reactions to the recipes contained in the cookbook.

Good Read Publishers and the editors have given up trying to determine the correct spelling of a word common to mysteries of all kinds. Is it who dun it, who-dun-it, who done it, whodunnit, or whodunit? You may vote for your favored spelling at cookbook@goodreadmysteries.com. No prizes will be awarded for your vote!

Table of Contents

Table of Contents

Table of Contents

Table of Contents

Table of Contents

Quick, Easy, Quirky, Saucy, & Even Pet Treats........157

Cozy Author Biographies 167

Table of Contents

Table of Contents

Table of Contents

Starters and Beverages

Crab and Artichoke Dip
From the Zoe Donovan Mystery series by Kathi Daley (page 184)

According to my Facebook page, which I share with Charlie, my half terrier/half mystery dog, we're in a relationship with our two cats, a huge orange tabby named Marlow and a petite black beauty named Spade. We are avid joggers and mystery buffs who own a wild and domestic animal rescue and rehabilitation shelter.

Crab and Artichoke dip is my best friend Levi Denton's favorite appetizer.

8 oz. cream cheese, softened
8 oz. Havarti cheese, grated
2 cans (approx. 14 oz. each) artichoke hearts, diced
8 oz. crab meat, fresh or canned
2 cups Parmesan cheese, grated
1 cup sour cream
2 tsp. horseradish (add more if you like it hot)

Mix and bake at 450 degrees for 30–45 min.; stir after 20 minutes.

Serve with baguette slices, tortilla chips, or crackers.

Cozy Food

Darla's Tortilla Rollups

From the Darla King series published by Wordsmiths4u by Rosalee Richland (page 223)

Square dancing takes a lot of energy, and dancers often bring snacks to a regular dance or hold a meal before a special dance. Darla's Tortilla Rollups are just the quick and easy type of snack Darla likes to fix to take to a dance.

6 regular flour tortillas (6-inch) or 3 large flour tortillas (12-inch)
2 bunches green onions, finely chopped
1 red bell pepper, diced
1/2 cup bacon bits (either real or artificial will work)
2 8-ounce pkgs cream cheese, softened
1 8-ounce container plain yogurt or sour cream
Optional to taste: 1 or 2 diced jalapenos with seeds removed (1 to 2 Tbsp)
Optional to taste: 1 cup chopped fresh spinach
To serve: Serve plain or add a dip of salsa, guacamole, tapenade, or pesto

Bring tortillas to room temperature and set aside. Combine cream cheese and yogurt (or sour cream) in large bowl. Stir until mixed and softened. Add remaining ingredients (except salsa etc.) and mix well. Spread mixture evenly over tortillas. Don't put too much or it will squish out when you roll them. Roll up each tortilla gently and stack in plastic wrap or air-tight container. Chill overnight. When ready to serve, use a sharp knife to cut 1/2-inch slices. (You can cut them ahead of time if you seal them tightly to keep from drying out.) Serve plain or with your choice of salsa, guacamole, pesto, tapenade, or dressing.

Makes about 60 roll-ups (because you sometimes lose the end cuts). Any remaining cream cheese mixture can be thinned with a little milk and served as dip.

Hummus for Celebrating

From *CATastropic Connections* by Joyce Ann Brown (page 180)

In *CATastrophic Connections,* from the moment Psycho Cat alerts Beth of her step-niece Adrianna's disappearance in Kansas City, the unassuming but feisty landlady must take action. Questioning construction company employees, encountering a witch doctor on the Virgin Islands, Beth follows clues she's afraid the police overlooked. Embezzlement and murder ensue. Shadowy characters intimidate Beth and her family at every turn. It's one thing for Beth to skirt danger on her own, but when her loved ones are threatened—Beth and Psycho Cat will fight to the end.

Will they be around to celebrate with hummus and pita?

1 can garbanzo beans (chick peas) drained
1/3 cup olive oil
¼ cup tahini
¼ cup lemon juice
1 clove garlic (or to taste)
1 tsp parsley flakes (or 2 T chopped fresh parsley)
1 tsp powdered cilantro (or 2 T chopped fresh cilantro)
½ tsp salt
1 tsp cumin
2 T (or more) water

Put all ingredients into a food processor or blender. Blend on high for several minutes. Add water until mixture becomes creamy. Transfer to a bowl and top with sundried tomatoes, roasted pine nuts, roasted red pepper slices, or more garlic. Serve on pita bread which has been fried in a little olive oil, on crackers, or with vegetable slices. Celebrate another cozy mystery solved.

Baba Ganoush
From the Local Foods Mystery series by Edith Maxwell (page 207)

In Edith Maxwell's Local Foods mystery series (Kensington Publishing), former software engineer Cam Flaherty grows organic vegetables on her farm in northeastern Massachusetts. She sells them to the local foods enthusiasts who belong to her farm-share program as well as to a tall intense chef. What she didn't plan on was encountering locally sourced murder, too.

When your garden or farm share yields more eggplants than you ever dreamed you'd want to eat, Baba Ganoush is a great solution. It makes a tasty vegetarian appetizer or sandwich spread, or even a topping for pasta. Serves two to twelve.

4 Asian eggplants
1/4 cup tahini, plus more as needed
3 garlic cloves, minced
1/4 cup fresh lemon juice, plus more as needed
1/2 tsp ground cumin
1/2 tsp salt
1 tablespoon extra virgin olive oil
1 tablespoon chopped fresh basil
1/4 cup brine-cured black olives, such as kalamata

Wash and stem the eggplants. Cube into one-inch pieces.
Combine all ingredients except olives in food processor. Process until smooth.
Serve at room temperature with olives on top and pita, crackers, or tiny carrots, or spread on a sandwich with a fresh tomato slice and lettuce.

Theo's Bean Dip
From the Quilted Mysteries, a series by Barbara Graham (page 193)

Theo Abernathy owns and operates a quilt shop and is married to the sheriff of tiny Park County, Tennessee. Her poor cooking ability is legendary. This bean dip recipe is so easy to prepare and tasty that it is a favorite of her friends and family. It is *always* Theo's assignment for game day gatherings.

1 Large can of refried beans
1 Cup sour cream
1 small can diced green chiles (mild)
½ tsp garlic powder
1 Cup grated longhorn or any mild cheddar cheese
Corn chips

Mix together the refried beans, sour cream, diced green chiles and garlic powder. Sprinkle the cheese on top. Cover with foil and bake at 350 degrees for 45 minutes. Serve with corn chips.

Cozy Food

Serves—2 teenage boys or 4 men or 8 women, if there are witnesses (otherwise everyone is as greedy as the teenage boys)

Pimento Cheese for Dummies
From the Cue Ball Mysteries series by Cindy Blackburn (page 175)

Jessie Hewitt, the star of the Cue Ball Mysteries, doesn't really think you're a dummy. But if you're not a southerner, you might be unfamiliar with this delicious spread. Jessie loves serving this to unsuspecting Yankees. Someone invariably asks if she spent all day pulling pimentos out of olives! Luckily, you can find chopped pimentos in the canned vegetables section of most supermarkets.

3 cups shredded sharp cheddar cheese
2 Tablespoon grated onion
1/2 cup minced pimentos, drained
1/2 cup mayonnaise
1 teaspoon Dijon mustard
1 Tablespoon milk

Mix all ingredients well. Cover and let "ripen" in the refrigerator overnight. Serve on crackers or celery as an appetizer for 6 – 10, depending on appetites. Or make sandwiches, cut into fours, all fancy-like. Also incredibly good on grilled steaks or burgers. It will be a hit!

As with ALL of Jessie's recipes, serve with champagne.

Gorgonzola, Spiced Walnuts and Port Wine Syrup
From the Italian Restaurant Mystery series by Shelley Costa (page 182)

Welcome to Miracolo Italian Restaurant, where thirty-something head chef Eve Angelotta runs the kitchen with a cool head and a passionate heart. But creating northern Italian cuisine that makes people swoon is just one of her talents. Suddenly a sleuth after discovering a corpse on the kitchen tiles, Eve turns up the heat to prove her grandmother's innocence and serve a killer their just desserts. She finds her cousin Choo Choo's Gorgonzola, Spice Walnuts and Port Wine Syrup dish just as appetizing as detective work.

3 cups port wine
1 TBS unsalted butter
1/2 c. walnut halves
1/2 tsp cayenne
1/2 tsp black pepper
1/2 tsp salt
2 tsp sugar
8 oz. Gorgonzola cheese

In a saucepan , bring the wine to a boil. Cook over medium heat until reduced to 1/2 cup, about 12-15 minutes. Allow to cool.

In an 8-inch saute pan, melt the butter over medium heat. Add the walnuts, cayenne, black pepper, salt and sugar and saute until well coated and lightly toasted, 2-3 minutes. Set aside to cool.

Divide the cheese among four plates and spoon nuts over each portion. Drizzle the wine syrup over each plate and serve with crusty bread. Serves 4. *Buon Appetito!*

Hawaiian Spam Musubi (Similar to sushi)
From The Islands of Aloha Mystery series by JoAnn Bassett (page 172)

This is a fun pupu (or appetizer) to serve at a Hawaiian-themed party or luau. It's not hard to make and although it looks like sushi it doesn't contain any raw ingredients. Spam is extremely popular in Hawaii. The people of Hawaii eat more Spam than any other place on earth! Pali Moon, the protagonist in the Islands of Aloha Mystery series was born and raised in Hawaii so she considers Spam one of the four major food groups.

2 slices Spam Classic
½ cup cooked short-grain rice (such as Cal-Rose)
1 Tbl. Soy cooking sauce (such as House of Tsang Sweet Ginger Sesame Sauce or Trader Joe's Soyaki)
1 sheet nori (black dried seaweed, the kind used for sushi)

Fry the Spam on both sides until lightly browned and crisp.
Place one-fourth of the rice in a musubi press. (You can order a Spam Musubi Press from Amazon.com.) or you can use a small can (such as the Spam can) with both ends cut off. Press the rice down tight.
Drizzle a bit of the sauce on top of the rice.
Cut a piece of the Spam to fit the size of the musubi press or the can and lay it on top of the seasoned rice.
Press down on the rice and Spam mixture until it is a compact block.
Remove the rice/Spam block from the press.
Lay the nori, shiny side up, and wrap it around the Spam mixture.
Cut each musubi into bite-size pieces.

Check out my Pinterest site to see what your finished musubi should look like: http://www.pinterest.com/joannbassett/hawaiian-food/pins/

Edna's Easy Herb Spread
From the Edna Davies mystery series by Suzanne Young (page 238)

Edna is the wife of a retired physician, mother of four and grandmother of seven. In her first adventure *Murder by Yew*, when she was suspected of killing her handyman, her herb concoction was shunned. By the time she solved her third murder in *Murder by Mishap*, this appetizer had become a favorite of her guests.

1/2 cup sour cream
1/2 cup cream cheese (whipped or softened)
1 Tbls fresh, chopped dill
1 Tbls fresh, chopped chives
2 Tsp fresh, chopped basil
1 pkg Water or rice crackers or toast rounds
Celery sticks (optional)

Note: freeze-dried herbs can be used, if fresh aren't available.

Cozy Food

Stir equal parts sour cream and cream cheese until well blended. Fold in the herbs. May be chilled or served at room temperature. Spread mix on crackers or toast rounds.

Suggested options include serving in a bowl as a dip with celery sticks.
Other herbs such as thyme, rosemary, garlic and marjoram may also be substituted, as your taste buds and your garden's availability dictate.
Makes 1 cup.

Dates with Goat Cheese and Basil
From the Tiara Investigations series by Lane Stone (page 229)

For the Tiara Investigations detectives, former Georgia beauty queens Leigh, Tara and Victoria, friends really are the family they got to choose. These recipes have been passed around so many times, who knows where they started.

Pitted dates
Goat Cheese
Basil – fresh
Optional – Prosciutto

Stuff the dates with goat cheese. Wrap in a basil leaf. And, if desired, with a slice of prosciutto. Broil for approximately three minutes.

Quince and Manchego
From the Tiara Investigations series by Lane Stone (page 229)

Quince (Look for this fruit at Whole Foods. If you absolutely can't find it, use pears.)
Manchego Cheese
Toasted, sliced almonds

Cut the quince and manchego into squares and stack two layers of each. Place a few almonds on each in a pinwheel or flower shape.

Pate du Chateau Blanc
From *A Dog Gone Murder* by Elaine Viets (page 233)

Good is not the word for Pate du Chateau Blanc. That's White Castle Pate. Belly bombers for the bon vivant. When you need recreational calories, cholesterol and fat, serve White Castle Pate.

You can read this recipe in my ninth Josie Marcus Mystery Shopper mystery, *A Dog Gone Murder,* (NAL, November 2014). Harry the Horrible, Josie's boss at Suttin Services, advises her to serve this to her new husband "and you'll thank me the next morning." Harry tells newlywed Josie to set the mood by lighting a White Castle scented candle.

Harry is fiction, but the candles are real. Google them and see for yourself.

15 White Castle Hamburgers, with pickles and onions.
3 raw bacon slices (optional)
1/2 cup sour cream

1/2 cup yogurt
chopped parsley for garnish
water

Take 15 whole White Castle hamburgers, including buns, pickle and onion. Blend the burgers in a blender, three at a time, scraping the sides and adding water as needed for blending. NOTE: Add the water first, then the burgers. I burnt out a blender trying to grind the burgers without the water.

Pour the mixture into a lightly buttered loaf pan. If desired, lay raw bacon slices in the pan first. Bake at 325 degrees for 45 minutes. Remove from pan and cool. Serve with a mixture of sour cream, yogurt and chopped parsley. Garnish with additional parsley, as desired.

Escargots with wine
From *Killer Surf* by Chris Forman (page 191)

This is a favorite of Ian Wallace, the kilt wearing food writer who keeps getting involved solving murders.

One can of snails
Half stick of butter
Three garlic cloves (minced)
¼ cup fresh parsley (chopped)
One cup red wine (Merlot or Pinot Noir)
Two tablespoons breadcrumbs (Panko would do)

Open the can of snails, drain and rinse well with cold water and pat dry. Place the snails and the wine in a small bowl and add the minced garlic and chopped parsley. Cover and marinate for two hours in refrigerator.
Place the snails in a small oven safe dish and pour in the marinade. Cut the butter into pats and spread on top. Bake at 450 degrees for twelve to fifteen minutes. They are done when the butter is boiling. Sprinkle the breadcrumbs on top.

Eat with fresh bread and make sure to soak up that delightful wine and butter sauce.

Stimulating Decaf Coffee
From *Murder in the Gazebo* (2013) by Chloe Evans (page 190)

Stuck with having to stick with decaf coffee? Maybe you find it a bit boring. This recipe for stimulating decaf coffee will change your mind.

Strongly flavored decaf coffee, such as Starbucks' "Gazebo" blend
½ t allspice
½ t vanilla
1 t cocoa powder

Brew coffee and add in other ingredients. Whisk briskly together to blend immediately before serving.

Cozy Food

Champagne Royale
From *Murder in the Gazebo* (2013) by Chloe Evans (page 190)

What would you order when you're having drinks with a prince? Champagne Royale, of course. But, you can try this easy recipe any time you want to celebrate almost anything.

Add 1 T grenadine syrup to a champagne flute, and fill with your favorite chilled champagne.

Limoncello
From the *Franki Amato Mysteries* by Traci Andrighetti (page 170)

Franki's not a big drinker, but she appreciates a good cocktail every so often. Okay, maybe more often than not. After all, it's hard fighting crime in NOLA. In general, her motto is, "When life gives you lemons, make Limoncello." But in extreme cases she revises it to, "When life gives you lemons, skip the 'making Limoncello' part and just go straight to drinking it." Here is Franki's recipe for three bottles of lemon heaven.

10 medium-sized Meyer lemons (15 if they're small)
1 quart Everclear (a brand of grain alcohol)
1 1/2 quarts water
2 3/4 pounds sugar

Wash and peel the lemons. Soak the lemon peels in three quarters of the Everclear for one to two months, storing the mixture in an airtight container in a cool, dark place.

When the peels are infused with the Everclear, boil the sugar and water until it makes syrup (about five minutes). Let the syrup cool, and then pour it into the lemon peel mixture along with the remaining Everclear. Store the Limoncello mixture in a cool, dark place for forty days. Then strain it using cheesecloth to remove the lemon peels before bottling the Limoncello. Serve chilled. *Salute!*

Tiki Goddess
From *Dying for a Daiquiri* by Cindy Sample (page 226)

After a tough day chasing deadly villains in Hawaii, it's time to relax on the beach with a cool tropical drink. Although the calorie count may be deadly, there's nothing tastier than Laurel's favorite TIKI GODDESS cocktail.

1 oz. pomegranate juice or ½ oz Pomegranate liqueur

1 oz. white rum
2 oz. pineapple juice
1 ½ oz coconut milk or cream of coconut

Pour mixture in a tall glass filled with crushed ice. Add pineapple wedge, maraschino cherry and umbrella. Party on!

Starters and Beverages

Deckchair Delight (Also known as Pina Colada)
From *Death Among The Deckchairs* by Karen Robbins (page 224)

Casey's second foray into sleuthing occurs when she takes a cruise to relax after all the excitement that happened in the first book. She falls asleep in a chair next to a nice young woman only to wake and find that the woman has been murdered. You may not want to use homemade sunblock after reading *Death Among The Deckchairs* but a nice Pina Colada on a summer day might get you to close your eyes and dream of cruising.

1 cup coconut milk
1 cup pineapple juice
4 tablespoons white sugar
8 cubes of ice
Optional 1/2 cup of rum (use a little rum extract, 1/4 tsp., if you want to go non-alcoholic)

In a blender, combine all ingredients and blend until smooth. Pour into glasses. Add an umbrella or garnish with a slice of pineapple and enjoy!

Makes 4 cups.

My Mother's Manhattan
From *Small Town Trouble* by Jean Erhardt (page 189)

Meet Kim Claypoole, restaurateur, reluctant heroine and amateur sleuth with moxie galore. "I'd had a feeling all along that this wasn't going to be my day. But I hadn't been prepared for things to go this badly ..."

From *Small Town Trouble*:

I figured she'd never hear me over the blaring TV, so I went on in. Bunky, my mother's aging Pekingese, jumped off the sofa where he'd been relaxing and watching the five o'clock news with my mother. Evelyn had an ice pack parked on her head. Headaches were no strangers to her. They were often brought on by her consumption of too many Manhattans.

2 generous shots of whiskey
¼ shot of dry Vermouth
Dash of aromatic bitters
3 ice cubes
Maraschino cherry

Place ice in the cocktail shaker. Add whiskey, Vermouth and bitters. Shake until chilled. Strain and pour into suitable glass. Garnish with Maraschino cherry.

Cozy Food

Murder on the Orient Espresso Martini
From The Maggy Thorsen Coffee Mysteries (just optioned for television) by Sandra Balzo (page 172)

When Agatha Christie's classic, *Murder on the Orient Express*, is re-enacted at a mystery-writers' conference, a night train into the Everglades takes a very wrong turn for tourist Maggy and her main squeeze, Sheriff Jake Pavlik. Luckily for everybody aboard, they have these babies to keep them warm!

Serves 2 (or 1, if you're seriously stressed)

1 oz. vanilla vodka
2 oz. Kahlua
2 oz. milk
1 oz. cold espresso

Shake with ice and serve in martini glass edged with chocolate syrup and dipped in finely crushed biscotti.

Soups and Crumbles

Eliza's Don't Spill the Beans Soup
From *Killing Time: An Eliza Gordon Mystery* (Hen House Press, 2012) by Amy Beth Arkawy (page 171)

1/2cup canned or 1/4 cup dried of each of the following:
Lentils, black beans, kidney beans, pinto beans and peas
4 strips bacon
2 cups onions; chopped
3 teaspoon garlic; minced (6 cloves)
5 cups of water
1 cup white wine or sherry
1 14.5 can peeled, diced tomatoes
Salt, pepper, cayenne pepper add Tabasco sauce (optional) to taste.

Cozy Food

In a small pan, cook bacon, drain and retain bacon fat. Crumble bacon bits, set aside. In a large stock pot, sauté onions and garlic in 2 Tablespoons of bacon fat. Add bacon, water, beans, peas, wine, tomatoes, salt and pepper. Bring to a boil, simmer covered for 3 hours, stirring occasionally. Add salt, pepper, cayenne and Tabasco to taste as needed. * May add water if soup is too thick.

This soup is so thick and hearty it will temporarily stifle loquacious gossips and tricky suspects. Makes ¾ gallon. Serves @ 16.

Easy-Peasy Mackinac Island soup
From *Gear For the Grave* (December, 2014) first book in CyclePath Mystery series by Duffy Brown (page 179)

Where biking takes a deadly turn. Shakedowns cover-ups and big fat lies keep bodies hidden on Mackinac Island and bike-riding tourist oblivious to it all.

From Duffy: I love Mackinac Island. No cars and with only horses, walking and bicycles for transportation folks work up quite an appetite. This soup and a chunk of crusty bread fits the bill on a cool autumn day looking out across Lake Huron or hunting for a killer.

In a big pot:
Brown 1 pound ground beef with 1 chopped onion, 3 cloves chopped garlic and 1 packet of Old El Paso Taco seasoning, and 1 packet of Hidden Ranch dressing.
Add 2 cans chopped tomatoes.
Add 1 can each undrained: hominy, yellow corn, black beans, pinto beans.

Simmer for as long as you have (smells great).

Serve with dollop of sour cream and sprinkle of shredded cheddar, chopped cilantro.

Timberland Shrimp Chowder
From the Zoe Donovan Mystery series by Kathi Daley (page 184)

According to my Facebook page, which I share with Charlie, my half terrier/ half mystery dog. When we aren't rescuing animals or solving murders, I volunteer at the senior center, where I horn in on their book club, and Charlie volunteers at the hospital, where he's a therapy dog. We both like to relax by cooking up something delicious or reading a good book in the converted boathouse we call home. Timberland Shrimp Chowder is my rich and gorgeous boyfriend Zak Zimmerman's favorite soup.

Base:
1 cube butter
½ chopped onion (or more if you like onion)
3-4 cloves garlic chopped
6 cups of peeled and diced potato (frozen hash browns work as well)
2 pounds cooked shrimp (any size, Rosie uses medium but she has used salad shrimp in a pinch.)
32 oz chicken broth (can use part chicken broth and part water if preferred)

Spices: amounts can be adjusted to accommodate taste.
¼ tsp chili powder
¼ tsp cayenne pepper

¼ tsp ground cumin
¼ tsp coriander
½ tsp nutmeg
½ tsp paprika
1 tsp salt
1 tsp white pepper

Melt butter in heavy pan. Sauté onion and garlic. Add potatoes and shrimp.
Cover with chicken broth (just enough to boil potatoes). Add spices.
Boil until potatoes are tender – this time will vary depending on the size of potato cubes

Cheese Sauce: While potatoes are boiling use a separate pan to make cheese sauce.
1 cube butter
4 oz cream cheese (1 small or ½ large package)
1 cup heavy cream
2 cups shredded cheddar cheese (do not use non or low fat)
2 cups grated parmesan cheese (or 1 cup parmesan and 1 cup Romano)

Melt butter in pan over med heat. Add cream cheese. Stir until melted. Add cream. Add cheese a little at a time. After potatoes are tender slowly fold cheese sauce into base. Stir constantly until well blended.

Mel's Famous Artery-Clogging Clam Chowder
From *The Honeymoon Cottage* first in the Pajaro Bay series by Barbara Cool Lee (page 202)

Welcome to Pajaro Bay, where mystery and romance mingle on the California coast. Readers praise the series for its "sweetness," its "excellent characterization," and say the books are "adorable, lively and like a warm hug."

Mel's Fish Shack is the most popular seafood joint in the village. His recipe for clam chowder includes fresh clams and heavy cream, and it's served in a sourdough bread bowl with a pat of butter on top. In case that's not artery-clogging enough, it comes with onion rings and fried calamari on the side.

The version of clam chowder here (straight off a very worn family recipe card) is much easier to make than Mel's (no shucking clams!), and much less unhealthy for your heart!

4 strips of bacon
1 sweet onion
6-7 potatoes
1 can clams
1 cup milk or cream
salt & pepper

Fry 4 strips of bacon until crisp in a large heavy soup pot (a "dutch oven" it says on the recipe card). Remove the bacon and then brown one finely chopped sweet onion (Vidalia or WallaWalla) in the bacon grease. Then add six or seven finely chopped potatoes (Idaho potatoes are nice and starchy for this), add water to cover potatoes, salt and pepper to taste (I always hate those recipes that say "to taste"–are you going to taste raw potatoes and see if they're salty enough? Just add a bit at this point and then add more at the end if you need to). Dump in one can of clams (yup, it says "dump"—very fancy recipe!). Crumble bacon over top.

Cook for 15 minutes. Mash with a potato masher. Add one cup of milk (or cream if you're feeling indulgent) just before serving (don't boil the milk; just heat gently).

That's it. It's very easy. While not quite like chowder made with freshly caught clams and whole cream, it sure tastes good on a foggy evening. Serve with San Francisco sourdough if you've got it (cornbread's good, too).

Enjoy!

Dispatcho Gazpacho
From *Murder in the Gazebo* (2013) by Chloe Evans (page 190)

The guests arrive for the early fall dinner in the gazebo. The first course is a wonderful chilled soup that takes advantage of the fresh local vegetables. But what gives it that very unique flavor? Try it to find out.

8 freshly picked tomatoes – quartered
1 red pepper – seeded
1 very young zucchini - peeled
Clove garlic – diced
1 T olive oil
1 t sugar
1 t salt
1 t balsamic vinegar
½ t cinnamon

Combine all ingredients in a blender to desired consistency. Chill and garnish with a basil leaf.

She Crab Soup/Bisque
From Allison Cesario Paton (page 219)

A rich crab bisque in roux-thickened fish stock and cream soup base seasoned with sherry and paprika.

5 tablespoons butter or margarine
1 cup green onion, minced
1 stalk celery, chopped
1 TBSP grated carrot
5 tablespoons all-purpose flour
2 cups fish stock or vegetable or chicken stock
2 cups milk or soymilk <u>plus</u> 1 cup heavy whipping cream (optional)
1 1/2 pounds crabmeat, flaked
1/4 cup sherry
1 1/2 teaspoons salt
1/4 teaspoon ground black pepper
½ teaspoon paprika or cayenne pepper
¼ teaspoon nutmeg

In a large pot, melt the butter over medium heat. Mince the green onions, celery, and carrots in food processor and then add to butter; cook, stirring occasionally, until vegetables are soft, about 5 minutes. Gradually add the flour and stir for 2-3 minutes until it is a smooth paste.

Keeping the mixture smooth, gradually add the stock and milk. Bring to a high simmer, whisking occasionally. Add the cream, crabmeat, sherry, salt and pepper, nutmeg and heat through. Ladle into bowls and garnish with a pinch of paprika.

Chilli Bean Soup

From the Amber Fox Mysteries by Sibel Hodge (page 195)

Amber Fox is an ex-cop turned insurance investigator who winds up working for her ex-fiancé, Brad Beckett. The only problem is, Brad thinks they've still got unfinished business in the romance department, making for a steamier working environment than Amber counted on.

Unfortunately, Amber is a disaster in the kitchen. In fact, the one and only time she ever actually used her oven was to cook a pizza, and she forgot to remove the plastic tray it came in, so she cooked that, too. Luckily for her, though, Brad knows the way to Amber's heart is through her stomach, so when he wants to get her all hot and steamy, this is the perfect spicy recipe to try to win her back!

Tip: If you want to use dried beans and cook them, instead of canned beans, then make sure you soak them overnight and cook them for 1 ½ – 2 hours until soft before adding them to the soup.

1 onion – diced
3 cloves of garlic – crushed and chopped
1 large carrot – peeled and grated
1 400 gr can of cannellini beans – drained and rinsed
1 400 gr can of red kidney beans – drained and rinsed
1 400 gr can of chopped tomatoes
2 tablespoons of dried oregano
1 tablespoon of ground cumin
¼ – ½ teaspoon of chilli flakes (or more, depending on the heat you like)
2 tablespoons of tomato puree
2 tablespoon of paprika
2 tablespoons of balsamic vinegar
1 – 2 tablespoons of cocoa powder
2 bay leaves
1 ½ pints (approx. 3 ¾ cups) of beef stock/chicken stock/vegetable stock/water
2 – 3 tablespoons of flat leaf parsley – chopped
Salt and pepper to taste
Olive oil for frying

Garnish: Mature cheddar cheese – grated (or a dollop of sour cream and chives)

Fry the onions until soft.
Add the rest of the ingredients, except for the parsley, and bring to the boil. Simmer for 35 – 45 minutes.
Stir in the parsley and pour into bowls. Top with grated cheese and serve.
Serves 4 – 6

* Gluten Free Option – Use gluten free balsamic vinegar and stock
* Vegetarian Option – Use vegetable stock/water/vegetarian cheese
* Vegan Option – Use vegetable stock/water. Omit the cheese or use vegetarian cheese
* Dairy Free Option – Omit the cheese or use non-dairy cheese

Cozy Food

Gumbo's a-brewing
From the Witchcraft Mystery series by Juliet Blackwell (page 176)

My mother's family was Cajun, so I grew up with dishes like gumbo, jambalaya, and crawfish etoufee. In my Witchcraft Mystery series, Lily Ivory whips up delicious Cajun fare for her friends and her familiar, a shape-shifting miniature potbellied pig. Whenever I write about Lily cooking, I can practically smell the air laden with familiar spices as her cauldron bubbles away on the stove …

Mom always used gumbo as an excuse to clean out the fridge, including all sorts of leftovers: assorted veggies, meats, etc., so feel free to improvise! But the classic family recipe is below:

1 cup all-purpose flour
3/4 cup bacon drippings, lard, or butter

1 cup coarsely chopped celery
1 large onion, coarsely chopped
1 large green bell pepper, coarsely chopped
2 cloves garlic, minced
1 pound andouille sausage, sliced
3 quarts water
6 cubes beef bouillon
1 tablespoon white sugar
salt to taste
Hot pepper sauce (2 tbsp or to taste)
1/2 teaspoon mixed Cajun seasoning, or to taste
4 bay leaves
1/2 teaspoon dried thyme leaves
1 (14.5 ounce) can stewed tomatoes (this is a controversial addition – a lot of people don't use tomatoes at all. If you want to leave them out, just be sure to add a little more water so it's not too dry.)
1 (6 ounce) can tomato sauce (see above)
2 teaspoons gumbo file powder
2 tablespoons bacon drippings, lard, or butter
2 (10 ounce) packages frozen cut okra, thawed
2 tablespoons distilled white vinegar
Chicken (pre-cooked) if desired
1 pound crabmeat or other shellfish, if desired
3 pounds uncooked medium shrimp, peeled and deveined
2 tablespoons Worcestershire sauce
Gumbo file powder

Serve over white rice; pair with cornbread and collard greens for a complete meal.

Make a roux by whisking flour and 3/4 cup bacon drippings together in a large, heavy saucepan (iron skillet is best!) over medium-low heat. It will become smooth with no lumps. Whisk constantly until the roux turns a rich mahogany brown color and smells like cookies – don't let it burn! Remember: A good roux is the secret to great gumbo! Remove from heat but continue whisking until mixture stops cooking.

Chop the celery, onion, green bell pepper, and garlic very fine. Stir the vegetables into the roux, and mix in the sausage. Bring the mixture back to a simmer over medium-low heat, and cook until vegetables are tender, 10 to 15 minutes. Remove from heat, and set aside.

Bring the water and beef bouillon cubes to a boil in a large Dutch oven or soup pot. Stir until the bouillon cubes dissolve, and whisk the roux mixture into the boiling water. Reduce heat to a simmer, and mix in the sugar, salt, hot pepper sauce, Cajun seasoning, bay leaves, thyme, stewed tomatoes, and tomato sauce. Simmer the soup over low heat for 1 hour; mix in 2 teaspoons of file gumbo powder about 45-minutes in.

Meanwhile, melt 2 tablespoons of bacon drippings in a skillet, and cook the okra with vinegar over medium heat for 15 minutes; remove okra with slotted spoon, and stir into the simmering gumbo. Mix in chicken (pre-cooked), seafood, shrimp, and Worcestershire sauce, and simmer until flavors have blended, 45 more minutes.

Gumbo really should be made a day ahead of time – it's always best after sitting overnight. But whether you eat it right away or the next day, reheated, stir in 2 more teaspoons of file gumbo powder just before serving over white rice.

Lazy Man's Vegetable Meatball Soup
From the "Cat in the Stacks" series by Miranda James (page 198)

When the weather turns cold and rainy, Charlie Harris gets a craving for soup. Usually vegetable soup. Usually his housekeeper, Azalea Berry, will make the soup, but on those occasions when Azalea isn't around, Charlie does it himself. He calls it "the lazy man's way." He buys a bag of seasoned meatballs out of the freezer section at the grocery store, 15-ounce cans of vegetables from the veggie aisle, and some chicken broth, dumps it all in the two-gallon crockpot, adds black pepper to taste, and lets it cook on high for about 3 hours. Yields about 8-10 bowls of soup.

In case you're wondering what veggies Charlie usually buys, here's the list:

2 cans of diced tomatoes (usually with spices added, like basil and garlic)
1 can of corn
1 can of Purple Hull peas
1 can of string beans
1 can of diced potatoes

He doesn't like okra, unlike many Southerners, so he doesn't add it. Others may want to add it, however.

Cozy Food

Peanut Butter Soup
From the Subbing isn't for Sissies Mysteries by Carolyn J. Rose (page 224)

Substitute teacher and accidental sleuth Barbara Reed gets little time for lunch at Captain Meriwether High School in Reckless River, Washington. This soup is easy to make, keeps for several days in the refrigerator, heats up in a few microwave minutes, and provides veggies and protein and a burst of heat to clear your head for the afternoon's challenges.

Chop into very small chunks (or save time and effort and use a food processor for smaller pieces)

4 (or more or less) jalapeno peppers
2-3 carrots
3 ribs of celery
1 small-medium onion
1 zucchini
A couple of cloves of garlic (more if you love garlic)

Saute in a little olive oil until tender and add:

2-3 cans of chicken stock – or vegetable stock

Simmer for about an hour, then add

½ cup peanut butter – or more for a nuttier taste – use creamy or chunky
½ cup or more chopped fresh tomatoes or a can of diced tomatoes
½ cup or more black beans
Pre-cooked pasta or rice if you like
Red pepper flakes if you want more heat

Cook, stirring occasionally, until peanut butter is mixed in and fresh tomato chunks soften.

Sierra's Pasta Ceci Soup
From *Alibis and Amethysts* by Sharon Pape (page 218)

In *Alibis and Amethysts*, the first book in Sharon Pape's Crystal Shop mysteries, Jaye Saylor moves to Sedona, Arizona to open a crystal shop near the so-called Psychic Vortexes. Her best friend, Sierra, follows her out west and opens a bakery she calls Cravings. When the owner of the other bake shop in town is found dead in Sierra's backyard, she becomes the prime suspect. The two friends are determined to find the real killer before the police arrest Sierra. They have the help of their Navajo friend, Daniel and a strange, little cat-like creature who's adopted Jaye. No one's seen anything like it before, but Daniel's grandmother comes from a long line of medicine women and she has a startling theory about the animal's origins.

Between work and searching for the killer, Jaye and Sierra have little time to cook. When they can't bear to eat another pizza, Sierra whips up the soup her Italian grandmother used to make. It's quick, easy and yummy!

One 46oz. can of tomato juice
One 19oz can of ceci beans (also called chick peas or garbanzo beans)

One package elbow pasta
1/4 green pepper, chopped
1-2 cloves garlic, crushed
Fresh parsley or one Tbsp dried parsley
Enough olive oil to barely cover the bottom of the soup pot

Serve with thick, crusty Italian bread and Romano cheese, shredded or grated.

1. Add olive oil to bottom of soup pot and heat over low fire.
2. When oil is hot, add green pepper and crushed garlic. Cover and saute on low until pepper is soft - five - ten minutes.
3. Add tomato juice and parsley and bring to gentle boil for 30 minutes.
4. Add ceci beans with their liquid and bring back to gentle boil.
5. Meanwhile, prepare elbow pasta (half cup per person - more if your family loves pasta.)
6. Allow diners to add their own cheese.

Serves 6 - 8 as a first course, 4-6 as a main dish.
Great with the Italian bread and a green salad

Stuffed Pepper Soup
From the kitchen of Gail Oust (page 217)

8 oz ground beef
1 (28 oz) can tomato sauce
1 (28 oz) can petite diced tomatoes
1 cup cooked white rice
2 cups (approx. 2) green peppers, chopped
1 can beef broth
2 T. Brown sugar
2 tsp salt
1 tsp pepper

In large saucepan, brown beef and drain well. Add tomato sauce, diced tomatoes, rice, green pepper, beef broth, brown sugar, salt, and pepper. Bring to a boil. Reduce heat, cover, and simmer for 40 minutes or until peppers are tender.

Buckskin Bread
From the Spadena Street mysteries by Marian Allen (page 169)

LeJune loves to cook, but only if there are no more than five ingredients and no more than seven steps to the recipe. This is one of her favorites.

2 cups self-rising flour
1 cup water

Mix. Put into a greased pie pan. Bake at 400 degrees Fahrenheit for 20 minutes. Wonderful with soup, or warm with butter melting all over it.

Serves four to six.

Cozy Food

Cornbread croutons
From the Imogene Duckworthy series by Kaye George (page 192)

When Hortense Duckworthy makes cornbread, there aren't often leftovers. She usually makes enough, though, that she can hide a few pieces for later. Yes, she eats some--Hortense loves to eat--but she also "repurposes" them, as she would say. Made into tasty croutons, she serves them to Saltlick police chief, Emmett Emersen, another gourmand (if that means a person who eats a lot).

Leftover cornbread, butter
Cut cornbread into 1-inch squares, brush with melted butter, and place on a baking sheet. Bake at 350° for 10 minutes or until golden brown.
Serves at least a dozen with 6 small cornbread pieces.

*adapted by Kaye George from *Southern Living*, FEBRUARY 2005

Salads and Dressings

Strawberry Surprise

From the Lina Townend and Griff Tripp series by Judith Cutler (page 182)

Lina leaves most of the cooking to her business partner and adoptive grandfather, Griff Tripp. Not so long ago, Griff had heart by-pass surgery, so Lina's had to do more in the kitchen. Because they both lead pretty sedentary lives, they make sure that they eat salad every day. Here is one of Lina's favourite recipes.

This serves four generously as a fun starter.

12 – 16 ripe strawberries roughly the same size
2 tsp balsamic vinegar
Freshly ground black pepper
1 Bag of mixed leaves
1 tbsp virgin olive oil
2 balls of buffalo mozzarella
1 packet of prosciutto Crudo de Parma

Hull and wipe the strawberries, place in a bowl and toss in the balsamic vinegar. Add plenty of pepper. Cover and set aside for half an hour or so. Do not refrigerate.

Toss the leaves in a little oil and place a handful in the middle of each serving plate. Tear the slices of prosciutto and drop them on top – it's meant to look casual so don't go for mathematical neatness.

Drain and slice the mozzarella balls and scatter them too.

Finally, drain and add the strawberries.

You may need more black pepper and a tiny amount of salt – but, remember, the prosciutto will contain salt.

Goldie's Bright Summer Salad
From the Animals in Focus Mysteries series by Sheila Webster Boneham (page 177)

Janet MacPhail, animal photographer and protagonist of the Animals in Focus mysteries, isn't much of a cook. Luckily for Janet, some of her friends are. Janet's next-door-neighbor and BFF Goldie Sunshine, for one, is always coming up with interesting new combinations, often using vegetables, fruits, herbs, and flowers (yes, flowers) from her fantastic organic backyard garden. Since Janet is *still* trying to lose those last ten pounds (okay, twenty), Goldie has stopped pushing her addictive breads and cookies at Janet in favor of some new salad combos. Extra bonus - if Janet can't finish the big bowl of salad, her Australian Shepherd, Jay, gets a treat. He loves salads! Leo the cat? He'll stick with catnip.

6 cups mixed spring greens (Bibb lettuce, romaine, arugula, etc.)
2 cups fresh flat-leaf parsley leaves
½ cup chopped fresh mint
1 cucumber
6 tender young asparagus spears
1 cup fresh blueberries
½ cup (1 ear) cooked & cooled sweet corn kernels
¼ cup toasted sunflower seeds
Raspberry balsamic vinegar to taste
Optional: extra virgin olive oil to taste

1. Tear washed-and-dried greens into bite-size pieces and place in large bowl.
2. Chop parsley and mint, and slice cucumber. Add to greens.
3. Wash asparagus spears, then snap the tough bottoms off. Cut into 1-inch pieces and add to greens.
4. Add blueberries, corn, and sunflower seeds.
5. Gently toss ingredients to mix.

Goldie allows her guests to dress the salad themselves. It's delicious with just a splash of the raspberry balsamic vinegar, or that plus a little olive oil.

This salad can become a more substantial side or light meal by mixing with two cups of cooked couscous (or a grain of your choice).

Salads and Dressings

Warm Pea and Lentil Salad
From the Lina Townend and Griff Tripp series by Judith Cutler (page 182)

Lina leaves most of the cooking to her business partner and adoptive grandfather, Griff Tripp. Not so long ago, Griff had heart by-pass surgery, so Lina's had to do more in the kitchen. Because they both lead pretty sedentary lives, they make sure that they eat salad every day. Here is one of Lina's favourite recipes.

This is a wonderful dish for when you want something that's really good for you but can't face another lettuce leaf. If you use frozen peas, it works well all the year round as a starter for four, or a filling lunch for two.

4 oz Puy lentils
4 oz shelled peas, fresh or frozen
3 tbsp olive oil
4 salad onions or 8 or 9 chives, chopped very finely
Juice of 1 lime
Freshly ground black pepper (and salt if necessary)
4 oz Feta cheese, diced
Wholemeal bread – wholemeal pitta is excellent – to mop up the dressing.

Wash the lentils – with a variety like Puy there is no need to soak them – and put them in a saucepan with enough water to cover them. Simmer for twelve or thirteen minutes – they should be tender, but still firm.

Meanwhile, using a small saucepan, cook the peas and onions or chives in the oil – about 10 minutes if you're using fresh peas, but only 5 if you're using frozen.

Drain the lentils and put on to individual plates. Tip over them the hot peas and the juices. Squeeze the lime over the little mound. Top with the diced feta, which is inclined to be salty, so do not add salt without tasting first. Grind black pepper over everything.

Eunice's Spicy Sweet Southern Summer Salad
From the Headlines in High Heels Mystery Series by LynDee Walker (page 234)

Ace crime reporter Nichelle Clarke subsists mostly on PopTarts, coffee, and grilled cheese sandwiches, but that doesn't mean she can't cook. She just rarely has time. Luckily, the features editor at the Richmond Telegraph is a whiz in the kitchen and loves to feed the newsroom—this salad is a summertime favorite of Eunice's because it even gets the guys at the sports desk to eat their veggies.

1 head of iceberg lettuce, cored and chopped
2 large tomatoes, chopped
15 ½ oz. can mild chili beans (Eunice loves Ranch Style, if you can find them)
2 cups shredded cheddar cheese
1 jicama, finely chopped
2 cups tortilla strips (Eunice swears by Fritos)
Sweet honey French dressing (Eunice uses Catalina)

Pour the lettuce, tomatoes, jicama, beans (with sauce), and cheese into a large salad bowl and toss. Divide evenly onto plates, top with chips and dressing, and serve immediately.

Cozy Food

Salmagundy
From the Tobias Campion books by Judith Cutler (page 182)

I doubt if the Rev Tobias Campion, being an aristocrat, could boil in egg. However, he's asked one of his closest friends, Mrs Maria Hansard, to help him find a recipe.

An intelligent hard-working dog assists in both Tobias' adventures so far. He goes by the name of Salmagundy. His owner jokes that this shows his ancestry is very mixed indeed, because a salmagundy is a plate made up of a wide variety of ingredients. Mrs. Hansard has helped me adapt it for the modern kitchen. The most important thing, she says, is that it should be attractive to the eye as well as the palate. She picked out a large round hors d'oeuvres dish, one with half a dozen segments radiating from the centre, as a suitable container. You may prefer to be more authentic, using a full size plate and inverting a soup-plate over it, arranging the ingredients in a gentle cone.

A bunch of well-washed watercress
Cooked breast of chicken, chopped into bite-sized pieces
Cooked ham, chopped into bite-sized pieces
Hard-boiled eggs, chopped
Cooked beetroot, chopped (you can use pickled beetroot but Mrs Hansard says the flavour is too coarse)
Grated carrot, dressed in vinaigrette
Cucumber, chopped
Pickled red cabbage
Parsley, some chopped, one sprig left whole
Capers, rinsed
Anchovy fillets (you may or may not prefer to soak them overnight in milk)

Lay the watercress over your plate as a base for everything else. If you are using an hors d'oeuvres dish, fill each segment with one of one of your main ingredients, making sure that the colours contrast nicely. You can do the same if you have used the plate/dish system, or you can arrange your ingredients in rings, ascending the little slope (you may need to paint it with melted butter to make the salad stick to it. Use the anchovy fillets to make a pretty lattice pattern, which you decorate further with the capers. Add a shake of the chopped parsley, and top the dish with the remaining sprig.

You may sprinkle the dish with a well-flavoured vinaigrette before you put it on the table, or pass the vinaigrette separately.

If you lack one or two of the ingredients, do not worry: you can replace them with attractive substitutes.

Mrs. Hansard reminds me that it is hard to say how many people this will serve, as it always appears as one of many dishes offered as a first or second course, and of course anything left over will be eaten by the servants. Let your serving dish size and the availability of ingredients guide you in your quantities, just as you would if you were preparing a twenty-first century buffet.

Salads and Dressings

Amelia's Fruit Salad with Sour Cream Sauce
From the kitchen of E.E. Kennedy (page 200)

This recipe is so easy that even Amelia Prentice, who generally subsists on canned soup and saltine crackers, is able to make a good version of it. It serves as a nice side dish when you're having Michigans.

The hardest part is choosing and carving the pineapple. All measurements are approximate except, of course, the pineapple. All ingredients are interchangeable except, of course, the pineapple.

Salad:
1 large, well-ripened pineapple (The pineapple should be a nice golden-brown on the sides and a leaf should pull easily out of the top.)
1 pint of strawberries
1/2 pint of blueberries
1 good-sized bunch of white grapes (The sweetest white grapes will be opaque and cloudy-looking.)
1 good-sized bunch of red grapes. (The best ones are firm and a deep red color.)
1 sweet apple (Red delicious is good)
1 ripe pear (Firm with just a little bit of "give")
Any other fresh fruit you choose. Note: Citrus and tart fruit doesn't usually work very well.
Some people like to include chopped nuts and/or shredded coconut. Not Amelia.

Wash everything thoroughly, even the pineapple.
Hull the strawberries and slice them in half. Examine the blueberries and discard the duds.
Pluck the grapes from their vines. Core the apple and pear and cut into in bite-size chunks. (You can leave the skin on, if preferred.)
Put all these fruits in a large attractive serving bowl and mix.
Carefully cut the top, bottom and outer layer from the pineapple.
Quarter it and cut out the tough center. Cut the pineapple into bite-size chunks, retaining the juice, if possible.
Add the pineapple to the fruit mixture and stir well, coating all the fruit with the pineapple juice.

Sauce:
1 pint sour cream.
Mint jelly or strawberry preserves (The "spreadable fruit" type works best.)

In a small, decorative bowl, blend the sour cream thoroughly with enough jelly for a pretty green color and refreshing mint taste.
Or blend in the preserves for a pretty pink color and a light, slightly sweet taste.

Serve the salad in small bowls and pass the sour cream sauce.
Serves about 10, depending on the amount of fruit you use.

Cozy Food

Pop Open the Bubbly Champagne Vinaigrette
From the Cue Ball Mysteries series by Cindy Blackburn (page 175)

According to Jessie Hewitt, every day without her ex-husband is a day worth celebrating. So Jessie makes a habit of drinking champagne—you guessed it—every day. Would this salad lover use any old white wine vinegar in her favorite salad dressing? Of course not!

2 cloves garlic, crushed
2 Tablespoons Dijon mustard
¼ cup champagne vinegar
2 Tablespoons fresh lemon juice
2 Tablespoons honey
2-3 dashes Tabasco sauce
1 Tablespoon finely chopped shallot
1/2 teaspoon salt
1 teaspoon pepper
1/2 cup olive oil

Put all ingredients in a glass jar, seal tightly, and shake really, really, well. Shake before each use. Recipe will dress 3 or 4 large green salads. Jessie prefers hers with romaine lettuce, tomatoes, and sliced avocado. But whatever veggies you prefer will pop beneath this dressing!

As with ALL of Jessie's recipes, serve with champagne. And yes, champagne DOES make a green salad healthier. Trust Jessie.

Allie's Perfect Salad
From *Maggie's Island* by Sharon Burch Toner (page 232)

In the fourth of the Maggie McGill Mysteries, *Maggie's Island,* Allie makes a wonderful salad. Here it is.

Red peppers, cut in strips
Pine nuts
Extra Virgin Olive Oil
Salad greens - arugula mixed with an herb mix
Feta Cheese, crumbled
Pear, cut in chunks
Croutons (made from French bread or purchased)

Coat pine nuts with olive oil and toast under broiler for 3-4 minutes, careful not to burn.
Coat red peppers in olive oil and roast for about 1 hour in 375° oven.
Arrange all ingredients on greens and serve immediately.
Dress with classic olive oil, balsamic vinegar and mustard dressing.

Dressing:
½ C White Balsamic Vinegar
1 tsp Dijon mustard
½ tsp Sugar
2 TBSP Extra Virgin Olive Oil
Sea Salt - taste to adjust amount
Ground pepper

Vigorously shake vinegar, mustard, sugar, salt and pepper in small jar. Add olive oil and shake again before serving.

The Poet's Recipe for Salad
From the Auguste Didier, Victorian Master Chef series by Amy Myers (page 212)

Auguste loves this recipe from the English wit and cleric Sydney Smith, 1771-1845. However Auguste has his own ideas (and for today's gourmets very sensible ones) on how it should be prepared. The most important diversion from the original is to omit the salt – the anchovies supply that.

Auguste's ingredients:
1 lb of potatoes
2 teaspoons of wholegrain mustard
3 tbsps good olive oil
1 tbsp wine vinegar
2 eggs yolks mashed
1 large shallot (or very mild onion or 3 scallions) cut very fine
3 chopped anchovies

These differ somewhat from the eloquent original which reads:

Two large potatoes, passed through kitchen sieve
Unwonted softness to the salad give;
Of mordaunt mustard, add a single spoon
Distrust the condiment which bites so soon;
But deem it not, thou man of herbs, a fault,
To add a double quantity of salt;
Three times the spoon with oil of Lucca crown,
Add once the vinegar, procured from town;
True flavour needs it, and your poet begs
The pounded yellow of two well-boiled eggs;
Let onion atoms lurk within the bowl,
And scarce suspected, animate the whole;
And lastly, in the flavoured compound toss
A magic teaspoon of anchovy sauce;
Then though green turtle fail, though venison's tough
And ham and turkey are not boiled enough,
Serenely full, the epicure may say-
Fate cannot harm me - I have dined today.

Auguste tells me he boils the peeled potatoes, and then puts them through a mouli-mix so that the resulting mash is light and fluffy. He then mixes in the mashed egg yolks and simply adds the other ingredients, using tinned anchovies rather than anchovy sauce, and onion to taste.

I don't know about you, but I find I rarely have green turtle in my fridge, so with Auguste's agreement I mould the resulting mash into balls and serve them on crisp lettuce leaves. They are nice warm (not hot) but are equally nice eaten cold – with cold meats or salad. It serves three or four people.

Cozy Food

Tomato-Bean Salad with Eggs
From the Local Foods Mystery series by Edith Maxwell (page 207)

In Edith Maxwell's Local Foods mystery series (Kensington Publishing), former software engineer Cam Flaherty grows organic vegetables on her farm in northeastern Massachusetts. She sells them to the local foods enthusiasts who belong to her farm-share program as well as to a tall intense chef. What she didn't plan on was encountering locally sourced murder, too.

Summer is a perfect time to make this scaled-down version of Salade Nicoise. It skips the tuna and the potatoes but is a great light meal accompanied by a loaf of sourdough and a glass of chilled Pinot Grigio. Serves six.

Salad:
2 lbs freshly picked slim green beans
6 eggs, hard boiled
Four medium size fresh tomatoes
2-3 T capers
1/2 c fresh parsley, minced

Dressing:
2 strips of fresh lemon peel, 1 by 2 1/2 inches each
1/4 t salt, plus more, if needed
1/2 T Dijon-type prepared mustard
1 to 2 T freshly squeezed lemon juice
1/2 c high-quality olive oil
Freshly ground pepper
Wash and trim the beans. Cut into two-inch pieces. Steam lightly until bright green and then chill in ice water. Drain and dry in a dish towel.
Cut the tomatoes into quarters.
Peel the eggs and carefully cut in half lengthwise.
Lay the beans in a shallow serving dish. Intersperse the tomatoes and eggs, cut side up, in an artful way.
Mince the lemon peel very finely with the salt, scrape it into the mortar or bowl, and mash into a fine paste with the pestle or spoon.
Beat in the mustard and 1 tablespoon of the lemon juice; when thoroughly blended start beating in the oil by droplets to make a homogeneous sauce—easier when done with a small electric mixer.
Beat in droplets more lemon juice and salt and pepper to taste.
Pour the dressing over the salad.
Sprinkle capers and parsley on top and add freshly ground pepper.
Serve at room temperature or chill if not serving soon.

Aunt Mary McGill's Wild Rice Salad with Apples
From Kathleen Delaney (page 185)

This salad is one of Aunt Mary's favorites and she serves it often. It goes with many types of meals, travels well, and she never has left overs.

For Salad:
1 cup wild rice
½ cup long-grained rice OR 1 pkg of mixed wild rice and white rice

2 stalks celery, chopped
1 onion, chopped
1 apple, peeled and chopped (Aunt Mary likes to leave the peel on the green ones as it provides a nice touch of color)
1 red bell pepper, chopped

For Dressing:
½ cup mayonnaise (Aunt Mary uses Hellmann's)
2 tsp Dijon mustard
1 garlic clove, crushed
¼ cup olive or safflower oil
1 Tbsp tarragon vinegar. If you don't have, substitute white wine vinegar and 1 tsp dry tarragon

Cook rice in 1 qt boiling water until tender, about 30 min. Drain, if needed and set aside to cool. Place rest of salad ingredients into bowl with rice and mix well. Combine ingredients for dressing, pour over salad and mix again. Chill 2-3 hrs before serving. Will keep up to 2 days in fridge, but you probably won't have any to left over.

Cold Quinoa Muffuletta Salad
From Out of the Frying Pan by Ellie Marks and Kelly Klepfer (page 202)

Fern Hopkins, art teacher with a classic style and a no-nonsense attitude buys local produce, or welcomes the bounty of others. She practices yoga and clean eating and is well versed on the newest super foods. This salad would be a choice she'd make at a local, organic restaurant where she'd prefer to sit alone, or at least across the restaurant from her sister-in-law roommate.

Follow the directions below for the basic quinoa. The amount of cooked quinoa will be slightly over 2 cups. And this salad will serve 4 - 8 depending on whether it's a main dish or side.
1 Cup quinoa
1/4 Cup dried mushrooms
1/4 Cup diced onion
2 Cloves garlic minced
2 Cups veggie broth

Toss all in a pan and bring to a boil. Turn down to simmer and cover and let simmer about 15 minutes.

Dressing:
3 TBSP lemon juice
2 TBSP olive oil
1/2 teaspoon garlic powder
1/2 teaspoon dried oregano
1/2 teaspoon of agave or maple syrup
1/2 teaspoon of yellow or brown spicy mustard
dash salt

Mix well.

Add the following:
1/2 Cup chopped mushrooms
1/4 to 1/2 Cup chopped green olives

1/4 to 1/2 Cup chopped kalamata olives
1/2 Cup shredded kale
The dressing
The cooked quinoa mixture

Mix well.

Kiki Lowenstein's Hoosier Daddy Kidney Bean Salad

From *Paper, Scissors, Death* by Joanna Campbell Slan (page 228)

This is cheap, filling and easy to make. Although you'll never find the recipe in a gourmet magazine, Kiki gets asked for it all the time. A picnic favorite, when made with low-fat mayo and egg whites only, this salad is a dieter's best friend. It's low-cal and high fiber.

1 can of red kidney beans
1/3 C. sweet pickle relish (more if you like)
2 hard-boiled eggs, chopped
¼ to 1/3 C. of mayonnaise (more if you like the salad soupier)
1 medium onion, chopped

Drain and rinse the kidney beans. (No, we don't know what that purple goop is in the bottom of the can, and we don't want to know either!)
Mix together the mayonnaise and pickle relish.
Add onion and beans to mayonnaise and relish.
Gently add the eggs.
Refrigerate.

Citrus Vinaigrette Salad Dressing or Marinade

From the Comfort Food series by Christine Wenger (page 235)

Trixie Matkowski, the owner of the Silver Bullet Diner in the small town of Sandy Harbor, NY, on the shore of Lake Ontario loves to make this refreshing dressing for the spring and summer. That's when she vows to go on a diet due to the fresh produce available. But soon, she's on the trail of a murderer and all thoughts of a diet disappear just like her New Year's resolutions!

This dressing is perfect on greens with or without fruit (mandarin oranges, strawberries, kiwi). And it also works as a marinade!

Dressing can be made one week ahead. Refrigerate. Shake before using.
Makes 1-1/2 cups, but can easily be doubled or tripled.

1 small shallot, finely chopped
3/4 cup olive oil
1/4 cup Champagne vinegar or white wine vinegar
3 tablespoons fresh lemon juice
2 tablespoons fresh orange juice
1/4 teaspoon finely grated lemon zest
Kosher salt, freshly ground pepper

Combine first 6 ingredients in a jar with a lid; season with salt and pepper if desired. Shake to blend.

Salads and Dressings

Sidney Marsh's Oh-SO-Easy Killer Coleslaw
From The Sidney Marsh Murder Mysteries series by Marie Moore (page 211)

Marie Moore's travel mystery series features Sidney Marsh, a young, New York based travel agent. Sidney came to Manhattan from Mississippi, fell in love with the Big Apple, and landed a job at a travel agency in Manhattan, Itchy Feet Travel. Based in New York, Sidney travels the world, working with her best friend and business partner, the flamboyant and fun-loving Jay Wilson. She doesn't have a lot of time to cook, so she adapts her mamma's Southern recipes to suit her fast-paced lifestyle. Here is one of them, and Mamma would tell you it's mighty good!

1 package chopped slaw mix OR 1 small cabbage, chopped fine
1 green bell pepper, cored, seeded and chopped. (If you like, add a red one as well!)
4 scallions chopped (white part only)
1 cup canola oil
½ cup apple cider vinegar
1 T. sugar or 3 packets artificial blue or yellow artificial sweetener
1/8 t. salt

Dump all in a 1 gallon plastic zip bag and toss to mix. Refrigerate until ready to serve, at least 30 minutes prior to serving. Drain well. May be made the day before. Great with anything fried, of course! 6-8 servings.

Cozy Food

Pasta and Casseroles

Pasta

Tom's Quick & Fragrant Pasta Sauce
From the Animals in Focus Mysteries series by Sheila Webster Boneham (page 177)

"I wanted to linger…where the aroma of simmering tomato and basil and something I couldn't identify wrapped itself around me like a warm embrace." So says fifty-something Janet MacPhail, animal photographer and protagonist of the Animals in Focus mysteries, when she first encounters this sauce in *Drop Dead on Recall*. Janet's idea of "cooking" is re-heated carry out, but that good-looking guy she met at the dog show is not just an animal lover and anthropology professor—he's also a genius in the kitchen (and at picking up take-out when time is short). Tom's also been known to share a bit of pasta with his Labrador retriever, Drake, and Janet's Australian Shepherd, Jay. Janet's cat, Leo, doesn't care.

2 24-oz jars of spaghetti sauce (Tom uses Newman's Own® Sockerooni™)
1 Tablespoon olive oil
½ pound bulk sweet Italian sausage
1 medium onion, chopped
1 small green pepper, chopped
Tablespoon oregano dried leaves

1 teaspoon dried tarragon leaves
¼ tsp garlic powder or fresh garlic to taste
1 packet sugar substitute OR tsp sugar
1 teaspoon Worcestershire sauce

Heat pasta sauce in 4-quart pan over medium heat.
Heat Tablespoon olive oil in large frying pan over medium heat.
In frying pan, cook chopped onion and green pepper (and garlic if using fresh) for about 5 minutes.
Add Worcestershire, oregano, and tarragon to the onions and peppers while they are cooking.
Add Italian sausage to frying pan and cook until cooked through, breaking it apart as it cooks.
Add this mixture to the sauce in the sauce pan.
Let simmer for at least 10 minutes.

Serve over cooked spaghetti or other pasta, or steamed vegetables such as zucchini or spaghetti squash. Top with grated parmesan or romano cheese as desired. Serves 4-6 people.

The tastiest Mac you ever did Cheese
From *The Day She Died* by Catriona McPherson (page 210)

When I made some teenaged friends of mine scratch mac for the first time they vowed never to eat the boxed stuff again. A win for real food!

Gus in *The Day She Died* makes mac and cheese for his children and he goes easy on the salt. It's one of the things that tells Jessie he's a caring dad. But for great mac and cheese you must a. use very mature cheddar and b. season boldly. Now is not the time to flirt with a low-sodium diet and, rest assured, the salt you add will not be more than gets put in the commercial brands.

2 oz of butter
¼ teaspoon olive oil
1 heaped tablespoon of multi-purpose flour
1 pint of full-fat milk
¼ teaspoon dry English mustard
1 lb extra-mature cheddar (Kerrygold's Irish in the black wrapper is good)
Salt and pepper
8 oz macaroni

Serves four

- Grate all of the cheese.
- Melt the butter and olive at medium heat in a thick-bottomed saucepan. (The oil stops the butter burning.)
- Add the flour to the melted butter and stir continuously. It will be a softish ball of paste that breaks up easily. If it sticks add more butter and keep stirring. If it's too soft to make a ball, add more flour.
- When the paste is bubbling hot, start adding the milk in small batches and stir like crazy. Don't worry about lumps; you can whisk them out.
- When all the milk is added turn up the heat and keep stirring/whisking without letting it stick to the pan base.

- After it starts to bubble, turn the heat down and add the mustard, half to three quarters of the cheese, and salt and pepper to taste. Keep stirring until the cheese has melted then set the sauce aside.
- You could check the seasoning now and add more salt if you think it needs it.
- Boil a big pan of water and salt it until it's as saline as the Mediterranean sea.
- Add the pasta and cook until it's al dente.
- Drain it thoroughly then mix it with the cheese sauce.
- Tip the mixed mac and cheese into a buttered casserole dish and sprinkle the rest of the cheese on top. Add a grind of pepper and a dash of salt (yes, more salt) and put under the broiler until the top is brown and bubbling.
- If you leave the cheese sauce until it's cool for any reason, the finished dish might need twenty minutes in the oven before broiling.

Maggie's Lasagna
From *Shadows at the Spring Show*, Antique Print Mystery series by Lea Wait (page 234)

Ingredients:
1 large can tomatoes (16 oz)
½ box (8 oz) lasagna noodles
10 oz box frozen chopped spinach, defrosted and drained
16 oz ricotta cheese
16 oz mozzarella cheese
16 oz chunky spaghetti sauce
Choices: one, some or all of:
     ½ pound fresh sautéed mushrooms
     2-3 small zucchini, sliced and sautéed
     2-6 cloves garlic, chopped and sautéed
     ½ lb browned ground beef
     6-8 oz sausage, cut in small pieces & browned
     1 large onion, chopped & sautéed
Oregano, pepper, garlic salt to taste
½-3/4 cup freshly grated Parmesan cheese

Cook noodles al dente, as directed on package. (Add a little oil to cooking water to keep noodles from sticking to each other or to pan.) Sautee any vegetables (as listed); brown any meat you'll be using. Slice mozzarella cheese.

Oil lasagna pan lightly. Season sauce with spices to taste. Cover bottom of lasagna pan with thin layer of spaghetti sauce. Cover with one layer of noodles. Layer meat, vegetables, spinach, ricotta, tomatoes, mozzarella, sauce, noodles. Repeat. After top layer of noodles, add rest of sauce and sprinkle top with grated Parmesan. Cover with aluminum foil. Cook at 350 degrees for 1-1/2 hours (depending on thickness) Remove foil for last half hour to allow top browning.

Lasagna is done when bubbly on sides and browned on top. Serves 6-12.

Maggie serves hers with garlic bread and a green salad. Can be made a day ahead and refrigerated.

Pasta and Casseroles

Not-Your-Sicilian Bolognese Sauce
From Angie's Papa in the Angelina Bonapart mysteries by Nanci Rathbun (page 222)

PI Angelina Bonaparte has plenty of experience with deception – and not just because of her former husband. In her job, she tracks down deadbeats and exposes unfaithful spouses. Then she's hired to prove a cheating husband innocent of the murder of his lover. As she and homicide Detective Wukowski work toward the same goal – discovering the truth – they realize their attraction for each other and must decide whether they are strong enough as individuals to work through her lack of trust and his fear of loss. This is a mystery with strong characters and touches of humor.

In my Angelina Bonaparte mysteries, it's a family tradition to gather on Sunday afternoon for a Sicilian-American meal. Angie's Papa makes spaghetti Bolognese (red sauce). I can't provide his delicious recipe, because I took fictional license in these novels - my family is mostly Norwegian and Irish, with some Dutch and German thrown in. I did learn to make a very simple, but tasty, Bolognese sauce, from my Irish-German mom.

1 pound ground chuck
1 large can (28-32 oz., depending on brand) tomato sauce
1 small red onion
1 TBSP Lemon-pepper marinade (this is a bottled spice, not a liquid marinade)
1 TBSP Italian herb seasoning (this is a bottled spice)
1 TSP salt
1/2 TSP pepper

Chop the onion and saute in olive oil. Brown the meat and drain the drippings. Combine onion and meat. Add tomato sauce. Swish a little water in the can and add to the pot. Crush the Italian seasoning in your hand to release the flavors, then add it and the lemon-pepper marinade to the pot. Add salt and pepper. Stir. Simmer for at least two hours - the longer it simmers, the more flavorful it will be. Taste after an hour, to see if more salt or pepper are needed. The sauce can be refrigerated or frozen. It will not lose texture or flavor. Enough for four servings of spaghetti.

Tagliatelle with Hazelnut Pesto
From The Italian Cooking Encyclopedia published by Annes Publishing Limited, UK. Submitted by Sylvia Massara (page 205)

Being from an Italian background, mixed with a sprinkle of Spanish blood, and being born in South America and transplanted to Australia as a young girl, I'm a bit like my favourite recipes—a bit of everything.

I have a love of food as do most Latin/Italians, but having little time to cook, I tend to let the protagonists in my novels do the cooking instead. The following recipe is one that comes from Mia Ferrari's repertoire, although she hasn't yet used this one in her novels. Despite this, Mia has cooked other yummy meals (and she loves eating!).

If you're a pesto enthusiast, hazelnuts make an interesting addition to this variation on the classic pesto.

Ingredients:
2 garlic cloves, crushed
25 g/1 oz/ 1 cup fresh basil leaves

25 g/1 oz/ 1/4 cup shelled hazelnuts
200g/7 oz/ scant 1 cup skimmed milk soft cheese
225g/8 oz dried tagliatelle
Salt and freshly ground pepper

Serves up to 4 people.

Cook's tip: If you buy fresh tagliatelle instead of dried, cook in boiling salted water for only 2-3 minutes until *al dente.*

Step 1 Place the crushed garlic, basil leaves, hazelnuts and cheese in a blender or food processor and process to a thick paste.

Step 2 Meanwhile, cook the tagliatelle in lightly salted boiling water for about 10 minutes until *al dente*; then drain well.

Step 3 Spoon the pesto into the hot pasta and toss lightly until melted. Grind over plenty of black pepper and serve hot.

BUON APPETITO!

Carbonara
From the Rebecca Mayfield Mysteries by Joanne Pence (page 220)

Rebecca Mayfield is a San Francisco Homicide Inspector. She's from Idaho and believes in doing her job and everything in her life "by the book," so much so that to her consternation, Richie Amalfi refers to her as "Rebecca Rulebook." And Richie is a ... what? Is he a crook or an out-of-the-ordinary businessman? A con man or really a nice guy? Rebecca isn't sure. This odd couple first met in a Christmas novella and now have their own series.

One thing Rebecca does know about Richie--he's a great cook. Here's his recipe for Carbonara:

1 cup diced pancetta (may substitute bacon or ham)
3 tablespoons olive oil
1 lb pasta noodles (in order of preference: linguine, vermicelli, angel hair, spaghetti)
5 eggs
1 cup grated or shredded cheese (Romano-Parmesan; or Parmesan)
1 cup heavy cream
1 diced green (spring) onion
Fresh black pepper to taste

Put lightly salted water in a large pot, and turn heat on high to bring it to a boil.

In a bowl or measuring cup, add eggs, cheese, and cream, stir together, and set it aside.

Using a large skillet or frying pan (electric works well), add pancetta and olive oil over medium heat until browned. When the pancetta is almost cooked, add the green onion, stir until the onion is tender, then lower the heat to keep it warm while the pasta cooks.

Add uncooked pasta to boiling water. When it is *al dente*, drain pasta well and add it immediately to the skillet. Add the liquid ingredients and fold it all together, mixing the ingredients so that all noodles are coated (using tongs to mix the pasta by lifting and stirring works well). Continue to cook over medium heat, stirring and lifting constantly, until the coating is set on all the noodles and the egg has cooked.

Transfer to a serving bowl, and add fresh black pepper to taste.

Theo's Pasta Slaw
From the Quilted Mysteries, a series by Barbara Graham (page 193)

Theo Abernathy owns and operates a quilt shop and is married to the sheriff of tiny Park County, Tennessee. While she is a fabulous quilter, a good mother and the occasional source of gossip that aids her husband's quest to find a killer; she is a wretched cook. This pasta dish is the only reliably edible salad she can prepare. Here's what she does.

1 pound uncooked linguini
1 ½ cups Cole slaw dressing
½ cup chopped purple onion
2 tsp prepared yellow mustard
1 pound package slaw mix (cabbage)
1 chopped green bell pepper

Break uncooked pasta into short lengths and cook according to package directions. Drain, rinse with cold water and drain again. Combine Cole slaw dressing, onion, and mustard. Add drained pasta and stir to coat. Cover tightly and refrigerate at least one hour and as long as eight hours. Just before serving, add cabbage, green pepper and stir to coat.
Serves 8.

Turkey (or Chicken) Tetrazzini
From the Hannah Ives Mystery series by Marcia Talley (page 231)

The Tranquility Garden at Calvert Colony is far from tranquil after Maryland sleuth, Hannah Ives, discovers the body one of its residents pinned to the ground with an ornamental glass sculpture. As she waits for the police to arrive her husband's words echo in her head: "Take care, Hannah. And no dead bodies, OK?", "Was I cursed," she wonders, "doomed to stumble over bodies for life, rerun after rerun like Jessica Fletcher on *Murder She Wrote*?" Over the course of fourteen novels, beginning with *Sing It To Her Bones*, Hannah has had to pay a lot of condolence calls, so whenever she whips up a batch of tetrazzini, she doubles the recipe and freezes half of it for later … just in case.

8 oz. spaghetti
¼ cup butter or margarine
¼ cup flour
1 cup turkey or chicken broth
1 cup heavy cream
¾ cup shredded Gruyere or Swiss cheese
2 T. cooking sherry
1 -6oz can sliced mushrooms, drained
2 ½ - 3 cups diced cooked turkey or chicken
1/3 cup grated parmesan
salt and pepper to taste

- Cook and drain spaghetti and keep warm.
- Melt butter in large saucepan and blend in flour. Gradually add broth and cream and cook, stirring, over low heat until smooth and thickened.
- Add cheese, mushrooms, turkey or chicken, and cooking sherry. Stir well.
- Salt and pepper to taste.
- Fold with spaghetti into shallow 2-qt. baking dish. Sprinkle generously with parmesan.
- Broil for 5 to 7 minutes until top is golden brown. Serves 6.

Ginny's Chicken Cacciatore (Polla alla cacciatore)
From *Chicken Caccia-Killer* by Liz Lipperman (page 203)

6 boneless, skinless chicken breasts cut into ½ inch strips
1-2 tablespoons seasoning salt
1-2 teaspoons pepper
1 cup all-purpose flour
3 tablespoons virgin olive oil
1 red bell pepper sliced lengthwise in small strips
1 orange bell pepper sliced lengthwise in small strips
1 yellow bell pepper sliced lengthwise in small strips
1 onion sliced lengthwise in small strips
2 tablespoons dried thyme
2 tablespoons dried basil
2 tablespoons dried oregano
2 tablespoons dried parsley
1 bay leaf
Salt and Pepper to taste
½ teaspoon red pepper flakes (optional)
1 can (15 ounces) tomato sauce
½ cup red wine
½ cup low sodium chicken broth

1 pound bag of linguine noodles
1 bag (12 ounces) Mozzarella cheese, shredded

Sprinkle first the seasoning salt and then the pepper on the chicken strips, then dredge in the flour to coat. In a large skillet, heat the olive oil and add the chicken. Cook 3-5 minutes on each side or until both sides are browned and then remove from skillet. In the same skillet, add the peppers and the onion to caramelize. Salt and pepper to taste. After several minutes, add the thyme, basil, oregano and the parsley. Then add the broth, tomato sauce and the wine. When it comes to a slow boil, cover and simmer for thirty minutes.

While sauce is thickening, cook linguine according to package directions. When it is ready, drain the water and place desired portion on a microwaveable plate. Next add about ¾ cup of the sauce (more if you like) followed by approximately ¾ cup vegetables (again, more if you like) and top each plate with ¾ cup Mozzarella cheese. Put in microwave for 30 seconds to melt the cheese. Yields 6 servings.

Hint: Adjust this to your personal serving size preferences. When I am being lazy, I use my favorite bottled spaghetti sauce instead of the homemade one. It works well, too.

Pasta and Casseroles

Date Night Chicken
Inspired by the Beauty Queen Mysteries by Diana Dempsey (page 185)
Ms America and the Offing on Oahu (Volume 1)

Happy Pennington works out and watches what she eats—a beauty queen pretty much has to do both—but she loves a tasty repast and an exotic cocktail. (In fact, delectable meals, decadent desserts, and adult libations feature prominently in the Beauty Queen Mysteries.)

Date Night Chicken is a wonderful easy casserole dish that can be prepared in advance and popped in the oven so a woman can sit back and enjoy her date night to its fullest—wearing a chic outfit and with cocktail in hand. Bon appétit!

(Serves two.)

2 or 3 chicken breasts, pounded thin if you prefer
2 or 3 slices prosciutto
2 or 3 slices Gruyère cheese
1/3 pound button mushrooms, de-stemmed, cleaned, and quartered
1 cup frozen peas
¼ pound unsalted butter, sliced thin
¼ cup lemon juice
salt
pepper
dried oregano

Pre-heat oven to 400 degrees.

Lightly season both sides of the chicken breasts with salt, pepper, and oregano. Lay a slice of prosciutto and a slice of Gruyère cheese on each breast and fold the breast in half, securing it with a toothpick if desired.

Arrange the breasts in a covered casserole dish. Pour the frozen peas around the breasts and do the same with the sliced mushrooms. Lightly season the vegetables with more salt, pepper, and oregano. Slice the butter thinly and dot the breasts and vegetables with it. Pour the lemon juice over everything.

Cover the casserole dish and place in the oven. Cook for 40 minutes, checking halfway through to add additional butter if desired.

Whole Wheat Penne with Good Stuff
From the Regan McHenry Mystery series by Nancy Lynn Jarvis (page 199)

There's nothing like some fast pasta after a long day of sleuthing and selling houses. This recipe is healthy, fast, good, and with some crusty bread on the side, a complete vegetarian meal.

12 oz whole wheat penne pasta, cooked according to package directions
1 T olive oil
1 small yellow onion, chopped
5 large cloves garlic, minced
¼ tsp. (more if you like heat) crushed red chilies
1 cup sliced mushrooms (white or baby bella)

1 bunch Swiss chard, washed and sliced (or use Kale)
1 bunch loose broccoli with leaves loosely chopped
½ cup vegetable stock or bullion
½ cup pitted Kalamata olives, roughly chopped
Salt and pepper to taste, if needed
Parmesan cheese (optional)

Cook pasta according to package directions until al dente. Heat olive oil in a large skillet over medium-high heat. Saute onion until translucent but not brown. Add garlic and crushed chili and sauté for thirty seconds. Add mushrooms and cook for 3 minutes. Add Swiss chard and broccoli and cook until Swiss chard is wilted.

Stir in vegetable stock, olives, and cooked pasta. Sprinkle with salt and pepper, if needed; sprinkle finely grated Parmesan cheese on top if desired; and serve. Serves 4.

Linguini with Roasted Vegetables & Shrimp
From the Seaside Knitters Mystery series by Sally Goldenbaum (page 192)

The seaside knitters—Nell, Izzy, Birdie and Cass—love to cook and to eat. Most summer Friday nights find them gathered with friends and family on the Endicott deck, enjoying Ben's martinis and grilled fish or Nell's famous pasta dishes.

Enjoy the flavor of the Seaside Knitters Mysteries! Serves 6.

1 package linguini
1 lb. shrimp (about 24 shrimp)
1 sweet onion, sliced thin
½ bunch fresh asparagus, tough end broken off and sliced into 2-inch pieces
1 red pepper, sliced thin
2 cups mushrooms, sliced
5 cloves minced garlic
½ cup pine nuts

4 T olive oil
1 T butter
1 T fresh lemon juice
½ tsp red pepper flakes
1 t white pepper
½ cup white wine
½ c fresh basil cut in strips
¼ Italian parsley
Salt & pepper
½ cup feta cheese

Toast pine nuts in dry skillet over medium-low heat about 3 minutes until golden brown. Watch carefully so they don't burn. Set aside.

Toss asparagus, red pepper, onion, mushrooms, garlic (3 cloves) in 2 T olive oil, spread out on baking sheet and roast in 400 degree oven for 15-20 minutes (onions should be golden brown). Vegetables may be substituted to match your taste. Nell uses whatever vegetables are fresh that day.

Salt and pepper shrimp, then sauté in 2 T olive oil plus 1 T butter & 2 chopped garlic cloves.
Remove shrimp and sprinkle with lemon juice; toss with vegetables.
Add basil and parsley to shrimp and vegetable mixture.

Add wine to shrimp juices and simmer until wine reduces in half. Add vegetables.
Toss with cooked linguini.
Sprinkle with additional basil, pine nuts, and feta cheese.
Salt and pepper to taste.

Sometimes Nell puts pasta into soup bowls, rather than tossing it with the vegetable mixture, then spoons the vegetable shrimp sauce over the pasta and adds cheese at last minute.

Add S&P and red pepper (for those who like spicy food) to taste.

Gnocchi a la Traci

From the Mitzy Neuhaus Mystery series by Traci Hilton (page 194)

Mitzy and Alonzo, and even Jane and Jake have had more than one dish of gnocchi—little Italian potato dumplings. There is something about this toothsome, satisfying pasta that makes me want to feed it to my darlings during their times of crisis!

The recipe that follows is adapted from a penne pasta, but I love it with the gnocchi too!

6 tablespoon butter, plus more for baking dishes
Sea salt
1 pound gnocchi (Italian potato dumpling pasta)
1 teaspoon olive oil
16 ounces grilled chicken sliced thin
1/2 cup flour
2 tablespoons flour
2 tablespoons minced garlic
6 cups whole milk
10 ounces white sliced white mushrooms
1/2 cup sun dried tomatoes (in oil) sliced
1 1/2 cups shredded provolone
1 cup grated Parmesan

Preheat oven to 400 degrees F. Butter two shallow 2-quart baking dishes. Prepare pasta according to directions—but to al dente so it can be baked.

In a 5-quart Dutch oven (I prefer cast iron!), melt butter over medium. Add flour and garlic cook over medium heat for one minute, while whisking. Add milk slowly, continuing to whisk. Bring to a simmer, whisking frequently. Add mushrooms and tomatoes. Cook 1 minute. Remove from heat and stir in the provolone and 1/2 cup Parmesan.

Add chicken and pasta to pot; season with salt and pepper.

Bake, uncovered, until top is golden and bubbling, about 25 minutes. Let stand 5 minutes before serving.

Cozy Food

Casseroles

Haute dish
From *A Stitch in Time* by Monica Ferris (page 190)

After writing *A Stitch in Time*, I was challenged to come up with a recipe for a hotdish prepared by an upper-middle-class character. Hotdish is, for non-Minnesotans, casserole. And casseroles are a tasty way of getting rid of small amounts of leftover meat by stirring it in with noodles, cheese, vegetables, and a can of cream of mushroom soup, and heating it in an oven until the top browns.
When Betsy Devonshire is taken to the hospital, her friends rally around by bringing food to her apartment so she won't have to cook. Some bring fruit baskets, some bring pies, but most bring hotdish.

Patricia Fairland wants to do the right thing. At the same time, her tastes are above canned cream of mushroom soup. So, according to the novel, her hotdish consists of "shrimp, peapods, and three kinds of cheese." I have never had a hotdish containing those three ingredients; that's why it's called creative writing.

Now I am faced with a book signing at which, for publicity's sake, hotdish is going to be served. And someone challenged me to produce an example of Ms. Fairland's hotdish. After some experimenting with high-end cheeses (Patricia doesn't have American Cheese in her kitchen, either), I came up with the following:

(NOTE: amounts are estimates)
1.5 TB Butter
.5 cup Flour
1.5 cups 2% milk
.5 tsp Chopped Garlic
1.5 cups Chopped onion (Vidalia or a sweet white)
2 TB Oregano, fresh
2 TB Basil, fresh
2 cups of cooked shell macaroni
1.5 cup Shrimp (cooked, but not canned), chopped, plus 4 whole ones
.5 cup Chardonnay wine
.5 cup Peapods cut in pieces
.5 cup Havarti cheese, chopped or grated
.5 cup Irish cheddar cheese, chopped or grated
.5 cup Parmesan cheese, chopped or grated
Salt & pepper to taste

Melt the butter in a pot and work in the flour. There should be enough butter melted to absorb the flour. Add the milk and stir until the mixture begins to thicken. Add the garlic and cheese and stir until it is melted. Add the herbs, salt, and pepper, stir. Pour into casserole dish, add the other ingredients except the whole shrimp and stir well, then arrange the whole shrimp on top.

Bake in a 350 degree oven for 30 minutes.

Pasta and Casseroles

Crescent Casserole
From Faye Burner, founding member of *The Sleuth Sisters* by Maggie Pill (page 221)

Faye is a born cook who likes to tinker with recipes. This one is easy to make, pretty to look at, and yummy, with simple ingredients that don't require a trip of an exotic foods store.

2 tubes of crescent rolls
Mix together
1 cup shredded American cheese
2/3 cup cream soup (broccoli, mushroom, celery, etc.)
½ cup chopped broccoli
½ cup chopped red pepper
¼ cup chopped water chestnuts
2 tbsp. chopped onion
1 can chicken white meat (drained), OR ¾ cup cubed, cooked chicken

Spread roll dough in a circle on a baking sheet with points touching in the middle. Spoon above mixture in a circle, leaving the center empty. Pull the crescent points back and seal them to the outer edge.

Bake at 375 degrees for 20-25 minutes. Slice and serve (six people)

Casey's Chicken Comfort Casserole
From *Murder Among The Orchids* by Karen Robbins (page 224)

In *Murder Among The Orchids*, Casey, who is a household manager, finds her boss dead in his greenhouse full of orchids. What killed Mr. Popelmayer, her employer is bizarre and the list of suspects grows as Casey and her new detective friend, Max Dugan, struggle to put the clues together. Is the murderer Priscilla his present wife or the ex-wife who was supposed to be dead? His daughter, Cattelya, whose boyfriend was of questionable character? Or perhaps Garo, the son with the gambling addiction? Casey makes this casserole to keep her hands busy and feed those who drop in.
2 1/2 cups uncooked wide noodles
4-5 cups cooked chicken, diced
2 cups chicken broth
1 can cream of mushroom soup
1/4 cup pimento
Small onion diced
1/2 lb. grated cheddar cheese
Small can of mushroom pieces
Seasoned croutons or sliced almonds

Mix all ingredients together in casserole dish saving some cheese back to sprinkle on later. Bake covered at 350° F for 30 minutes stirring once. Uncover and sprinkle the rest of the cheddar cheese on top along with either the croutons or almonds. Return uncovered to oven and continue baking until cheese on top bubbles. Serves 6-8.

Cozy Food

Lazy Lobster Casserole
From the kitchen of Pamela Kelley (page 200)

This recipe is for a Lobster Casserole that our family traditionally has every Christmas Eve. It's simple and delicious, and is best made with fresh lobster. If that's not easy to come by where you live, you can substitute shrimp and/or scallops or any white flaky fish. This topping is what forms the base of many seafood stuffings at restaurants all over Cape Cod, MA where I grew up and worked during my college years.

1 pound fresh lobster meat, chopped into roughly 1 inch pieces
1 stick of butter
1 sleeve of Ritz crackers
2 tablespoons sherry (optional)
2 tablespoons chopped, fresh, flat parsley

Melt 3/4 stick of butter in a small bowl. In a medium casserole dish, place lobster, and pour half the melted butter over and stir to coat. Add Ritz crumbs and parsley to the remaining melted butter. Mix well, and then pat over top of lobster meat, until evenly coated. Cut remaining butter into small pieces and dot over top of stuffing. Drizzle sherry evenly over the top, and bake for about 25 minutes at 300 degrees.

Keisha's Noodle Casserole
From the Kelly O'Connell Mystery series by Judy Alter (page 169)

Kelly O'Connell never thought real estate was a dangerous profession. But while updating early-twentieth-century Craftsman houses in an older neighborhood in Fort Worth, Texas, she stumbles over a skeleton and begins unraveling an old murder, tracks down a serial killer, fights against a big box store in her neighborhood, and challenges a drug ring to save an abused child. Kelly's not much of a cook, but her assistant, Keisha, makes this casserole for Kelly and her two daughters.

First layer:
1 lb. ground beef
1 14 oz. can diced tomatoes
1 8 oz. can tomato sauce
2 cloves garlic, crushed in garlic press
1 tsp each sugar and salt (do not omit sugar)
Pepper to taste
Brown ground beef in skillet. Drain grease and return to skillet. Add tomatoes and tomato sauce, garlic, sugar, salt and pepper. Simmer 20 minutes, until it thickens a little. Spread in a 9 x 13 pan.

For noodle layer:
5 oz. (approximately—they don't come in this size pkg.) egg noodles
3 oz. cream cheese
1 c. sour cream
6 green onions chopped, with some of the tops included

Topping:
1½ c. grated cheddar

Cook egg noodles and drain. While the noodles are hot, stir in cream cheese, sour cream, and green onions. Spread over meat mixture. Top with grated cheddar, bake 35 minutes at 350 or until bubbly and cheese is slightly browned.

Supposed to serve 8, but you'll be lucky if you can feed six with it. Freezes well.

Ivy's Lazy-Day Casserole
From The Ivy Malone Mysteries by Lorena McCourtney (page 207)

The Ivy Malone Mysteries (*Invisible, In Plain Sight, On the Run, Stranded*) by Lorena McCourtney.

Ivy Malone never intended to be a senior sleuth, but then something she never expected happened to her. She realized she had aged into invisibility. But she quickly decides "invisibility" can be a handy asset as she sets out to solve the mysteries of the dead bodies that seem, all too often, to turn up in her life. Ivy likes to cook, but she isn't into complicated gourmet recipes, so this is one of her favorites.

1 pound ground beef
1 tsp. salt
1 (10 oz) package frozen peas, partly thawed
1 ½ cups sliced celery
3 green onions, tops included
3 oz. can of sliced mushrooms
1 can cream of mushroom soup
Couple of handfuls of potato chips, tortilla chips, or Chinese noodles (whatever you like)

Brown ground beef and salt in a skillet. Spread in a baking dish, scatter uncooked peas, celery, and green onions over the meat. Mix mushrooms and their liquid with the soup and pour over the mixture. Coarsely crush the chips and sprinkle on top. Bake 35-45 minutes at 350 degrees. Makes 4 servings.

Main Course Dishes

Chicken & Turkey

Eliza Gordon's 'Healthy' Killer Cajun Chicken Wraps
From *Dead Silent: An Eliza Gordon Mystery* (Cozy Cat Press, 2013) by Amy Beth Arkawy (page 171)

3 tablespoons Cajun seasoning
1 tablespoon flour
1 teaspoon paprika
12 oz. boneless, skinless chicken breast, cut into strips
4 medium tortillas
½ small red onion, thinly sliced
2 cups mixed filed green, arugula, spinach or your choice lettuce
4 teaspoons low fat mayonnaise or low fat Ranch dressing
1 teaspoon lemon juice
4 oz. cheese (optional); choose cheddar, American, or for extra zing pepper jack

Combine 3 tablespoons seasoning mix, flour and paprika. Season chicken with salt, pepper and dredge in seasoning mixture. Coat a large, non-stick pan with cooking spray. Over medium-high heat add chicken to pan, sautéing until fully cooked, about 1-2 minutes per side. Remove chicken from heat, set aside. Combine mayonnaise or Ranch dressing), lemon juice, and ½ teaspoon Cajun seasoning for dressing. On each tortilla, spread 1 teaspoon dressing; add onion slices and greens. Top with chicken pieces, approximately 2 per tortilla and cheese (optional) and wrap. Serves 4.

Sichuan Chicken
From *A Capital Murder* in Noir Nation: International Crime Fiction No. 4 (2014)
Submitted by Chloe Evans (page 190)

2 chicken thighs, sliced thin, marinated in:
2 tablespoons soy sauce
1 ½ tablespoons cornstarch
1 tablespoon sherry
1 teaspoon chili oil
¼ cup chopped HOT pepper
½ cup peanuts, chopped fine

Fry chicken in oil for 1 minute. Add peppers and fry 1½ minute. Combine nuts with:
1 tablespoon soy sauce
1 tablespoon sherry
½ tablespoon vinegar
1 teaspoon sesame oil
1 teaspoon sugar
¼ teaspoon salt
¼ cup water
1 teaspoon cornstarch

Add this mixture to pan and cook 2 more minutes.

Cashew Chicken
From the Bogey Man Mysteries by Marja McGraw (page 208)

In the Bogey Man Mysteries (four books in this series), Chris Cross is a dead ringer for Humphrey Bogart. He walks the walk and talks the talk, and inadvertently becomes involved in mysteries. Pamela (his wife) discovers a version of Cashew Chicken when she's injured and her mother-in-law brings it to her while she's recovering. They have a young son who frequently manages to involve himself in the mysteries, too. Even though these stories take place today, they include slang from the 1940s.

NOTE: This can be made ahead of time and refrigerated until time to bake. Don't add croutons or cashews until time to bake.

5 chicken breasts, cooked and diced
1 can sliced water chestnuts
2 cans mushroom soup (undiluted)
1 cup mayonnaise
1 tsp. lemon juice
2 cups herbed croutons

1 cup frozen peas (raw)
½ cup cashews
½ cup chicken broth, if needed

Mix all ingredients except cashews, adding chicken broth if mixture is too thick. Place in 9"x13" pan and top with cashews.

Bake at 350º until bubbly (about 30-40 minutes)

Carrie's Chicken Pie
From *A Wedding to Die For* by Radine Trees Nehring (page 214)

A Wedding to Die For. In this novel, most everyone's mind is on Carrie and Henry's wedding until attempted murder, a successful murder, a bombing, and, in the middle of it all, the birth of a baby, disrupt plans. But in the meantime Carrie wants to prove to Henry that she can prepare comfort food. So, here is her recipe.

1 16-oz bag frozen mixed vegetables
2 ready-made frozen or refrigerated pie crusts
1 can cream of chicken soup
1/4 cup milk (approximately)
2, 4 1/2 or 5 oz cans white chicken meat, cut into bite-sized pieces
1/2 tsp pepper
1/2 cup chopped onion

Heat oven to 375 degrees

Thaw frozen mixed vegetables in microwave (about three minutes). Mix all ingredients but pie crusts and milk together. Add amount of milk needed to make desired creamy consistency. Spoon mixture into bottom crust, top with second crust. Pinch edges, cut vents. Place on baking sheet in 375 degree oven and bake for 35-45 minutes, or until crust is golden brown.

Four to six servings.

Chicken with Green Olives and Cranberries
From *Bone-A-Fied Delicious with Recipes from Zinnia's Finest Chefs* by Carolyn Haines (page 194) et al.

This is a recipe I really enjoy. Since I don't eat beef or pork any more, I'm always looking for different ways to cook chicken and fish. This recipe is in Sarah Booth Delaney's section of *Bone-A-Fied Delicious, Recipes from Zinnia's Finest Chefs*. This is a cookbook I put together with my friends assuming the "voices" of my characters. It's a fund raiser for Good Fortune Farm Refuge, an animal sanctuary and spay/neuter fund that I run. The cookbook is 515 pages and over 700 recipes and can be purchased on my website www.carolynhaines.com or at www.goodfortunefarmrefuge.org

1¼ lbs. boneless, skinless chicken breasts (or thighs, if you prefer)
1 tsp. extra-virgin olive oil
1 c. chicken broth
½ c. red wine vinegar
½ c. chopped green olives

½ c. dried cranberries
Freshly ground black pepper

Wash and pat dry chicken. Heat oil in skillet over medium-high heat. Add chicken and cook until browned, about 2 minutes per side. Add broth and vinegar and bring to a simmer. Add olives and cranberries and pepper. Reduce heat to low. Cover and cook until chicken is tender and no longer pink in the center (about 15 minutes). Put chicken on plate and spoon sauce over it. Serve immediately.

Pedro's Green Chile Chicken Enchiladas
From the Charlie Parker Mystery series by Connie Shelton (page 227)

Fans of my Charlie Parker series often ask me where Pedro's restaurant in Albuquerque is located. Sorry, it's a fictional place. But that doesn't mean that you can't make Charlie's favorite dish at home. The green chile sauce is a longstanding tradition in New Mexico, and you can make it as spicy or mild as you wish, simply by using hot or mild chile. For a true New Mexican meal, serve these with margaritas and make Samantha Sweet's easy flan for dessert!

Enchiladas:
1 recipe green chile sauce, below
8 corn tortillas
1/4 c. vegetable oil
2 chicken breast halves, cooked and shredded
1/4 c. finely diced onion
1 c. shredded cheddar cheese
lettuce and tomato, chopped, for garnish
sour cream (optional)

Make the sauce and keep it warm. Heat oil in a skillet, then quickly dip each tortilla in the hot oil for a few seconds, turning once with tongs, then placing on paper towels. You want the tortilla to be soft, not crispy. Place 2-3 tablespoons shredded chicken and a sprinkling of diced onion along the center of each tortilla and roll it up. Place the rolled tortillas in a baking dish, top with the sauce and cheddar cheese. Bake at 350 degrees about 15 minutes or until cheese is melted. [Alternately, place two rolled tortillas on each dinner plate, top with sauce and cheese, and microwave 30-45 seconds to melt the cheese.]

Garnish with a dollop of sour cream and chopped lettuce and tomato. Typically, in New Mexico these would be served with refried beans and Spanish rice on the side.

Makes four servings, two enchiladas each.

Pedro's Green Chile Sauce:
1 T. shortening or vegetable oil
1/2 c. chopped onion
1 c. chopped green chile (canned is fine, any "hotness" that you like)
1 c. chicken broth
1/4 t. garlic powder
2 T. flour
1/2 t. salt (if chicken broth is salty, start with less and taste before adding the full amount)

Heat shortening in saucepan, sauté onions until glossy. Add green chile, garlic powder and chicken broth. Bring to a boil. Stir the flour into a small amount of cold water in a cup until smooth, then gradually stir the flour mixture into the boiling chile sauce. It will thicken pretty quickly. Taste, and add salt if desired.

(For an added touch, I usually add about 1/2 cup diced tomato. You can also add a little chopped leftover beef or pork.)

Simmer 15 to 20 minutes so the flavors will blend well, then serve over enchiladas, burritos or any Mexican dish that needs a sauce. Makes approximately 4 servings.

Chicken Cacciatore with Mushrooms and Olives
From the Dead Red Mystery series by R.P. Dahlke (page 183)

I'm too Busy Writing the Next Dead Red Mystery to Cook, so I use the crock pot to slow cook this savory meal and win compliments!

3 lbs boneless, skinless chicken thighs
½ cup flour
Salt and pepper to taste
3 T. olive oil
1 large red onion sliced thin or diced
1 (8 oz) can tomato sauce
1 (14 1/2 oz) can diced Italian tomatoes
½ lb sliced Portobello mushrooms (I add regular sliced mushrooms to make up the ½ lb)
1 green bell pepper finely chopped
4 cloves garlic minced
½ cup sliced black olives
¼ cup chopped celery
1 tsp kosher salt
½ cup Sangiovese wine
1 tsp crushed red pepper flakes

- Heat the olive oil in a heavy skillet.
- Combine the flour, salt and pepper in a gallon sized zip-lock bag. Add the chicken thighs and toss to thoroughly coat.
- In the skillet, brown the chicken on all sides.
- Place the sliced onions on the bottom of a large crock pot or slow cooker.
- Add the browned chicken thighs.
- Combine all the rest of the ingredients. Stir together and pour over the chicken.
- Cook on low heat 7 to 9 hours (or on high 3 to 4 hours).

Prepare your favorite pasta the way you like it (I like it also with mashed potatoes) and serve the cacciatore over it with a lovely bottle of Sangiovese (I find the Sangiovese at Fry's. It is Italian, made by Bolla).

Serves 6 people.

Main Course Dishes

Thad's Favorite Chicken
From *Maggie in White* by Sharon Burch Toner (page 232)

In *Maggie in White,* the chef, Caroline takes this dish, ready to heat up from the freezer. Not only is it easy and delicious, but it can be started early in the day and finished just as the guests arrive or, as Caroline did, make it ahead, freeze it, and have it ready in less than an hour.

8 boned and skinless chicken thighs
8 slices prosciutto
1 C Chevre (goat cheese)
1 TBSP finely chopped basil
1 TBSP finely chopped Italian parsley
1 C red wine
1 C chicken stock
2 TBSP brown sugar

Mix herbs with softened goat cheese. With a sharp knife make slits in chicken thighs to form pockets. Spoon cheese mixture into pockets of thighs. Wrap each thigh in a prosciutto slice. Secure with toothpick or string.

In large skillet bring wine and chicken stock to a boil and stir in sugar. Add chicken thighs to skillet. Simmer for about 20 minutes until chicken is tender and juices run clear. Remove chicken and set aside.

Boil sauce until reduced and thickened. Remove string/toothpicks and slice chicken. Pour sauce over to serve. Serve with quinoa or cous-cous.

Emmy Winning Chicken entree
From the Dead Red Mystery series by R.P. Dahlke (page 183)

Soap Star, Leila Standiford, cooks an Emmy Winning Chicken entree!

4 Skinless Boneless Chicken Breasts
¾ C. mayonnaise
½ C. Grated real Parmesan cheese
1 T. No salt seasoning such as Mrs. Dash
1 T. Garlic powder
Fresh Italian Parsley for garnish

- Pre-heat oven to 425F.
- Layer Chicken in shallow glass baking dish.
- Mix together mayo, Parmesan, Garlic powder and Seasoning and spread it over the chicken. Garnish with parsley.
- Bake 45 min. to an hour until brown and bubbling.
- Serves 2-4 people. Can be doubled.

Cozy Food

Pru Marlowe's chicken with mushrooms
From the Pru Marlowe Mystery series by Clea Simon (page 227)

Pru Marlowe isn't what you'd call a domestic type. In fact, she'd snarl at you for suggesting it. Still, a girl's got to eat – and a girl with a cat knows better than to try to survive on bourbon and potato chips. With that in mind, Pru's rather fond of this little recipe. And any men who come by? They can do the dishes.

1 lb. chicken thighs
1 T olive oil
2 cloves garlic, chopped
1 tea dried thyme (or a few sprigs fresh)
several cups sliced mixed mushrooms (portabello, shitake, and domestic white mushrooms make a great mix)
3 cups wine (red, white, whatever you've already opened)
½ cup dried tomatoes

In a good-sized casserole or Dutch oven, heat the olive oil and brown the chicken, remove from pan.

In the oil/chicken drippings, sauté garlic until fragrant, but not burned.

Add the mushrooms and stir, until they are nicely coated and starting to wilt.

Replace the chicken, skin side up, and dust liberally with the thyme, salt and pepper.
Add the tomatoes and then the wine.

Cover and let simmer for at least 45 minutes.

Serve over pasta or with a crusty French bread. And more wine, of course.
Serves two hungry souls.

Turkey Meatloaf
From Allison Cesario Paton (page 219)

1 lb. ground turkey
½ cup parsley, chopped
1 carrot, grated
½ teaspoon salt
A dash of ketchup
1 egg, slightly beaten
1 cup seasoned breadcrumbs
2 stalks celery, chopped fine (opt.)
1 small onion, chopped
¼ teaspoon pepper
¼ cup milk or soymilk

Preheat oven to 350 degrees. Mix together turkey, breadcrumbs, parsley, celery, carrot, onion, salt, pepper and dash of ketchup. Add egg and milk and mix well. Can be microwaved in glass dish for 10-12 minutes or bake in conventional oven 40 to 45 minute until loaf is firm to touch. Serve warm with good ol' mashed sweet or white potatoes and fresh green beans. Leftover can be refrigerated overnight, sliced, and served cold with slabs of homemade sourdough bread as a sandwich with Dijon mustard and horseradish, or just plain as a workingman's pate.

Fish & Seafood

Ted's Smoky Mountain Rosemary Trout
From *Deep Trouble* by Jean Erhardt (page 189)

From *Deep Trouble*:

My restaurant partner and sometimes best friend, Mad Ted Weber paddled up next to me and pointed out a large trout that was jumping out ahead of us. The fish shot up out of the middle of the river maybe three more times, wriggling in the air like he was saying hello.

"I feel like grilling tonight," Ted said, gliding alongside in his inner tube, sipping beer. "Fresh rosemary stuffed trout, white beans with lemon and spoon bread, enjoyed with a chilled, stony Chablis."

"I love it when you talk dirty." I was already smelling the outdoorsy aroma of trout sputtering on the grill.

"Who said you were invited?"

"Who else would come?"

"Good point."

2 tablespoons extra-virgin olive oil
4 whole dressed trout (about 10 ounces each), head and tail on
8 sprigs fresh rosemary
2 shallots, thinly sliced
2 lemons, sliced into 1/4-inch-thick rounds
Coarse salt and freshly ground pepper
Nonstick cooking spray

Brush trout with olive oil. Stuff rosemary sprigs and lemon slices inside of the fish. Season to taste with salt and pepper.

Preheat a grill to medium-high. Spray a grill basket large enough to hold 4 fish with nonstick cooking spray. Arrange fish in grill basket.

Grill until just cooked through and firm to the touch, 5 to 7 minutes per side.

Serves 4.

Cozy Food

Bob's Shrimp Etouffe`
From *Deadly Reunion* in the Cealie Gunther series by June Shaw (page 226)

3 lbs. chopped onions
1/3 block of butter or margarine
1/3 C. vegetable oil
1 t. salt
1 t. black pepper
½ t. corn starch
1 ½ lbs. medium shrimp
In a heavy pot combine all ingredients except corn starch and shrimp. Cook over medium heat until onions caramelize. (About ½ - 2/3 hr.) Add shrimp and corn starch. Cook until shrimp are pink and look done, about 20 minutes. Eat in a plate over cooked rice. Feeds 6 to 8. So good it'll make you want to slap your mamma!

Annapolis Fish Stew
From the Hannah Ives Mystery series by Marcia Talley (page 231)

When Annapolitan and sleuth, Hannah Ives is in the mood for crab cakes, she goes to McGarveys; when she hankers after traditional Irish stew, it's Galway Bay. But, when the wind blows cold off the Chesapeake Bay and fish stew is on the menu, Hannah takes a brisk walk down Prince George Street to City Dock, where sea-going vessels have docked for centuries and where, since 1788, the Market House has been providing "all accommodations necessary for the reception and sale of provisions." After warming her hands on a cappuccino at City Dock Coffee, Hannah heads for the Annapolis Fish Market to select fresh fish for her popular stew.

8 cups water
3 medium potatoes, peeled, cut into ¼ in. cubes
3 medium turnips, cut into ¼ in. cubes
4 large carrots, cut into ¼ in. cubes
3 medium or 2 large leeks, thinly sliced (both white and green parts), thoroughly rinsed in cold water
2 celery stalks, thinly sliced (including tops)
2 pounds any firm-fleshed ocean fish such as grouper, cod, halibut, porgy or whiting, cut into 2 inch chunks
4 generous sprigs fresh cilantro (coriander) chopped
1 tsp. black pepper
½ tsp. salt or to taste

Put water and vegetables in a large pot, bring to boil and simmer for 10 minutes. Add fish and seasonings and simmer for 30 minutes more. Serve topped with garlic bread crumbs, if desired. Delicious with white rice.

Makes 6 – 8 servings.

The author says if she doubles the recipe, it'd be enough to serve all twelve co-conspirators in her wild and wacky serial novels, *Naked Came the Phoenix* and *I'd Kill for That.*

Main Course Dishes

Tilapia Baked with Shrimp Sauce

From Chef Victor Cirrincione, Riderwood Village, thanks to Eileen Haavik McIntire (page 209)

Eileen Haavik McIntire's 90s Club mystery series features 90-year-olds at Whisperwood Retirement Village in central West Virginia. Whisperwood is like many retirement villages around the country offering a lifestyle and amenities similar to living on a cruise ship, including excellent dinners every night of the week. The 90s Club at Whisperwood might look forward to this tasty dish in their dining room, but it comes from Chef Victor Cirrincione at Riderwood in Silver Spring, MD. The recipe is scaled down to serve four.

1 lb. Tilapia filet, skinless, fresh or frozen
1 tsp. Chardonnay wine
1 oz. margarine or butter blend
2 ½ tsps. ground paprika
Parlsey flakes to taste
¾ cup + 1 Tbsp. heavy whipping cream
1 ½ tsps. shrimp soup base, no MSG
1 tsp. canned tomato paste
2 ½ tsps. cornstarch
1 Tbsp. sherry wine
6 ¾ oz. shrimp, tails off, steamed.
1 ½ tsps. lemon juice

Place thawed fish in a 2" deep pan.
Combine white wine and melted butter and ladle over fish.
Sprinkle paprika and parsley over fish.
Bake uncovered at 350 degrees F. for about 8 to 10 minutes, ensuring that an internal temperature of 145 degree F. has been reached. Keep hot until ready to serve.

For sauce: Heat cream to a low boil and add the shrimp base. Allow this to come to a boil. Thicken with mixture of cornstarch and sherry, stirring until consistency is thick and smooth. Stir in steamed shrimp and lemon juice. Keep hot until served.

To serve: Place 1 piece of fish on dish and ladle sauce on top.
Yield: 4 servings.

Eggplant Supreme à la Bob

From *Deadly Reunion*, the first book in the Cealie Gunther mystery series by June Shaw (page 226)

Spunky widow Cealie Gunther wants to rediscover herself, but her hunky lover Gil Thurman opens "Seafood Delights" Cajun restaurants wherever she travels. And Cealie is horrible at avoiding tempting dishes and men.

During her journey, she discovers and needs to solve murders before she and some people she loves become the killers' next victims.

4 eggplants
1 lg. onion chopped
½ lg. bell pepper chopped
2 cloves garlic minced

Cozy Food

2 T. cooking oil
1 lb. crabmeat
1 lb. small shrimp
1 c. seasoned breadcrumbs
salt and pepper to taste
melted butter or margarine

Heat oven to 350°. Cut eggplants in half and parboil 25–30 minutes. Carefully remove pulp of the eggplants with a spoon so as not to break the skin. Set the skin aside on a shallow baking pan. Mix cooking oil, eggplant pulp, onions, bell pepper, and garlic in a heavy pot and sauté about 20 minutes. Add crabmeat, shrimp, and salt and pepper. Cook 20 minutes more. Fill eggplant shells with the cooked mixture. Top with bread crumbs and drizzle melted butter on top. Bake until topping is brown. Will serve 8 happy people.

Vegetarian

Rory's Spinach and Mushroom Quiche
From *To Sketch a Thief* by Sharon Pape (page 218)

In book two of my Portrait in Crime mystery series, *To Sketch a Thief*, Rory is having her family over for their first dinner in her new home. Although most people hosting a dinner might be worried about the food turning out okay, Rory has two bigger concerns. Will Hobo, the huge, furry mutt she adopted when his owner was murdered, and federal marshal Zeke Drummond, the ghost who shares her house, turn the evening into a crazy free-for-all?

Rory is making her Spinach and Mushroom Quiche as a side dish. She loves this recipe, because all the flavors are so well-balanced. Plus, it's easy to make.

One 9" frozen, unbaked, deep dish pie crust
One 10oz. package frozen spinach, cooked and well drained
One large can slice mushroom, well drained
8 oz. shredded Swiss cheese
1/2 cup mayonnaise
1/2 cup milk
2 eggs, beaten
2Tbsp. flour

1. Preheat oven to 350 degrees.
2. Take pie crust out of the freezer and set aside.
3. Combine all the ingredients in a large bowl and mix together.
4. Pour the mixture into the pie crust.
5. Bake for 40-45 minutes or until it is set (no longer wet in the center.)
6. Allow to cool for 20-30 minutes. Serves 8-10 as a side dish.

TIP: the secret to this recipe is draining the spinach and mushrooms extremely well. Using a sieve to press the liquid out of the cooked spinach helps.

This quiche also works well as a main dish for lunch or brunch, along with salad or soup. Serves 4-6.

Nichelle's Pasta Pomodoro
From the Headlines in High Heels Mysteries by LynDee Walker (page 234)

When crime reporter Nichelle Clarke has time to cook, pasta and veggies is a comfort-food favorite. This easy dish is heavenly with farm-fresh summer tomatoes.

10 oz. package of thin spaghetti or angel hair pasta
4 cups chopped fresh tomatoes
Olive oil spray
3 T fresh or freeze-dried basil
2 cloves fresh garlic, minced
1 cup shredded parmesan cheese

Prepare the pasta according to package directions. While it cooks, spray a large skillet with olive oil and let it heat for about 2 minutes. Pour in tomatoes, garlic, and basil. Cook over medium heat, stirring constantly until the tomatoes partially reduce to form a light sauce (5-10 minutes, there should still be chunks of tomato in the pan). Drain pasta and toss with sauce. Top with cheese and serve.

Vegetarian Meatballs
From *Dying for a Clue* by Judy Fitzwater (page 191)

My sleuth, Jennifer Marsh, is a vegetarian. In one of my books, *Dying for a Clue*, she makes chicken and dumplings without chicken for a church supper. Technically, I suppose that's just dumplings, but it's a funny scene. I'm not a vegetarian, but I have several friends who are and that sometimes makes cooking for them a challenge. I have a couple of really good recipes stashed away for dinners to serve them. When I was writing my cooking column for a weekly newspaper in rural North Carolina, I interviewed local residents, wrote up brief bios for each of them, and featured their favorite recipes. One lady, a vegetarian, gave me this recipe for Vegetarian Meatballs. They really do taste like meatballs, and if you don't tell the meat eaters they're vegetarian, they'll never know. Yummy! The sauce I use over them is to-die-for and can be used over real meatballs, as well.

3 eggs, beaten
1 clove garlic
¼ cup quick oats
½ cup chopped pecans
1 medium onion, chopped
2/3 cup shredded cheese (Cheddar or your favorite variety)
4 slices bread, broken up (Remove the crusts and put them in the toaster for a few seconds to dry them out a bit)
½ tsp. salt

Mix together all ingredients and form into balls. (This can be messy, but hang in there. The results are worth it.) Brown in a lightly greased skillet. Place in a baking dish. Top with sauce. Bake for 30 minutes at 350 degrees.

The Best Meatball Sauce Ever:
¾ cup ketchup
½ cup water
¼ cup vinegar

1/3 cup packed brown sugar
1 ½ Tbsps. minced onions
1 tsp. prepared mustard
Salt to taste
4 tsps. Worcestershire Sauce
6 drops Tabasco

Mix all ingredients together and pour over browned vegetarian meatballs or cooked meatballs. If using real meatballs, cook for 30 minutes in single layer at 350 degrees, then cover in sauce and bake for 30 more minutes.

Beef & Pork

Stabbed Kabobs
From the Leigh Girard Mystery series by Gail Lukasik (page 204)

Intrepid reporter Leigh Girard lives in the resort community of Door County, Wisconsin, where to the chagrin of the local police, her ability to solve murders is as unfailing as a Saturday night fish boil. Admittedly not much of a cook, in a pinch, Leigh has been known to whip up a tasty kabob. After a long day of hunting down murderers, she finds stabbing meat with sharp, pointy skewers very therapeutic. Here's the recipe Leigh uses.

1½ pounds of beef. You can substitute shrimp for the beef or use both.
4 medium onions quartered
2 peppers cut in 1½ inch squares
Cherry tomatoes
½ pound medium sized mushrooms.

NOTE: Leigh strongly suggests you buy the mushrooms from a grocery store. As she discovered in her first book, *Destroying Angels*, even seasoned mycologists sometimes make mistakes when gathering mushrooms in the woods.

Sauce:
½ cup lemon juice
½ cup olive oil
¼ teaspoon salt
¼ teaspoon pepper
¼ teaspoon garlic powder
½ teaspoon oregano

Marinate meat and vegetable for ½ hour in the sauce. Then alternate meat and/or shrimp on skewers. Push meat close together if you want juicy meat and leave spaces between if you want crisp and well-done meat. Cook 10-30 minutes over grill, depending on desired degree of doneness. Serves four.

Jillybean's Tacos

From the Edna Davies mystery series by Suzanne Young (page 238)

When Edna visits her son in Colorado, she is troubled that her daughter-in-law doesn't seem to enjoy Edna's dinners. When she realizes that New England recipes simply are too bland for someone used to the flavors of Mexico and the southwestern United States, Edna encourages her eight-year-old granddaughter Jillian (nicknamed "Jillybean") to teach her how to make spicier dishes.

1 pkg taco shells (12 count)
1 lb. lean hamburger
1 pkg dry taco seasoning
3/4 cup water
1 medium tomato, diced
1 1/2 cups shredded iceberg lettuce
1 1/2 cups shredded cheddar cheese
1 small onion, coarsely chopped (optional)
2/3 cup guacamole or avocado slices (optional)
Sour cream (optional)

In a medium frying pan, brown the hamburger and drain. Add the taco seasoning and water. Cook, stirring often, until the mixture thickens, approximately 5 minutes.

Divide the hamburger mixture among the taco shells, top with diced tomato, shredded lettuce and cheese -- and other toppings, as desired.

Suggested option: For vegetarian tacos, heat a can of refried beans to use instead of hamburger. Serves 4.

Tacos Buenos

From the kitchen of Melissa Bourbon Ramirez (page 222)

These tacos are not only tasty, they stretch the meat, thereby helping your budget. Whether our budget needs stretching or not, we make our tacos like this because they are just too good not to.

Tacos:
1 pound ground beef
3 potatoes, chopped
3 carrots, chopped
3 cloves garlic, minced
3 tomatoes, finely chopped (or tomato sauce)
1/2 onion, finely chopped
1 1/2 tsp salt, to taste
1/4 – 1/2 tsp cumin
1/4 bunch cilantro, chopped, for garnish (optional)

Brown beef in large frying pan. Remove and drain excess fat. In same frying pan, sauté onion and garlic until onion is translucent, about 5 minutes. Return meat to pan. Add potatoes, tomatoes (or tomato sauce), carrots, salt, and dash of pepper. Cover and simmer for about 20 minutes, or until potatoes are tender.

Cozy Food

Taco Shells:
Heat oil in a frying pan. Fry desired amount of corn tortillas, using tongs to create a taco shell shape. Drain on paper towels.

To Serve:
Fill each taco with meat/potato filling. Top with:
Parmesan cheese
Shredded Jack or Cheddar cheese
Sour Cream
Lettuce
Tomatoes

Shepherd's Pie
From the Bad Hair Day mystery series by Nancy J. Cohen (page 182)

Marla Vail is a hairstylist and salon owner who solves crimes in between cutting and coloring her customers' hair. She lives in South Florida where passions ignite under sultry temperatures and wackos move down for the warmth. Warming Marla's life is her new husband and his teenage daughter in the latest title, *Hanging By A Hair*. This means cooking meals fit for a family. Here's one of the recipes Marla might make for dinner.

2 lb. prepared garlic mashed potatoes
8 oz. sliced mushrooms
2 Tablespoon olive oil
1 to 1-1/2 lb. lean ground beef
1 medium onion, chopped
1 Tablespoon chopped garlic
2 Tablespoon flour
12 oz. jar Heinz fat-free beef gravy or any leftover gravy
1/4 cup chopped fresh parsley
½ teaspoon dried marjoram
14-1/2 oz. can peas and carrots, drained
1 Tablespoon Worcestershire sauce
4 oz. shredded cheddar cheese

Microwave potatoes as directed but omit adding milk or butter. In heavy large skillet, sauté mushrooms in oil and remove when wilted. Add beef, onion, and garlic to same skillet and cook on medium high heat until beef is browned. Add flour and stir. Add mushrooms, gravy, parsley, marjoram, peas and carrots, and Worcestershire sauce. Simmer until mixed through. Transfer beef mixture into 9-inch square greased baking dish. Spoon mashed potatoes over beef layer. Sprinkle with cheddar cheese. Bake at 350 degrees for 15 minutes or until bubbly. Serves 4-6.

Suspenseful Camp Stew
From the Working Stiff Mystery series by Kerri Nelson (page 214)
(recipe created by Kerri's hubby named Stu)

Mandy Murrin is a small town girl from Millbrook, Alabama and she loves to eat. Good thing she's back home where good meals are readily provided by her interesting neighbor Ms. Lanier. This creation of delicious meats and veggies is full of savory goodness to entice your senses and satisfy your belly. And while there are many different variations of this recipe, I think most locals will agree that this is a creation indigenous to the River Region of Alabama. Second heapin' helpins' are **not** optional!

1 lb. smoked pulled pork, chopped fine (We use a Dixie Butt—them Yankees call it a Boston Butt!)
1 average sized chicken breast, cooked through and chopped fine
29 oz. can tomatoes petite diced (undrained)
½ cup water
15 oz. can of whole kernel corn (undrained)
15 oz. can of lima beans (undrained)
1 large or 2 medium potatoes (peeled and diced small/petite)
½ cup of ketchup
2 oz. Worcestershire sauce
½ tsp. black pepper
½ tsp. crushed red pepper
1 Tbsp. Tabasco (or hot sauce of your choice)
1½ Tbsp. brown sugar
¼ bag of frozen cut okra (optional)

Combine all ingredients in a Dutch oven and cover. The amount of ketchup and Worcestershire noted above is approximate and can be adjusted to taste, but a guideline is that upon mixing the stew it should attain a slightly red color—use too little and the stew will have something of a gray pallor. Cook over medium or medium low heat for 1 to 1½ hours minimum. Stir every 5-10 minutes and re-cover promptly. Potatoes should be cooked though. If you'd prefer the stew thicker, remove the stew from heat following cook time and leave the cover off for 15 minutes or so to thicken. Serve with Saltine crackers. Serves 6-8.

Pork Tangine
From the Regan McHenry Mystery series by Nancy Lynn Jarvis (page 199)

Most of what Realtor and foodie Regan McHenry cooks doesn't take long to prepare—she has to be quick what with after-dinner listing presentations and responding to phone calls that may put her in peril—but you'd never know it with this dish; it's good enough for company dinner.

One rack of pork ribs cut into individual pieces with a bone in each piece.
1 cup beef or vegetable broth
½ cup dried peaches cut into one inch chunks
½ cup dried cherries
1 bunch scallions chopped. (Include some very tender green parts as well as the white part)
4 small sweet red or orange peppers chopped in large chunks
½ tsp cinnamon
1 tsp. cumin
½ tsp turmeric
¼ ginger

Brown ribs in a dry pan over medium-high heat. Add beef broth, dried peaches and cherries, scallions and sweet peppers and spices. Cover and cook over medium heat until pork is cooked through, adding water if ingredients become dry. Best served with cous-cous or rice. Serves 4.

Cozy Food

Schnitz und Knepp (Ham with Dried Apples and Dumplings)
From *Assaulted Pretzel* by Laura Bradford (page 178)

In *Assaulted Pretzel* (book 2 in my Amish Mysteries), Claire Weatherly has heard so much about the Amish dish, Schnitz and Knepp, that she can't wait to try some at the annual Amish Food Festival in Heavenly, PA. Unfortunately, before she can try some, English toymaker, Rob Karble, is murdered right in the middle of the festival and Claire finds herself in full-blown sleuth-mode.

Here's what she missed out on (at least until the end of the book)...

Ham with Dried Apples:
3 pounds smoked ham with bone
4 cups dried tart apples (*see notes below*)
3 tablespoons brown sugar
1 large onion, finely chopped

Dumplings:
2 cups sifted all-purpose flour
1/4 teaspoon salt
4 teaspoons baking powder
3 tablespoons unsalted butter
1 large egg, beaten
1/2 to 2/3 cup milk

In a large pot, cover ham with cold water. Bring to boil, reduce and simmer for 2 hours or until ham is tender. Meanwhile, put apples in bowl and cover with water. Soak for at least 2 hours. Remove ham from bone and cut into medium pieces. Return ham to pot. Add apples with most of apple liquid. Add brown sugar and onion. Cover and simmer for 30 minutes.

For dumplings, sift or whisk together sifted flour, salt and baking powder. Cut in butter with two knives or pastry cutter. Stir in egg. Gradually add enough milk to make a moist, fairly stiff dough, gently stirring just enough to bring it together. Drop dough by tablespoons into simmering stew. Cover tightly and simmer for 12-15 minutes, or until dumplings are done. Serve immediately. This serves 6 to 8.

Veggies and Side Dishes

Sweet Potato Casserole with Pecan Topping
From *Bitter Chocolate*, book 2 of the Hot Chocolate cozy mystery series by Dawn Greenfield Ireland (page 197) and consumed by the Alcott characters in the story.

Lila Mae Alcott, the middle-aged chocolate heiress of Houston's River Oaks, can't believe it when Amelia, her house manager and cook returns from the grocery store on her day off to find a dead body on the kitchen floor. The entire Alcott clan rushes to Amelia's house and are shocked when they discover the identity of the murder victim. Great food soothes the nerves while the mystery is solved.

4 cups peeled and chopped sweet potatoes
1/2 cup sugar
2 eggs, beaten
1/2 teaspoon salt
4 tablespoons soft butter
1/2 cup milk
1/2 teaspoon organic vanilla extract

For topping:
1/2 cup brown sugar, packed
1/3 cup flour
3 tablespoons soft butter
1/2 cup chopped pecans

Preheat oven to 325 degrees F (165 degrees C). Boil sweet potatoes until tender. Drain and mash. In a large bowl mix together the remaining ingredients (NOT the topping) until smooth. Place in a 9 x 13 greased baking dish.

In a medium bowl, mix the brown sugar and flour. Cut in the butter until the mixture looks like little pea-sized clumps. If you do not have a pastry cutter, try taking two butter knives and running them through the mix until the butter is completely cut into the flour/sugar mix. Stir in the pecans. Sprinkle the mix over the casserole. Bake for 30 minutes or until the topping is lightly brown.

If you have leftovers, you must have done something wrong. We practically had our heads in the casserole dish! I plan to double the recipe next time.

Perfectly Pleasing Popovers
From Allison Cesario Paton (page 219)

3 TBSP butter
1 cup all-purpose flour
1 cup milk
1 teaspoon salt
2 eggs

Preheat oven to 400 degrees. Divide the butter between six 6-ounce greased custard cups and put those on a metal tray into the oven to melt the butter.

Meanwhile, in specific order in the blender: first the milk, flour and salt, then the eggs, until all is smooth; do not overbeat. Remove the pan of cups; quickly fill each custard cup 1/2 full.

Bake for exactly 40 minutes. Immediately remove from cups and serve piping hot in a warmed dish-cloth napkin-lined basket, covering the steaming popovers….enjoy!

Ivy's Parsnip Pie
From *The Blackwoods Farm Enquiry* by Ann Purser (page 221)

Ivy Beasley's Parsnip pie: This is a favourite of Ivy Beasley, elderly sleuth and resident, recently married, in Springfields Luxury Home in Barrington, Suffolk. She has recently married for the first time, and is living in blissful marital state with husband Roy. Her series of books, Ivy Beasley's Enquiries, most recent *The Blackwoods Farm Enquiry*, is about to be/already is published, and her friend Lois Meade (series Lois Meade Mysteries) has a new addition 'Scandal at Six'.

The recipe was handed down from Ivy's rather dreadful mother, and has been voted Best Recipe in Springfields annual competition.

Ivy says it is adaptable, and you can use cream instead of milk, and for the faint-hearted, use butter liberally in the parsnip puree.

4 medium sized parsnips
full cream milk
1 large egg
2 ozs fresh butter
4 ozs Cheddar (or similar) cheese
Salt, pepper to taste

Prepare 8" pastry flan case: 4 ozs flour (plain or SR) Roy prefers the pastry made with Self Raising flour. Lighter, he says.

2 ozs butter or healthier buttery fat
Salt
Ice cold water to mix

Peel and cube parsnips and boil until soft, add butter.
Mash with fork, but do not process. When thick and smooth-ish, mix in milk (or cream), grated cheese, beaten egg (beaten with a fork or whisk), salt and pepper. The mixture should not be sloppy, and not too smooth. Spoon mixture into flan case and place in a medium to hot oven, for thirty minutes or when the top should be a golden yellow. Ivy says she always finishes it off by placing it on the floor of the oven to thoroughly cook the pastry base.

I say to her that she has split an infinitive, and she says that next time she cooks parsnip pie, I'd better watch out. She also says she never weighs or measures her ingredients, but goes by the look of the thing. However, she hopes the above will suffice.

Ivy has figured in all three of my crime novels, The Round Ringford stories of village life; the Lois Meade Mysteries, and last but not least, the Ivy Beasley Enquiries. Ivy and Roy, together with Gus and Deirdre, these last two younger members of the team, have solved some interesting cases, and I am sure one of these days all four are going to turn up at my front door and demand an explanation.

Buttermilk Gnocchi
From Mina's Adventure series by Maria Grazia Swan (page 229)

Mina Calvi, twenty-something Italian transplant to California may not know how to cook, but she sure likes to eat. When she visits her home town in Veneto, Italy, she decides to change all that, and what better way to do it than trying out new foods?

You won't find recipes in my books, not until Mina gets serious about cooking, that doesn't mean we don't talk home cooked Italian food. This is a regional recipe from the province of Vicenza. It is so regional that the main ingredient Fioretta* could not be found in Arizona so I substitute with Buttermilk. Therefore, instead of Gnocchi con la Fioretta* we will call this Buttermilk Gnocchi.

Gnocchi (dumplings):
3 cups of flour
3 cups of buttermilk (I use low fat)

Cozy Food

Sauce:
1 stick on unsalted butter (8tbsp)
10 sage leaves (fresh) washed
¼ teaspoon of nutmeg

Stir together flour and buttermilk to smooth consistency, like a custard.

In a large pot boil 4/5 quarts of water, salt to taste. When the water is boiling drop teaspoons of the buttermilk mixture, one at the time. When they float back to the surface they are done. Scoop them up and drain them well in a colander. Serve with the butter sauce and a sprinkle of Parmesan cheese.

Sauce. Melt the butter in a saucepan, drop the sage and the nutmeg, and let the butter brown and the leaves turn crisp before spooning over gnocchi. Enjoy.

*Fioretta is the watery milk left after the making of Ricotta and must be used right away.

Sweet Potato Casserole
From Marilyn Levinson (page 203)

I always make this sweet potato casserole for Thanksgiving. It's tasty, and a big favorite with my family. What's more, it's basically healthy. For Passover, I use matzoh meal instead of bread crumbs. This year my son's girlfriend told her mom to get the recipe from me.

Cut up 4-6 medium sized sweet potatoes and cook in microwave until soft.
When cool, remove skin and mash sweet potatoes.

Add and mix well with sweet potatoes:
3 eggs, beaten
1/4 cup of bread crumbs
2 teaspoons of vanilla
1 teaspoon of dried parsley
1/2 teaspoon of paprika
1 teaspoon of cinnamon
2 tablespoons of brown sugar
1/2 cup of melted butter
1 teaspoon of onion powder
1/4 cup dried cranberries (optional)
1/4 cup of cut up dried apricots (optional)
salt and pepper to taste

Pour into greased casserole and sprinkle sliced almonds on top.
Bake in 350 degree oven for 30-45 minutes.

Roasted Vegetables
From the Regan McHenry Real Estate Mystery series Nancy Lynn Jarvis (page 199)

Regan McHenry would love to spend time in her garden, but being an active Realtor and amateur sleuth keeps her busy. She settles for growing citrus trees and deer-proof rosemary and lavender. She grows basic herbs in a protected kitchen garden, too.

1 small sweet white onion quartered
1 bunch broccoli broken into florets
½ head of cauliflower broken into florets
1 red bell pepper sliced into stripes
Carrots, preferably baby (if using big carrots, cut into chunks no longer than three inches and no thicker than ½ inch)
Seasonally, you can also add fresh turnips, beets, zucchini, baby red potatoes all cut to ½ inch thickness
2 Tbls olive oil
Juice from 2 Meyer lemons
2 tsp fresh rosemary
1 clove garlic, minced
¼ tsp salt
¼ tsp pepper
Chopped fresh parsley and basil to taste

Preheat oven to 375 degrees. Wash, dry, and prepare vegetables you have selected. Place them in a bowl and toss with oil, lemon juice, rosemary, garlic, salt and pepper. Arrange on in a single layer on a baking sheet and save any leftover olive oil mixture. Roast in oven for 20 to 30 minutes or until crisp-tender. Remove and put in a bowl, top with parsley, basil and leftover olive oil mixture. Toss and serve. Refrigerated leftovers are good thrown into a salad the next day. Serves 4.

Yorkshire Pudding
From the Kate Shackleton 1920s mystery series by Frances Brody (page 178)

This savoury dish is traditionally served as part of Sunday dinner. Being a true Yorkshire woman, Kate's housekeeper will serve Yorkshire pudding with onion gravy before the main meal. This will surprise Kate's visitors from other parts of England, where the pudding would be on the same plate as the main course of meat and two veg. Serves 4.

4 oz plain or self-raising flour
¼ teaspoon of salt
1 egg
½ pint of milk

Sieve flour and salt into a basin, make a well in the centre, add the egg and begin mixing, adding the milk gradually. Continue stirring the dry flour and add the milk until a smooth batter results. Beat hard for about 5 minutes to break all lumps and to introduce as much air as possible. Stir in the remainder of the milk. Leave the batter to stand for half an hour. Prepare a shallow baking tin (8¾ x 6 inches). Put ½ ounce of dripping, lard or vegetable fat into the tin and heat until it gives off blue smoke. Stir batter thoroughly. For a good result, it should be the consistency of single cream, so you may need to add more milk. Pour all the mixture into the tin, alternatively, half fill small tins.

Bake on the second shelf of a hot oven, 230°C, 450°F, Gas mark 8 for about 30 minutes for a large pudding, 20 minutes for smaller ones.

Cozy Food

Cheddar Green Onion Biscuits
From the Imogene Duckworthy series by Kaye George (page 192)

Imogene's Uncle Huey is running Huey's Hash in Saltlick, TX, as the first book opens. The biscuits that Clem, Huey's excellent cook, makes bring people in from the surrounding towns of Cowtail and Bootstrap. When Immy quits as one of his waitresses, she's thrilled that she can branch out and do something else, but her mother doesn't see it that way. Nor does Huey. Unfortunately, Huey meets his maker early in the book and the fate of the diner is unsettled. But this biscuit recipe lives on.

2 1/4 c. Bisquick
6 T. butter, chopped coarsely
1 1/2 t. minced garlic
6 oz. grated sharp cheddar cheese
3 green onions (or scallions) chopped finely
1 c. buttermilk

Cut butter into Bisquick until the texture of coarse crumbs. Stir in cheese, onions, and garlic. Add buttermilk and stir just enough to mix. Do not overmix.
Drop onto greased cookie sheet or pizza stone by heaping teaspoonsful.
Bake at 400 degrees for 15-18 minutes or until golden brown.
Makes nearly 4 dozen.

Optional: Add 4 oz. coarsely chopped green chili or jalapeno peppers.

adapted by Kaye George from
http://www.mysisterskitchenonline.com/2006/07/06/cheddargreen-onion-biscuits/

Hot Rice
From The Jennifer Marsh Mysteries by Judy Fitzwater (page 191)

Hi, I'm Judy Fitzwater and I love a good mystery. I also love to eat. My first paid writing gig was doing a food column for a weekly newspaper—and covering superior court. Food and mystery—two of my favorite things. So when I started to get serious about fiction, I created a Southern heroine, Jennifer Marsh, who is a part-time caterer and an aspiring mystery writer who finds herself being drawn into the real world of murder and mayhem. Jennifer's kept me close to my Southern roots. I adore homemade biscuits and gravy, cheese grits, banana pudding—all those heavenly, bad-for-you things my mother used to cook. I'm sharing a favorite rice recipe with you that my whole family loves. It's spicy and delicious!

1 cup rice
Chicken broth
1 cup sour cream (lite is fine.)
1 ½ Tbsps. pickled jalapeno peppers, seeded and minced
1 ½ Tbsps. jalapeno juice
1/3 cup creamy Italian or ranch dressing
8 oz. shredded Monterey Jack cheese
Paprika

Cook rice according to package directions substituting chicken broth for the water. Combine all ingredients except cheese. Pour half of the mixture into a greased 2-quart casserole dish. Top with half the cheese. Add the rest of the rice mixture and top with remaining cheese. Sprinkle with paprika. Bake uncovered at 350 degrees for 30 minutes. (For a less spicy flavor, reduce peppers and juice to 1 Tbsp. each.) This dish freezes well. 8 servings. Enjoy!

Spicey Dicey Onion Rings
From Out of the Frying Pan by Ellie Marks and Kelly Klepfer (page 202)

Zula Hopkins, sister-in-law to Fern, lives life to the fullest. Full volume, full color spectrum and full on senses and usually all at the same time. Zula can whip up a dinner party better than most folks can boil water. Clues explode, hearts pitter-patter, and tensions soar during a dinner party where these little gems were served.

1/3 Cup garbanzo bean flour (besan)
1/3 Cup water (use 1/4 cup and add a 1/2 TBSP at a time until you get consistency for the batter you want, you may need less)
1/2 TBSP lemon pepper or lemon garlic blend or lemon peel/fried garlic
1/4 teaspoon sea salt (additional for cooked rings if desired)
1 1/2 teaspoon garlic powder
1 1/2 teaspoon of dried parsley
1/2 TBSP brown or yellow mustard
1/2 TBSP lemon juice
1 1/2 teaspoon of siracha sauce or pepper sauce of choice

Combine dry ingredients until well mixed, add 1/4 cup of water to the wet ingredients and stir into the dry. Add more water if needed. You don't want watery nor so thick it's gooey. Just dippable.

Slice a medium onion.

Heat oil on a stove top or in a deep fryer. When hot add the dipped rings. When the rings are golden either flip if you don't have enough oil to cover the top of the onions or remove and place on paper towels to absorb the grease. Sprinkle with salt if desired. (serves 2 - 4)

Roasted Red Peppers
From *Killer Surf* by Chris Forman (page 191)

This is a favorite of Ian Wallace, the kilt wearing food writer who keeps getting involved solving murders.

Take a few nice red peppers and wash them. Put them on the grill at high heat and cook, turning so that all sides get cooked, until the skin is blackened. Put them in a paper bag and close them up. Let them sit until cool, about thirty-minutes. At this point the skin will just come off with your fingers. Slice to the size you want and use them in salads, on burgers, or as a side dish. You can also add some olive oil and garlic to them.

Cozy Food

Desserts and Pies

Desserts

Bribe Your Best Buddy French Chocolate Mousse
From the Cue Ball Mysteries by Cindy Blackburn (page 175)

Got a chore you need help with? A garden to plant, a room to paint, a cat that needs babysitting while you're on vacation? Bribe your favorite chocoholic buddy with this to-die-for dessert. Jessie Hewitt, who can barely change a light bulb without written instructions, makes this mousse anytime she needs help from her favorite chocoholic friend, Karen Sembler. Handy that Karen lives in the condo downstairs. Also handy that Karen is so handy. The woman can fix anything. She comes running (tool belt on hips) anytime Jessie promises mousse.

6 ounces bittersweet chocolate, chopped
3 Tablespoons unsalted butter
3 large eggs, separated (this recipe uses raw eggs, so please don't serve to elderly people or children!)
1/2 teaspoon cream of tartar
1/4 cup plus 2 tablespoons sugar
1/2 cup heavy cream
1/2 teaspoon vanilla

Melt chocolate and butter in a double boiler. Remove from heat and let cool slightly. Then whisk the egg yolks into the chocolate mixture, 1 at a time, whisking until smooth after each addition.

While chocolate melts, in another bowl, beat the egg whites until foamy. Add cream of tartar and beat until soft peaks form. Gradually beat in 1/4 cup sugar and continue beating until stiff peaks form.

Rinse off beaters and in yet another bowl, beat the heavy cream until it begins to thicken up. Add remaining 2 tablespoons sugar and vanilla and continue beating until the cream holds soft peaks.

Now that you've got each step prepared, put it all together. Using a spatula, gently fold the chocolate mixture into the egg whites/meringue. Then fold in the whipped cream. Don't overwork the mousse, but make sure all the chocolate from the bottom of the bowl gets incorporated.

Divide the mousse into 6 of your prettiest dessert cups. Cover and refrigerate 4 hours. Your helpful buddy whom you're bribing for favors will want to lick her dessert cup clean! As with ALL of Jessie's recipes, serve with champagne.

Dark Chocolate Torte with Grand Marnier
From *Maggie's Ghost* by Sharon Burch Toner (page 232)

At the conclusion of *Maggie's Ghost*, Maggie hosts a come one, come all housewarming party. She has the party food catered, but she and her neighbor, Lulu make the dessert - four of the following tortes:

12 sinfully delicious servings

2 2/3 cups semisweet chocolate chips (16 ounces), divided
1 cup (2 sticks) salted butter, divided
1/4 cup unsweetened cocoa powder
1 teaspoon instant espresso powder or instant coffee powder
5 large eggs
1 cup sugar
4 TBSP Grand Marnier
Fresh mint sprigs

Preheat oven to 350°F.
Rub 9-inch-diameter spring form pan with butter; line bottom with parchment.
Melt 1 ⅔ cups chocolate chips and ¾ cup butter in saucepan over low heat and stir until smooth. Whisk in cocoa and espresso. Cool 10 minutes.

Using electric mixer, beat eggs and sugar in large bowl on high speed until thick, about 6 minutes. Fold in chocolate mixture. Pour batter into prepared pan.

Bake torte until dry and cracked on top and toothpick inserted into center comes out with some moist batter attached, about 42 minutes. Cool in pan on rack 1 hour (center will fall). Using spatula, press raised edges so top is level. Cut around pan sides; remove sides. Place plate atop torte and invert onto plate. Remove pan bottom; peel off paper, and cool torte completely.

Stir remaining 1 cup chocolate and ¼ cup butter in small saucepan over low heat until smooth. Whisk in Grand Marnier. Cool ganache 20 minutes. Pour ganache into center of torte. Smooth top with spatula, allowing some of ganache to drip down sides. Refrigerate uncovered until glaze is set, about 1 hour. (If kept refrigerated, can be made up to 3 days ahead.)

Cut torte into wedges. Garnish with mint and raspberries.

Cozy Food

Crème Brulée
From the Murder Packs a Suitcase mystery series by Cynthia Baxter (page 173)

Like Mallory Marlowe, the travel writer in my Murder Packs a Suitcase mysteries, I've worked as a travel writer. A restauranteur I once interviewed gave me this recipe for classic crème brulée, which was originally created by a well-known chef in New York. Yet while this creamy French dessert always impresses people, it's ridiculously easy to make. Most of the work is done before guests arrive, too. And while heating the top with a blowtorch just before serving is a dramatic touch, caramelizing the top can be done just as efficiently in the broiler. (Just don't let it burn – a little *too* much drama!)

Makes 5-6 servings.

4 egg yolks
4 Tbsps sugar
1 pint (16 ounces) heavy cream
¼ to ½ tsp vanilla
Brown sugar

Preheat oven to 300 degrees.

Whisk eggs yolks and sugar by hand until creamy. Heat heavy cream until almost boiling (using the microwave is fine), then stir it into the mixture along with the vanilla. Let mixture sit for 5 to 10 minutes.

Pour mixture into 5 or 6 shallow ramekins. Put ramekins into a cookie sheet (the kind with edges) that contains hot water. Slide into oven.

Bake at 300 degrees for 30 minutes. Then rotate pan 180 degrees and bake another 15 minutes. (Bake a total of 45 minutes.) Cool and refrigerate.

When it's time to serve, sprinkle brown sugar on top (avoid clumps) and broil a few minutes to caramelize. Check it often!!!

Tips: Make sure the heavy cream is REALLY hot and be sure to rotate the pan while baking.

Pumpkin Crème Brulee
From *Unseemly Pursuits: A Concordia Wells Mystery* by K.B. Owen (page 218)

This autumnal treat is a favorite at the Masquerade Ball, hosted by Hartford Women's College every Halloween. But Professor Concordia Wells wonders if the lure of delicious desserts will be enough to distract the student pranksters this year, especially when the unpopular Lady Principal Grant - nicknamed "The Ogre" - is on the warpath once again.
(4 servings)

1 1/2 cups heavy cream
1 tsp cinnamon
¼ tsp ground cloves
½ tsp ginger
½ tsp freshly grated nutmeg
5 egg yolks

½ tsp vanilla extract
¼ cup pumpkin puree, fresh or canned
1/3 cup granulated white sugar
1 tablespoon light brown sugar, firmly packed
For sugar shell top (*optional*): 4 tsp granulated white sugar

Preheat oven to 325 degrees (Fahrenheit). In a saucepan, whisk cream, cinnamon, cloves, ginger, and nutmeg over medium-low heat for 3-5 minutes, until bubbles form around edges of saucepan and steam rises from the surface. DO NOT BOIL. Take pan off the heat and set aside for 15 minutes.

Meanwhile, whisk together egg yolks, vanilla, pumpkin puree, and sugars (except that reserved for sugar top) in a large bowl until ingredients are fully incorporated. Add cooled-off cream mixture. Strain all of it through a fine mesh sieve, and evenly divide into four ramekins (8-10 oz size).

Hot water bath: place ramekins in a large baking pan, and pour boiling water into the pan (around the ramekins) until water is halfway up the sides of the ramekins. Cover with aluminum foil and bake in the oven for 30 minutes, or until set. It may still be a little jiggly in the middle, but that will set as it cools. Carefully remove ramekins from hot water bath.

Once they have cooled to room temperature, cover with plastic wrap (don't touch the wrap to the surface of the custard) and chill in the fridge.

Optional: just before serving, sprinkle 1 tsp of white sugar over top of each custard and either use a small kitchen torch to carmelize the surface, or put ramekins on a baking sheet and set it under the boiler for a minute or two, until the sugar is melted and the top is browned. Let cool briefly, and serve.

Nana's Cream Puffs

From *Corpse of Discovery,* A Portland Bookmobile Mystery by B.B. Cantwell (page 180)

Hester Freelove McGarrigle, the librarian on the Portland City Bookmobile, relieves the day's stresses by cooking the comfort food from her youth like these amazing cream puffs. The first time she made them, though, the recipe instruction "drop a rounded tablespoonful" didn't seem like enough – she ended up with 4 creampuffs the size of human heads…

Heat oven to 400F. Makes a dozen normal sized or 4 bigger than your head sized servings.

Heat to a rolling boil in a saucepan:
1 cup water
½ cup butter
Stir in all at once
1 cup sifted flour
Stir vigorously over low heat until mixture leaves the pan and forms into a ball—approx 1 minute—remove from heat and beat in thoroughly, 1 at a time: 4 eggs.

Beat the mixture until smooth and velvety. Drop a rounded tablespoonful onto a baking paper lined baking sheet. Bake until dry –approx 45-55 minutes.

Custard Filling:
Mix in saucepan

Cozy Food

1 cup sugar
1 teaspoon salt
2/3 cup flour
Stir in
4 cups milk

Cook over medium heat stirring until it boils. Boil one minute. Remove from heat. Stir a little over half of this mixture into 8 egg yolks (or 4 whole eggs) that are lightly beaten. Blend the mixture back into the saucepan. Bring just to the boiling point and then cool. Blend in 4 teaspoons vanilla.

Thin Chocolate Icing:
Melt together over hot water
1 square unsweetened Baker's chocolate
1 teaspoon butter
Remove from hot water and blend in
1 cup sifted confectioners' sugar
2 Tablespoons boiling water
Beat until smooth.

To make up the cream puffs:
Slice the top off a cooled cream puff. Gently pull out any soft stands from the interior. Fill with Custard Filling. Place top back and spoon Thin Chocolate icing over the top. If icing gets too thick, add a few drops of boiling water to it. Refrigerate cream puffs.

West Riding Pudding
From the Kate Shackleton Yorkshire-based 1920s mystery series by Frances Brody (page 178)

Sleuth Kate Shackleton has developed a reputation for finding missing persons. She hasn't yet invited a client to join her in eating comfort food, but when she does this will be the perfect dessert pudding. Kate's housekeeper will be more than ready to produce this traditional dish and serve with hot custard.

6 ozs self-raising flour
3 ozs sugar
3 ozs butter or margarine
3 tablespoons jam
Few drops of vanilla essence
2 eggs
Little milk to mix

Butter a pie dish. Put the jam at the bottom. Work the butter and sugar together until creamy, beating in each egg separately. Fold in the sieved flour as lightly as possible, adding a little milk if necessary. Lastly add vanilla essence. Put the mixture on the top of the jam and bake in a moderate oven of 350°F, 180°C, Gas mark 5 for approximately 1½ to 1¾ hours until the pudding is golden brown and firm.

Desserts and Pies

Maple Bread Pudding
From *Threads of Evidence*, the Mainely Needlepoint series by Lea Wait (page 234)

Angie Curtis' grandmother, Margaret Curtis, loves to cook for friends and family. In *Threads of Evidence*, in the Haven Harbor Mainely Needlepoint series, she makes this elegant but comforting bread pudding out of northern New England ingredients when Angie is trying to reconstruct the 1970 murder of a young woman whose killer may still be in Haven Harbor … ready to strike again.

2 ½ cups light cream
4 eggs, separated
¾ cup pure maple syrup
Pinch of salt
Pinch of nutmeg
5-6 cups day-old French or Italian bread, cut into cubes
Whipping cream, optional

Pre-heat oven to 350. Heat baking pan ½ filled with hot water.

Scald cream. Set aside to cool. Combine and beat together egg yolks, maple syrup, salt. Slowly stir cream into egg mixture. Beat egg whites to peaks. Fold into custard mixture. Spread bread cubes in buttered 1 ½ quart baking dish and pour custard mixture over them, mixing lightly. Sprinkle nutmeg on top.

Place baking dish in pan of hot water. Bake in preheated oven 40-45 minutes or until knife inserted in center comes out clean.

May be served warm or cool … Margaret Curtis prefers is warm, and often adds a bit of whipped cream to the top.

Serves 6-8

(Don't Let Lady Macbeth Near The)Lemon Posset
From the Dandy Gilver series by Catriona McPherson (page 210)

You can't really ask for a better pedigree than a dessert being mentioned in Shakespeare, can you? "I have drugg'd their possets, that death and nature do contend about them, whether they live or die." (Macbeth, Act II, Sc2).

While I'm sure that Dandy Gilver's cook – the devoted Mrs. Tilling – would be more likely to make syllabub (which is tricky) or soufflé (which is really tricky) I've always preferred flashy results from little effort. Lemon posset is too easy for words but goes down a storm. I've never served it to someone and not been asked for the recipe.

20 oz of heavy cream
5 oz sugar
Two drops vanilla extract
2 large lemons

Serves six
Serving suggestion: this is delicious with fresh shortbread.

- Grate the zest off the lemons and juice them.
- Reserve half the zest – ideally in long strips but it doesn't matter.
- Put the cream, sugar and vanilla into a heavy-bottomed saucepan and bring to the boil.
- Add the lemon juice and the other half of the zest and whisk.
- Bring back to the boil and keep whisking for about half a minute until the mixture changes consistency. The sound of the whisk will become more muffled.
- Remove from the heat and pour into six glasses or teacups. (I like to serve this in pretty cups and saucers at lunchtime and in elegant glasses at dinnertime.)
- Cool slightly, then add the reserved zest to the tops as decoration and chill in the fridge for at least three hours before serving.

Samantha Sweet's Mexican Flan
From the Samantha Sweet mystery series by Connie Shelton (page 227)

In her delectable pastry shop, Sweet's Sweets, Samantha Sweet bakes up some fabulous treats. This is an easy one you can make at home; the basic version was first given to me by a friend in Mexico. For the best flavor, I use Mexican sugar and Mexican vanilla, but results are still great with the regular varieties.

3/4 c. plus 1/4 c. Mexican sugar (azucar) or refined white sugar
3 eggs
1 can sweetened condensed milk
1 can evaporated milk
1/2 t. Mexican vanilla or pure vanilla extract

Preheat oven to 325 degrees. Have an 8" pie plate or casserole dish ready.

Pour the 3/4 cup sugar into a small saucepan over medium heat. Stir constantly until the sugar liquefies and turns brown. Quickly pour the melted caramelized sugar into the pie plate, swirling it to coat the bottom. It will harden quickly as it cools but it becomes liquefied again after the flan has baked.

In a mixing bowl, blend eggs and both types of milk together with a whisk, then slowly mix in the 1/4 c. sugar, then the vanilla. Whisk until smooth. Pour mixture over the caramel in the pie plate. Place the pan on a cookie sheet to catch any boil-over. Bake about 1 hour 25 minutes. Check for doneness by inserting a knife just to the side of center—it should come out clean.

When cool, invert onto a serving plate and cut slices, if desired, or simply scoop it out of the pie plate. Spoon the runny caramel over the custard. Makes 6 to 8 servings.

Easy as a Peach Cobbler
(for your dessert enjoyment or as an ingredient in the Peach Pie Shake)
From the Working Stiff Mystery series by Kerri Nelson (page 214)

1 cup Bisquick
1 cup milk
½ tsp. nutmeg or cinnamon
½ cup butter
1 cup granulated sugar
1 large can sliced peaches (or 2 cups fresh peaches)

4 Tbsp. peach syrup (if you use the canned peaches only)

Heat oven to 375 degrees. Melt butter in 8x8 square or round baking dish. Combine all other ingredients (except peaches) in a mixing bowl (it may be a little lumpy from the Bisquick). Remove baking dish with melted butter and pour the butter into your mixing bowl ingredients and stir. Pour all mixing bowl ingredients into hot baking dish. Add peaches and then return dish to oven. Bake 45-55 minutes until top is bubbling and golden brown. Serves 6-8.

Ricotta Dream Dessert
From *Intrigue in Italics* by Gayle Wigglesworth (page 236)

In *Intrigue in Italics*, the third adventure in the Claire Gulliver Mystery series, Millie, Claire's mother, attends an elite cooking school in the hills of Tuscany. While Millie learns Italian cooking and puzzles over the strange events occurring in the class, Claire spends her time exploring Florence where she sees a good friend who she had last seen at her funeral. Of course Claire has to solve the mystery.

This dessert was the specialty of the chef who hosted the cooking school and it could be your specialty too. It's elegant and simple, perfect for a light dessert after a wonderful meal. If you want to read the book and help solve the mysteries you can purchase the book via the links on my Author page.

1 cup of Ricotta Cheese
2 tablespoons of sugar or two packets of Splenda
½ teaspoon of Almond Extract
¼ cup of Sliced Almonds for garnish
Optional:
½ cup of cherries, raisins, or strawberries soaked in enough liquor such as Frangelica, or Amaretto to cover them. Soak for at least two hours before serving.

Mix the Ricotta, sugar and flavoring together
Chill for one or two hours
Spoon into dessert dishes, sprinkle with toasted almonds and serve
Optional:
Spoon fruit over top and sprinkle with almonds
Serve.

This makes two servings. If using fresh Ricotta, when you can find it, you may want to press it through a strainer to eliminate any lumps.

Variation: Ricotta con le Fragole
Follow the above recipe then before chilling and finishing add the following:

½ cup strawberries soaked in enough sweet white wine to cover them for 2 hours prior to serving
Carefully mix into Ricotta mixture (see above recipe)
Fold 1 egg white beaten to stiff peaks into cheese/strawberry mixture
Chill and serve sprinkled with sliced almonds

Cozy Food

Lemon Mystery
From the Miss Dimple Kilpatrick series by Mignon F. Ballard (page 171)

Sugar was rationed when I was growing up during the war years in the 1940's, but our mother somehow managed to save enough ration stamps to provide dessert as often as possible. Lucky for us, desserts were her specialty, and my sister and I would race one another home after school to try to get that last luscious mouthful. One of our favorites was a pudding cake she called Lemon Mystery.

Although my character, first grade teacher, Dimple Kilpatrick, claims that too many sweets are harmful to your health, I happen to know she keeps Hershey bars hidden in her desk drawer at Elderberry Grammar School, and when Odessa Kirby, who cooks for Phoebe Chadwick's boarding house where she lives, serves this special treat, Miss Dimple, along with the other teachers who are fortunate enough to live there, doesn't hesitate to dive right in.

Enjoy!

2 tablespoons butter
1 cup sugar
4 tablespoons all-purpose flour
1/8 teaspoon salt
juice and grated rind of 1 lemon
3 egg yolks
3 egg whites, beaten
1 ½ cups whole or 2% milk

Preheat oven to 350 degrees. Cream butter. Add sugar and mix well. Add flour, salt, rind and juice of lemon. Stir in egg yolks mixed with milk. Fold in beaten whites and pour into a 1 ½ or 2 qt. baking dish. Set in a shallow pan of hot water and bake for 45 minutes. Can be served with sweetened whipped cream but is almost as good without it.

Serve cool to 6 normal people or 4 of my relatives.

Limoncello-Mint Sorbetto
From the *Franki Amato Mysteries* by Traci Andrighetti (page 170)

Although Franki would prefer to drink her Limoncello, she's certainly not averse to eating it. Like most Italians, she's passionate about *gelato* (ice cream) and, in this case, *sorbetto* (sorbet). And because she's Sicilian in origin, she's partial to anything with lemon. Here is Franki's recipe for eight servings of cold, lemony goodness.

2 cups water
1 1/3 cups sugar
1/2 cup Limoncello
1 cup fresh lemon juice (about 6 large lemons)
1/2 cup chopped fresh mint
lemon slices or blackberries for garnish (optional)

Combine the water, sugar and Limoncello in a saucepan over medium-high heat. Bring to a boil, stirring until the sugar dissolves. Remove from heat and add the lemon juice and mint. Cover and chill in the refrigerator.

Desserts and Pies

When the juice mixture is chilled, strain through a sieve into a bowl. Discard the solids. Pour the mixture into the freezer can of an ice-cream maker and freeze according to the manufacturer instructions. Or, freeze the mixture in a freezer-safe container, stirring frequently to aerate. Cover and freeze for one hour or until firm.

Serve the sorbetto with blackberries or lemon slices, if desired. *Buon appetito!*

Charlotte Russe

From *Dangerous and Unseemly: A Concordia Wells Mystery* by K.B. Owen (page 218)

Although Professor Concordia Wells finds herself a reluctant amateur sleuth – who knew the students and staff were capable of such mayhem at a respectable women's college? – she is an avid lover of desserts. One of her favorites is *Charlotte Russe*, a 19th century custard-and-spongecake dessert created by the French in honor of the Russian Czar. Of course, when one is wearing a tightly-corseted gown at the Seniors' Spring Dance, it's difficult to eat very much of it.
(8-10 servings)

1 packet unflavored gelatin, mixed into ½ cup cold water
1 cup granulated white sugar
4 eggs, separated into whites and yolks
4-6 tablespoons of the liquor of your choice (bourbon, whiskey, sherry or grand marnier work well)
2 cups whipping cream
20 ladyfingers
Garnish: fresh fruit of your choice - strawberries, peaches, berries, orange slices, etc.

Cook gelatin and water mixture on low heat until gelatin is dissolved; remove from heat to cool a bit.

Meanwhile, beat sugar and egg yolks until incorporated and smooth. Whisk in liquor.

Whisk in gelatin until incorporated into the egg yolk mixture.
In a separate bowl, beat egg whites until stiff (don't overdo it; you don't want them to be dry). Fold egg whites into the egg yolk/gelatin mixture.

In a separate bowl, beat whipping cream into soft peaks. Gently fold into the rest.

Line a glass bowl (3 qt size) with lady fingers (split them first, nice sides facing out). Fill gently with the cream mixture, being careful not to dislodge the lady fingers. Cover; chill overnight (at least 8 hours).

If desired, garnish with fresh fruit just before serving.

Cozy Food

Gluten-free Pumpkin Cheesecake with Caramel Sauce
From the kitchen of Nancy J. Parra (page 219)

Filling:
4 8oz packages of cream cheese
1 ½ cups granulated sugar
4 eggs
1 cup canned pumpkin
2 tsp pumpkin pie spice
1 tsp cinnamon

Caramel Sauce:
2 tablespoons butter or margarine
1/3 cup Light corn syrup
1/3 cup packed brown sugar
1/3 cup heavy whipping cream
1 tablespoon of spiced rum (optional)

Heat oven to 300°F. Spray 9-inch springform pan with cooking spray.

In large bowl, beat cream cheese and granulated sugar with electric mixer on medium speed until light and fluffy. Beat in eggs, one at a time, just until blended. Spoon 3 cups of the mixture into pan; spread evenly. To remaining cream cheese mixture, add pumpkin, pumpkin pie spice and cinnamon; mix with wire whisk until smooth. Spoon over mixture in pan.

Bake 1 hour 15 minutes to 1 hour 25 minutes or until edge of cheesecake is set at least 2 inches from edge of pan but center of cheesecake still jiggles slightly when moved. Run small metal spatula around edge of pan to loosen cheesecake. Turn oven off; open oven door at least 4 inches. Let cheesecake remain in oven 30 minutes. Cool in pan on cooling rack 30 minutes. Cover loosely; refrigerate at least 6 hours but no longer than 24 hours.

In small saucepan, heat brown sugar, corn syrup and 2 tablespoons butter to boiling over medium-low heat, stirring constantly. Boil 5 minutes, stirring occasionally. Stir in whipping cream; heat to boiling. Remove from heat; stir in rum. Cool until warm.

Just before serving, run small metal spatula around edge of pan; carefully remove side of pan. Top individual slices with warm sauce and a dollop of whipped cream. Cover and refrigerate any remaining cheesecake.

Pies

Ruth Miller's Shoo Fly Pie
From the Amish Mysteries by Laura Bradford (page 178)

Next door to Heavenly Treasures, is Ruth Miller's Shoo Fly Bake Shoppe. It's one of the more popular shops on Lighted Way thanks to the amazing baked treats Benjamin and Eli's sister, Ruth, sells.

Desserts and Pies

Shoo Fly Pie is, of course, the shop's signature dessert.

This is her recipe and it makes 2 pies (use whatever pie crust recipe you prefer in order to make two 8-inch unbaked crusts):

Crumb Mixture:
2 c. flour
3/4 c. brown sugar
1/3 c. margarine
1/2 tsp. nutmeg
1 tsp. cinnamon

Syrup Mixture:
1 c. molasses
1/2 c. brown sugar
2 eggs
1 c. hot water
1 tsp. baking soda, dissolved in the hot water

Mix crumb ingredients together until crumbs are formed. In separate bowl, mix syrup ingredients together. Pour 1/2 of syrup into each pie shell, then top each with crumbs, using 1/2 on each. Bake at 400 degrees for 10 minutes. Reduce heat to 350 degrees and bake for 50 more minutes. Cool completely before cutting.

Pecan Pie (yummy)

From *Pearls and Poison* (March 4, 2014) Book three in the Consignment Shop Mystery series by Duffy Brown (page 179)

Some elections are pure murder.

A dead opponent is one way to win an election … unless you wind up in jail for the murder.

Gloria Summerside is trailing in the poles but front-runner as a murder suspect when her mud-slinging opponent is poisoned. Is someone out to frame Judge Guillotine Gloria? Will she be the one behind bars this time? Can her daughter find the real killer or will they have adjoining cells?

From Duffy: I love Southern cooking, especially Savannah southern cooking. The city is best visited if you eat your way across it. When I was there I got the very best … and easiest … pecan pie recipe ever and I'm here to pass it on to you. This is the pie Auntie KiKi makes for Thanksgiving dinner.

9" unbaked pie crust (if in a hurry Pillsbury in the fridge section)
1 cup light corn syrup
1 cup firmly packed dark brown sugar
3 eggs slightly beaten
1/3 cup butter melted
½ tsp salt
1 tsp vanilla
1 cup pecan halves (or walnuts)

Heat oven to 350.

Cozy Food

Combine corn syrup, sugar, eggs, butter, salt, vanilla and mix well. Pour into crust, sprinkle with nuts and bake for 50 min till knife comes out clean. Cool. Add whipped cream, cinnamon or caramel ice cream is great.

And when you take that first bite think of me.

Yum-Yum Pie

From Barbara Evans, founding member of *The Sleuth Sisters* by Maggie Pill (page 221)

Barb isn't much of a cook, but she does like a good dessert that's easy to make. She doesn't own mixing bowls or other baking tools, but she has a blender, so this recipe suits her fine when her sweet tooth calls for something good.

Combine in a blender:
2 eggs
1 cup milk
¾ cup sugar
½ cup flour
2 tbsp. melted butter
½ tsp. vanilla
½ tsp. nutmeg
½ tsp. salt

Blend on high for 20 seconds. Pour into greased pie plate. Sprinkle with 1 cup coconut. Bake at 350 degrees for 35-40 minutes. Slice and serve (six people)

Key Lime Pie

From The Dream Club Mysteries by Mary Kennedy (page 201)

Lucinda Macavey, a prim and proper Savannah lady in The Dream Club Mysteries, firmly believes that the way to a man's heart is through his stomach. Whenever she entertains a "gentleman caller," she serves this delicious pie. It's light and delicious, the perfect ending to one of Lucinda's fabulous dinners.

1 (14 oz ounce can) of sweetened condensed milk. Be sure to buy condensed milk, not evaporated.
1/2 cup Key Lime juice. Lucinda likes to use fresh limes, but you can use bottled juice.
3 egg yolks
One graham cracker crust. This doesn't have to be home-made, Lucinda usually buys one at the grocery store.

Preheat oven to 325 degrees
Mix the sweetened condensed milk, lime juice and egg yolks. Pour mixture into graham cracker crust.
Bake until set, about 40 minutes. Be sure to chill it well before serving.
Serves 8.

Hawaiian Chocolate and Coconut (Haupia) Pie

From The Islands of Aloha Mystery series by JoAnn Bassett (page 172)

Desserts and Pies

This is a truly "pull-out-all-the-stops" dessert based on a heritage sweet served in Hawaii—haupia pudding. If you really want to impress your friends or family with a Hawaiian-style dessert that will leave you groaning for more, give this a try!

1 9-inch <u>unbaked</u> pie crust
1 cup milk
1 (14 oz.) can coconut milk
1 cup white sugar
1 cup water
½ cup cornstarch
1 ¼ cups semi-sweet chocolate chips
1 ½ cups sweetened whipped cream

Preheat oven to 350 degrees (175 C.) Bake the crust for 15 minutes or until golden brown and then let it cool.
In a saucepan whisk together the milk, coconut milk and 1 cup of sugar. Bring to a boil.
In a bowl, dissolve the cornstarch in the water.
Reduce the coconut mixture to simmer and whisk the cornstarch mixture into the coconut mixture. Stir the mixture over low heat until it starts to thicken, about 3 minutes. Take it off the stove.
In a glass bowl microwave the chocolate chips just until melted (about 1 minute or less). Divide the still-warm coconut mixture into two bowls. Mix melted chocolate into one-half of the coconut mixture and spread it on the bottom of the baked pie crust.
Pour the remaining coconut mixture on top and spread it smooth.
Refrigerate for at least an hour before serving.
Cover top of cooled pie with the whipped cream and decorate with chocolate shavings, if desired.

Mr. Appleton's Apple Pie
Featured in *Cupcakes, Pies, and Hot Guys* by Pamela DuMond (page 188)

I discovered this recipe a long time ago and have modified it over the years until it is now the. Best. Apple Pie. Ever.

Two 9" pie crusts
Eight medium to large Granny Smith apples
½ cup dark brown sugar, packed
¼ cup granulated sugar
One ¼ teaspoon ground cinnamon
Juice of one lemon
Just under 1 tablespoon vanilla extract (Recommend the real stuff, not artificial.)
½ teaspoon salt
Slightly under 1/3 cup all-purpose flour
Three tablespoons (almost ½ stick) unsalted butter

Mr. Appleton's Secret Concoction:
Four tablespoons granulated sugar
Almost ¾ cup all-purpose flour.
Two tablespoons unsalted butter
Almost ½ cup butterscotch chips

Cozy Food

Egg Wash:
One egg
Almost two tablespoons water

Peel and slice apples ¼ inch thick. In a separate large bowl combine and mix the flour, brown sugar, granulated sugar, cinnamon, lemon juice, vanilla and salt. Place apple slices in this mixture and stir.

Melt the butter in a large sauté pan. Add apple-flour-sugar and stir until the apples are soft. Avoid burning. Remove from heat and cool.

Preheat oven to 350 degrees. Pre-bake the <u>bottom</u> piecrust for 10 minutes. (Don't pre-bake the top crust.)

Combine ingredients in Mr. Appleton's Secret Concoction. Mix thoroughly.

Whisk the egg wash in a small bowl.

Place cooled apple mixture in pre-baked piecrust. Top with Secret Concoction. Place the reserved piecrust on top of pie. Crimp edges to seal the pie. (Don't have too much top crust hanging down from pie edges as it will fall and burn off during baking.) Smooth egg wash onto top crust. Make four or five slashes in top crust to allow pie to vent.

Yield: Depends on how thinly you slice those pieces. Between 8 to twelve slices.

Place pie in oven. Bake for 45 minutes. Check on it once in a while to make sure the top isn't burning. Remove and let cool for 30 minutes before serving. Goes great with fresh vanilla ice cream.

(Note. For those who like it less sweet? Cut back a little on the sugar.)

Cherry Cream Cheese Pie
From the cookbook of the mother of Leighann Dobbs (page 187)

When I was growing up, we each got to pick the kind of cake or dessert we wanted on our birthdays. I always picked the cherry cream cheese pie even though I didn't like the actually cherries and used to pick them off (I still do that). My mother used to laugh that out of all the desserts I could pick, I'd choose this one because it is so easy to make! This recipe comes from her collection.

1 pckg unfilled ladyfingers
3 0z cream cheese
3/4 cup sugar
1 teaspoon vanilla
1/2 pt. whipping cream
1 can cherry pie filling

Line a 9" pie plate bottom with split lady fingers (break them in half if needed).
Line the sides of the pie plate with half lady fingers sticking up with the rounded sides up.
Soften the cream cheese and add the sugar and vanilla, mix well.
Beat the cream until stiff and fold into the cream cheese mixture.

Spread over the lady fingers.

Spoon the cherry pie filling on top.

Chill overnight. (I remember it was like torture to see that pie chilling in the fridge and knowing I couldn't eat it until the next day!)

THE Pumpkin Pie

From Birthday Dinner by Donna Andrews (page 170)

When my mother first tried this recipe, she quickly realized that it was at least three times as much work as an ordinary pumpkin pie, and the ingredients were pretty darned expensive, too. So she asked us if we liked it enough that she should make it again. Our collective "yes!" was so resounding that we've had the pie nearly every Thanksgiving since, and often at Christmas, too. And since it's made with amaretto, which, like cyanide, smells of almonds, I used it as a potential murder weapon in my story "Birthday Dinner," published in Death Dines In, a short story anthology edited by Claudia Bishop and Dean James and published in 2005. But since the anthology's out of print . . . here it is. THE Pumpkin Pie. Also known as Mother's Sinfully Rich Pumpkin Pie

1 9-inch pie shell, cooled

(Mother will forgive you if you buy a precooked one. Or if you don't tell her, she'll never guess. Both pastry and graham cracker crusts work nicely.)

1 envelope unflavored gelatin

½ C praline liqueur or Amaretto

16 ounce can of pumpkin

4 egg yolks, lightly beaten

½ C packed brown sugar

½ C granulated sugar

¼ C butter or margarine, melted

1 teaspoon ground cinnamon

½ teaspoon salt

¼ teaspoon ground cloves

4 egg whites

1/8 teaspoon cream of tartar

¾ C whipped cream. Yes, real cream.

Soften gelatin in liqueur, set aside.

Heat pumpkin and all ingredients through cloves in a saucepan over medium heat. Stir constantly until lightly boiling and slightly thickened. Remove from heat. Beat in gelatin mixture. Cool, but do not allow to harden completely.

Whip the cream until stiff. Beat the egg whites, cream of tartar and a pinch of salt until stiff peaks form. Fold egg whites and whipped cream into pumpkin mixture. Pour into pie shell, mounding in center. (You may have to pour part in, let it harden a bit, and then fill the rest. It makes a <u>very</u> full pie.)

Garnish with more whipped cream.

Cozy Food

Cakes, Cupcakes, and Frostings

Bûche de Noël, Yule Log

From the Cutthroat Business mysteries by Jenna Bennett (page 174), featuring realtor and recovering Southern Belle Savannah Martin in Nashville, Tennessee.

Bûche de Noël is the French name for a Christmas cake shaped like a log. When Savannah and her boyfriend Rafe have Christmas dinner with the Martin family in *Contingent on Approval*, the Cutthroat Business holiday novella, *Bûche de Noël* is the dessert to cap the meal, as befits a family whose roots are French.

Traditionally, *Bûche de Noël* is dusted with confectioner's sugar to resemble snow on a log, and often, a fork is dragged through the icing to create the illusion of bark. The *Bûche de Noël* is commonly decorated with mushrooms made from marzipan or meringue (edible), and with evergreen sprigs (not).

Cakes, Cupcakes, and Frostings

Here's what you need to do:

Preheat oven to 375 degrees F. Line a 10x15 inch jellyroll pan with parchment paper. It can help to spray the paper with cooking spray to avoid sticking.

Meanwhile, get going on the filling:

2 cups heavy cream
½ cup confectioner's sugar
½ cup unsweetened cocoa powder
1 teaspoon vanilla extract

In a large bowl, whip all four ingredients together until thick and stiff. Refrigerate.

For the cake:

6 egg yolks
½ cup granulated sugar
1/3 cup unsweetened cocoa powder
1 ½ teaspoons vanilla extract
1/8 teaspoon salt
6 egg whites
¼ cup granulated sugar

In a large bowl, use an electric mixer to beat egg yolks with 1/2 cup sugar until thick and pale. Blend in 1/3 cup cocoa, 1 1/2 teaspoons vanilla, and salt. In large glass bowl, using clean beaters, whip egg whites to soft peaks. Gradually add 1/4 cup sugar, and beat until whites form stiff peaks. Immediately fold the yolk mixture into the whites. Spread the batter evenly into the prepared pan.
Bake for 12 to 15 minutes in the preheated oven, or until the cake springs back when lightly touched. Dust a clean dishtowel with confectioner's sugar. Run a knife around the edge of the pan, and turn the warm cake out onto the towel. Remove and discard parchment paper. Starting at the short edge of the cake, roll the cake up with the towel. Cool for 30 minutes.

Unroll the cake and remove the towel. Spread the filling to within 1 inch of the edge of the cake. Roll the cake up again with the filling inside. Place the cake seam side down onto a serving plate, and refrigerate until serving. Dust with confectioner's sugar before serving.

You can frost the cake with chocolate buttercream if you want, and go for a bark look by dragging a fork or other kitchen implement through the frosting.

Gingerbread Cupcakes with Cinnamon Cream Cheese Frosting
From *Cupcakes, Paws, and Bad Santa Claus* by Pamela DuMond (page 188)

During the course of writing a cupcakes mystery series, I've met a lot of bakers and sampled their goods. (Woe is me --the research is so difficult.) One of the best bakers as well as the funniest and kindest persons I've met is Laura DeVries from Cupcakes-A-Go-Go in Madison, Wisconsin. She donated this recipe for *Cupcakes, Paws, and Bad Santa Claus.* (FYI – they ship cupcakes and cakepops 2nd day to all parts of the country. Check her out on Facebook or at http://www.cupcakesagogo.com/)

Cozy Food

Prep Time: Around 25 minutes
Baking Time: 18 – 22 minutes
Yield: 18 cupcakes

1.5 cups stout beer
1 tsp. baking soda
1 small box vanilla instant pudding mix
1 cup sour cream
1/3 cup dark molasses
1.5 cup light brown sugar
.5 cup granulated sugar
3 cups all-purpose flour
3 tbsp. ground ginger
1 tsp. baking powder
1 tsp salt
.5 tsp. ground cinnamon
.5 tsp. finely ground black pepper
4 eggs
2/3 cup vegetable oil
2 tbsp. finely grated fresh ginger

1. Preheat oven to 350 degrees. Place baking cups into cupcake pans.
2. Bring the stout to a boil in a medium saucepan over medium heat, stirring occasionally. Remove from the heat and stir in the baking soda (mixture will foam up). When foaming subsides, stir in molasses, brown sugar and granulated sugar until dissolved; set aside.
3. Whisk flour, ground ginger, baking powder, salt, cinnamon, pepper and pudding mix together in a large bowl. Set aside.
4. Transfer the stout mixture to a large bowl. Whisk in the eggs, oil, sour cream and grated ginger until combined. Whisk the wet mixture into the flour mixture in thirds, stirring until completely smooth after each addition.
5. Fill baking cups 2/3 full and bake 18 – 22 minutes. Cupcakes are done when a toothpick inserted into the center comes out clean.
6. When cupcakes are completely cooled, top with cinnamon cream cheese frosting.

Cinnamon Cream Cheese Frosting:
1 package 8 oz cream cheese, softened.
4 tbsp. butter softened
1tsp. pure vanilla extract
1 pkg. (16 oz.) powdered sugar
1- ½ tsp. ground cinnamon

Using a hand mixer or stand mixer, beat cream cheese and butter until smooth. Add vanilla and cinnamon. Add powdered sugar gradually and beat until light and fluffy.

Blueberry Pound Cake
From *Mud to Ashes* by Gayle Wigglesworth (page 236)

Empty nester, Karo Meisner, reinvented her life by moving to the beach, where her adopted dogs found a woman's body in the surf, which ultimately led to nationwide notoriety and nearly cost her life.

Cakes, Cupcakes, and Frostings

In *Mud to Ashes*, Karo is trying to build a new life so whenever someone dropped in she tried to pull something scrumptious from the freezer to serve with her coffee or tea. Frequently it would be this Blueberry Pound Cake. No wonder she made such good friends and gained a reputation for being a great cook. If you would like to follow Karo's adventures in making a new life for herself, you can purchase the book via the links on my Author page.

3 sticks or 3/4 lb of butter
3 cups granulated sugar
5 large eggs or 6 small eggs
3 cups flour
1 teaspoon vanilla
½ teaspoon lemon extract or 1 teaspoon grated lemon peel
½ teaspoon almond extract
1 cup minus 2 tablespoons of ginger ale or similar soda
2 cups fresh or frozen blueberries

Using a mixer cream butter until it is light and fluffy.
Mix in sugar and continue to beat.
Add eggs one at a time until batter is smooth.
Beat in one cup of flour.
Add the extracts and a small amount of ginger ale.
Continue beating.
Add the rest of the flour and ginger ale a little at a time until batter is completely mixed and smooth.
Add blueberries.
Pour in to 2 loaf pans or one Bundt or tube pan which has been sprayed with PAM.
Bake in a pre-heated 275° oven for 1 hour and 45 minutes or until a toothpick inserted in the middle of the cake comes out clean.

This cake freezes well.

Aunt Nettie's Blueberry Cake with Lemon Sauce
From *Shadows of a Down East Summer*, Antique Print Mystery series by Lea Wait (page 234)

Aunt Nettie may be in her 90s, but she's a tough Mainer. She knows what she likes, and she cooks with local Maine ingredients. In *Shadows of a Down East Summer* (the Antique Print Mystery series) she cooks her famous Maine Blueberry Cake for her nephew's gal, Maggie Summer, who is visiting … and trying to solve a mystery that involves Winslow Homer, women who posed for him in 1890, a contemporary local artist, and Aunt Nettie's best friend.

Cake:
1/3 cup butter, at room temperature
1 ½ cups sugar
2 eggs at room temperature
½ cup milk
1 ¼ cups flour
½ teaspoon salt
½ teaspoon vanilla
2 teaspoons baking powder
2 cups wild blueberries (fresh or drained frozen) mixed with ½ cup flour

Butter sheet cake pan or two 8-inch cake pans. Pre-heat oven to 375 degrees.
Cream together butter and sugar. Beat eggs, and add to creamed mixture. Add vanilla and milk. Stir. Then add flour, salt and baking powder. Mix thoroughly. Add blueberries. Stir gently, until berries are covered with batter. Pour into prepared pan(s) and bake 20-25 minutes, until toothpick inserted in middle of cake comes out clean. Cool. Cut in squares and pour lemon sauce on top when served.

Lemon Sauce:
1 ½ cups sugar
2 Tablespoons cornstarch
2 Cups boiling water
4 Tablespoons butter
Juice of 1 lemon
¼ teaspoon nutmeg

Mix sugar and cornstarch. Gradually add boiling water. Boil 5 minutes, stirring constantly. Remove from heat and add lemon juice, butter, nutmeg and salt. Stir well. Pour over individual pieces of blueberry cake. Sauce may be served hot or cold. Refrigerated, it will keep several days, and may be reheated before serving. Aunt Nettie prefers to serve it warm.

Pippi O'Brien's Chocolate "Dumpster" Cake (Chocolate Dump Cake)
From *Murder for Bid* and *Murder on Consignment* by Susan Furlong Bolliger (page 177)

When not helping the police solve crimes, Pippi O'Brien spends her days perusing garage sales, consignment shops and … yes, dumpster diving for castoffs she can upcycle and resell for profit. All this work leaves little time for baking. So, when in need of a delectable dessert for a special occasion, Pippi turns to this easy-peasy recipe:

1 box of yellow cake mix
16 ounces of sour cream
12 ounces of chocolate chips
4 eggs
½ cup of oil
1 small package of instant chocolate pudding

Just dump in all the ingredients into a lightly greased Bundt pan, stir and bake at 350 degrees for 1 to 1 ½ hours!

Triple Chocolate Mousse Cake
From *Chocolate Mousse Attack* by Sally Berneathy (page 174)

A friend gave me a wonderful recipe for Triple Chocolate Mousse Cake. However, it was about fifteen pages long and took half a day to make! I modified and simplified the recipe then included it in *Chocolate Mousse Attack*.

Grease with butter a 9 inch springform pan at least 3 inches high. Preheat oven to 325 degrees.

Make layers in order.

Bottom Layer:
6 tablespoons butter

7 ounces bittersweet chocolate (60% chocolate)
2 teaspoons vanilla extract
4 large eggs, separated
1/3 cup packed brown sugar, crumbled to remove lumps

Melt butter and chocolate in large bowl in microwave in two 30 second segments, stirring after each. Allow mixture to cool slightly, about 5 minutes. Whisk in vanilla and egg yolks. Set aside.

Beat egg whites at medium speed until frothy. Add half of brown sugar and beat until combined, about 15 seconds. Add remaining brown sugar and beat at high speed until medium soft peaks form.

Fold beaten egg whites into chocolate mixture. Transfer batter to prepared spring form pan, smoothing top.

Bake until cake has risen, is firm around edges, and center has just set but is still soft (center of cake will spring back after pressing gently with finger), 13 to 18 minutes. Transfer cake to wire rack to cool completely, about 1 hour. (Cake will collapse as it cools.) Do not remove cake from pan.

Middle Layer:
2 tablespoons cocoa powder
5 tablespoons hot water
7 ounces bittersweet chocolate (60% chocolate)
1-1/2 cups cold heavy cream
1 tablespoon sugar
1/8 teaspoon salt
1/2 teaspoon vanilla

Combine cocoa powder and hot water in small bowl; set aside. Melt chocolate in large bowl in microwave in 30 second segments, stirring after each one. Cool slightly, 2 to 5 minutes.

Whip cream, sugar, vanilla and salt until soft peaks form.

Whisk cocoa powder mixture into melted chocolate until smooth. Fold whipped cream into chocolate mixture. Spoon mousse into springform pan over cooled cake. Refrigerate cake at least 15 minutes while preparing top layer.

Top Layer:
3/4 teaspoon powdered gelatin
1 tablespoon water
6 ounces white chocolate chips
1 1/2 cups whipping cream
1 teaspoon vanilla
Shaved chocolate or cocoa powder (optional)

In small bowl, sprinkle gelatin over water; let stand at least 5 minutes. Place white chocolate in medium bowl. Heat ½ cup cream in microwave, about 45 seconds, until hot but not boiling. Add gelatin mixture and stir until fully dissolved. Pour cream mixture over white chocolate and whisk until chocolate is melted and mixture is smooth, about 30 seconds. Cool to room temperature, stirring occasionally.

Whip remaining cup cream until soft peaks form. Fold whipped cream into white chocolate mixture. Spoon white chocolate mousse into pan over middle layer. Smooth top. Return cake to refrigerator and chill until set, at least 2 hours.

Garnish top of cake with chocolate curls or dust with cocoa. Run thin knife between cake and side of springform pan; remove side of pan. Cut into slices and serve.

Gram's Chocolate Bundt Cake
From the Blue Plate Café Mystery series by Judy Alter (page 169)

When Kate Chambers' beloved Gram dies suddenly, Kate inherits Gram's café in the small town of Wheeler, Texas. She leaves a promising career as a paralegal in Dallas to run the café, never dreaming she'll run into a prickly police chief, a drug dealer, a swindler, and more than one murder. When things are peaceful, Kate serves this cake in the café.

1 box cake mix (Kate usually uses chocolate, but you could use vanilla, lemon, etc.)
1 box instant pudding (complimentary to cake flavor)
½ c. oil
4 eggs
1½ c. sour cream
Sugar and cinnamon

Mix together everything but sugar and cinnamon. Spray Bundt pan with Pam or similar coating. Mix cinnamon and sugar and sprinkle on all sides of prepared pan. Add the batter, evening it out as much as possible (it's a thick batter), and top with cinnamon and sugar. Bake at 350° for 50 to 60 minutes (check with a long kebab skewer or something similar); it often has to cook longer. Cool five minutes and remove from the pan. DON'T WAIT ANY LONGER. Run a knife around edges of pan and tunnel in the middle, and then top with a plate, invert, and gently shake to remove the cake from the pan.
Serves 12.

Deep in the Black Forest Cupcakes
From *Murder in the Gazebo* (2013) by Chloe Evans (page 190)

Who doesn't love chocolate? Deep in the Black Forest Cupcakes are easy and deeply chocolate and satisfying. Melanie admits to being a chocoholic so she bakes up this special treat every time she needs to treat herself or her friends.

1 package dark chocolate cake mix, with eggs, oil and water as prescribed on the package
2 C raspberry preserves
Canned white frosting (good quality)
Mint leaves and fresh raspberries for garnish

Prepare cake mix according to package directions, adding 1 c of raspberry preserves to cake batter. Spoon into buttered muffin tin and bake according to package directions. Remove from baking tin onto cooling rack. When cool, top with canned white frosting mixed with another cup of raspberry preserves. Top each cupcake with a fresh raspberry and mint leaf.

Cakes, Cupcakes, and Frostings

Devils' Food Cake
From Devil's Food Cake by Josi S. Kilpack (page 201)

When I chose the title "Devil's Food Cake" for the third book in my culinary mystery series, I went on the hunt for the perfect recipe to include in the book. As I experimented I wished I could find one as good as the regular chocolate cake recipe I'd been raised with. Eventually I did some research and learned that the difference between Devil's Food Cake and regular chocolate cake was baking soda. A quick look at my Grandma's recipe showed that low and behold it had baking soda! All along my favorite chocolate cake was exactly what I was looking for. The frosting was shared by one of the members of my Test Kitchen and is a perfect pairing.

Devil's Food Cake:
1 cup sour milk (1 cup milk + 2 teaspoons white vinegar or lemon juice OR use 1 cup buttermilk)
2 cups flour
2 cups sugar
2/3 cup unsweetened cocoa
1/2 teaspoon salt
2 eggs
1 cup vegetable oil
1 teaspoon vanilla
1 cup boiling water
1 teaspoon baking soda

For sour milk, mix milk and vinegar in a small bowl. Set aside for five minutes. In a large bowl, mix together all ingredients except the water and baking soda. Mix until batter is smooth. Add the soda to the boiling water (kids love this part because it bubbles). Add soda/water mixture to batter. Mix well—batter will be thin. Pour batter into a greased and floured 9x13-inch pan and bake at 350 degrees for 35 to 45 minutes or until middle is set.

If using round cake pans, grease pans very well and cut a round of wax paper to fit inside the bottom of the pans to prevent cake from sticking when removed.

Let cake cool five minutes in pans before turning out onto a wire rack.
Serves 12.

* Shawn (i.e. Mint-aholic) likes a teaspoon of mint extract added to the batter.

Sandra's Chocolicious Frosting:
1/2 cup butter
2 tablespoons shortening
1 cup baking cocoa
8 ounces cream cheese
3 cups powdered sugar
1 teaspoon vanilla

Melt butter and shortening. Whisk in cocoa and stir until smooth. Let cool until it is cool enough to touch. Add cream cheese and mix thoroughly. Add powdered sugar and vanilla. Mix well. Will cover two 9-inch layers or a 9x13 cake.

Cozy Food

Self-Frosted Cake
From the Sandi Webster Mysteries by Marja McGraw (page 208)

The Sandi Webster Mysteries (six books in this series) involve a female private eye who's somewhat of a chocoholic (she takes after her author). She tends to eat sweets, chocolate in particular, when she's stressed, scared, happy or sad – even when she's confused. This cake is sweet and she'd probably be bouncing off the walls while she waited for it to bake and cool.

Cake:
1-1/3 cup flour
1 cup sugar
2-1/2 tsp. baking powder
¾ tsp. salt
½ cup shortening
2/3 cup milk
2 eggs
1 tsp. vanilla

Topping:
½ cup chocolate syrup
½ cup warm water
1/3 cup sugar

- Measure flour by spooning into cup and leveling off.
- Mix all ingredients except topping. Beat at medium speed.
- Spread batter evenly in greased 2 qt. casserole.
- Mix Topping. Spoon evenly over batter and place in pre-heated oven.
- Bake at 350° for 40-50 minutes.
- Cool 1-2 minutes. Loosen edges with knife and turn out upside down on cake plate.

221b Bakery 'Barbe a queue' BabyCakes (courtesy of the Maney Bros.)
From the Finn Sherlock series by Pamela Rose (page 225)

Finn Sherlock is justifiably proud of Sherlock's Home Mystery Bookstore and the adjoining 221b Bakery. Putting her failed marriage behind her, along with her identical twin, Echo, and her beloved Uncle Oz, she immerses herself in the rarefied world of mystery books and delectably sweet treats named for famous mystery writers and/or their sleuths. Too soon the haven she has designed for herself unravels as murder rears its ugly head. Finn confronts this unwelcome intrusion into her newfound bliss via the only means she knows: becoming an amateur detective worthy of the crime fiction she purveys.

Streusel Topping:
¼ cup brown sugar
1 Tlbs. butter
½ Tsp. cinnamon
¼ cup of cooked maple sausage tidbits (approx. 2 cooked links broken into tiny pieces)

Cut butter into brown sugar and cinnamon. Add in maple/sausage tidbits. Don't overdo; mixture is supposed to be crumbly.

Cakes, Cupcakes, and Frostings

Cupcake Batter:
1-3/4 cups all-purpose flour
¾ cup cocoa
2-1/4 Tsp. baking powder
1/8 Tsp. salt

Whisk above ingredients together and set aside

2 sticks softened butter
1 Cup white sugar
¼ Cup brown sugar
2 eggs
1 Tsp. maple flavoring
3/4 Cup milk
¼ Cup honey BBQ sauce
Beat 2 sticks of softened butter together. Add sugars and beat in. Beat eggs and add to mixture with the maple flavoring and the BBQ sauce. Beat in flour mixture, alternating with the milk until smooth mixture is achieved.

Pour into lined muffin tins (18) and top with sprinkling of maple/sausage streusel.

Bake in 350 degree oven for 21-23 minutes depending upon variance in oven temp.

BBQ Buttercream Icing:
3 sticks butter, softened
1 Tlbs. bacon grease (optional)
2 Tsp. vanilla extract
1 ½ to 2 pounds confectioners' sugar, sifted
2 Tlbs. honey BBQ sauce
3-4 Tlbs. heavy cream or milk
Maple syrup for drizzling

In a large mixing bowl, cream butter and bacon grease until fluffy. Add vanilla, BBQ sauce and 2 tablespoons of heavy cream or milk. Slowly add in confectioners' sugar, and continue creaming until well blended.

Blend on low speed until moistened. Add an additional 1 to 2 tablespoons of heavy cream or milk until you reach the desired consistency. (More confectioners' sugar may also be added at this point if required.) Beat at high speed until frosting is smooth and fluffy.

After BabyCakes have cooled, pipe icing onto cupcakes until they look like ice cream cones. Drizzle sparingly with maple syrup over the top.

*Note: adjustment in cream and confectioners' sugar depends upon whether or not bacon grease is used. It should be noted that the bacon drippings were part of the original Hogs & Heads recipe, but the buttercream is still good without it.

Cozy Food

Limoncello Cake with Limoncello Syrup and Lemon Glaze
From the Franki Amato Mysteries by Traci Andrighetti (page 170)

Besides Nutella, of course, Franki's favorite food of all time is cake—with icing. (Incidentally, "Let them eat cake" is her favorite quote, even though rumor has it that Marie Antoinette actually said "Let them eat *brioche*.") And baking Limoncello into a cake is her idea of Italian-American nirvana. Here is Franki's recipe for an utterly lemontastic Limoncello-lemon cake with syrup. And glaze.

Cake:
non-stick cooking spray
1 1/2 cups all-purpose flour
1 1/2 cups cake flour
1 Tbsp baking powder
1 tsp salt
2 3/4 cups powdered sugar
1/2 cup lightly packed, finely grated lemon zest
1/2 cup vegetable oil
2 sticks unsalted butter, softened
3 large eggs, room temperature
3 large egg yolks, room temperature
3 Tbsps Limoncello
2 Tbsps lemon extract
3/4 cup heavy cream

Limoncello Syrup:
1/4 cup sugar
1/4 cup fresh lemon juice
1 Tbsp Limoncello

Glaze:
1 cup powdered sugar
2 Tbsps fresh lemon juice
1 tsp almond extract

Preheat the oven to 350 degrees. Coat a ten-inch Bundt pan with non-stick cooking spray. Dust the pan with flour.

In a large bowl, combine the all-purpose flour, cake flour, baking powder and salt. Sift the ingredients and set aside.

Using a stand mixer, add the vegetable oil, butter, powdered sugar and lemon zest. Beat on medium speed until the mixture is pale yellow (about four minutes). Add the eggs, Limoncello and lemon extract and continue to beat on medium speed for one minute. Add the flour mixture and heavy cream in three alternating batches, starting and ending with the flour.

Pour the batter into the Bundt pan. Bake on the middle rack of the oven for one hour, rotating the pan after thirty minutes. When the cake is done, cool in the Bundt pan for thirty minutes. Then turn the cake onto a cake plate.

While the cake is cooling, make the Limoncello syrup. Place the sugar, fresh lemon juice and Limoncello in a small saucepan. Heat over a low heat to dissolve the sugar. Remove from heat and cool slightly. Poke holes in the top of the cake with a skewer, and brush the syrup all over the cake.

When the cake has cooled completely, make the glaze. Place the powdered sugar, fresh lemon juice and almond extract in a bowl and stir until smooth. Pour the glaze on the top of the cake, letting it drizzle down the sides. Allow the glaze to set, and then serve. *Delizioso!*

Hot Grudge Sundae Cake with Dark Chocolate Fudge Sauce

From Mysteries a la Mode by Wendy Lyn Watson (page 235) and from the Pet Boutique mysteries by Annie Knox

Tally Jones from the Mysteries a la Mode and Izzy McHale from the Pet Boutique mysteries lead very different lives. They have two things in common, though: neither one has much time to spend in the kitchen, and they both love ice cream. While they're both perfectly content with a pint and a spoon, this recipe saves the day on more special occasion: it's deliciously easy yet fancy enough to serve at a dinner party. It's also versatile, so feel free to put your own spin on it.

2 c. chocolate wafer (or chocolate graham) crumbs
5 ½ Tbs. butter, melted
2 pints coffee ice cream
2 c. Cool Whip
1 - 7 ½ oz. jar marshmallow fluff
1 jar caramel topping
toffee bits (for garnish)

Combine crumbs and melted butter. Press onto the bottom and up 1 inch of the sides of a lightly oiled 10-in springform pan (I use butter to grease). Freeze for at least 30 minutes. Meanwhile, make the fudge sauce (below); soften ice cream; and fold fluff and Cool Whip together.

When the crust comes out of the freezer, spread the ice cream. Drizzle with caramel sauce. Top with fluff/Cool Whip combination. Drizzle on more caramel and sprinkle with toffee bits. Serve with Dark Chocolate Fudge Sauce.

Dark Chocolate Fudge Sauce:
1 ½ c. heavy cream
2/3 c. brown sugar
4 oz. good bittersweet chocolate
3 oz. unsweetened chocolate
½ stick of butter
1 ½ tsp. vanilla (or up to 3 Tbs. liqueur, if you want a flavored sauce … Frangelico goes well with this particular combination of flavors)

Bring cream and sugar to a very low boil, whisking occasionally. Continue to boil whisking until sugar dissolves. Remove from heat, then whisk in chocolate, whisk in butter, and finally whisk in vanilla or liqueur.

Alternative Flavor Combination: As mentioned above, this is a very versatile recipe. My favorite variation is to replace the coffee ice cream with mint chocolate chip, do away with the caramel sauce, and replace the toffee with crushed peppermint candy. Find a way to make your favorite flavor work!

Cozy Food

Carrot Cake
From the Murder Packs a Suitcase mystery series by Cynthia Baxter (page 173)

The heroine of my Murder Packs a Suitcase mysteries, travel-writer Mallory Marlowe, is a busy woman, dashing off to one vacation destination after another. I'm also pretty busy, so I appreciate crowd-pleasing desserts that are easy to make plus absolutely foolproof. This moist, flavorful carrot cake always fills the bill. Like most cakes, it can be made in a large sheet, in square or round layers, or even as cupcakes. It also freezes well. (And the white cream cheese frosting can be dyed with food coloring, making it perfect for a birthday cake or any other special occasion cake.)

Makes one 9 x 13 inch cake.

2 cups flour
2 cups sugar
2 tsps baking powder
2 tsps baking soda
1 tsp salt
2 tsps cinnamon
1 ¼ cups vegetable oil
3 cups (about one pound) grated carrots
4 eggs
½ cup chopped nuts
2 tsps vanilla
Cream cheese frosting

Preheat oven to 350 degrees.

Combine first six ingredients in a large mixing bowl and beat for 2-3 minutes. Add oil, then carrots, then eggs one at a time, continuing to mix well. Stir in vanilla, then nuts.

Pour batter into greased and floured pan. Bake at 350 degrees for 50 to 60 minutes. Cool completely in pan before frosting.

Cream Cheese Frosting:

8 ounces cream cheese
½ cup (1 stick) butter
4 cups confectioners sugar

Beat cream cheese and butter until light and fluffy. Gradually add confectioners sugar, continuing to beat until well mixed. Spread over cooled cake.

Classic New York Cheesecake
From the Reigning Cats & Dogs mystery series by Cynthia Baxter (page 173)

Like the heroine of my Reigning Cats & Dogs mystery series, veterinarian Jessica Popper, I live on Long Island. Here in the sprawling suburbs of New York City, we're lucky enough to be very much influenced by the Big Apple—including its fabulous food. New York Cheesecake is a luscious dessert that now appears on menus all over the country (and the world!). But while there are endless variations, this recipe is for the classic version—rich, dense, and velvety-smooth. And although some people think making cheesecake is complicated, it's surprisingly easy. (It's also best if it's made the day before it's served.)

Serves 12.

Crust:
1 ½ cups cookies (butter cookies, Social Teas, Oreos, etc.)
2 Tbsps melted butter

Cheesecake Filling:
32 ounces cream cheese
¾ to 7/8 cup sugar
2 Tbsp cornstarch
1 egg
1 tsp vanilla
½ cup heavy cream
Preheat oven to 450 degrees. Spray 10" springform pan with Pam.

Using a blender or a rolling pin, crush cookies. Mix in melted butter until moistened. Press into bottom of springform pan to make crust.

Whip heavy cream (you are making unsweetened whipped cream); set aside. In a mixing bowl, beat cream cheese until light and fluffy. Gradually add combined sugar and cornstarch. Beat in egg, then vanilla and heavy cream.

Pour filling into springform pan. Bake at 450 degrees for 30 minutes.

Remove from oven (even though it looks wet and uncooked). Cool on rack for 3 hours (it continues to "bake"). Refrigerate.

Remove from refrigerator a half hour before serving. Serve with berries, caramel or chocolate sauce, nuts, whipped cream, or whatever creative garnish you can come up with.

Bacardi Rum Cake
From The Main Street Murder series, set in North Carolina's western mountains, by Sandra Balzo (page 172)

Life in Sutherton has always revolved around Mama Philomena's restaurant on Main Street. Sadly, second-generation "Mama," Phyllis Balisteri, has inherited neither her mother's recipes nor her cooking ability along with the restaurant.

In the first book of the series, *Running on Empty*, Phyllis has resorted to serving the dishes that sustained her as a child at home, even while Philomena was dishing up authentic Italian cuisine for the rest of the town: convenience foods and the brand name recipes found on the backs of boxes, cans and bottles.

Here's one classic the Sutherton locals would kill—or, at least, wound--for:

Bacardi Rum Cake:
1 cup chopped pecans or walnuts
1 18 1/2 oz. package yellow cake mix

3 3/4 oz. package Jell-O Instant Vanilla Pudding mix
4 eggs
1/4 cup water -- cold
1/2 cup Wesson
1/2 cup Bacardi Dark Rum (80 proof)

Glaze:
1/4 lb. butter
1/4 cup water
1 cup granulated sugar
1/2 cup Bacardi Dark Rum

Preheat oven to 325 degrees. Grease and flour 10-inch tube or 12-cup Bundt pan. Sprinkle nuts over bottom of the pan. Mix all cake ingredients together. Pour batter over nuts. Bake 1 hour. Cool. Invert on serving plate. Prick Top. Drizzle and smooth glaze evenly over top and sides. Allow cake to absorb glaze. Repeat until all glaze is used up.
Glaze: Melt butter in saucepan. Stir in water and sugar. Boil 5 minutes, stirring constantly. Remove from heat. Stir in rum. Serves 10-12.

Myrtle's Better than Sex Cake
From *Beef Stolen-off* by Liz Lipperman (page 203)

1 package German chocolate cake mix
¾ cup hot fudge sauce
¾ cup caramel sauce
¾ cup sweetened condensed milk
12 ounces extra creamy nondairy whipped topping such as Cool Whip
4 Heath Bars (1.4 ounces each), chopped

Prepare the cake mix according to package directions and bake in a 13-by-9-by-2 pan 32-37 minutes or until toothpick inserted in the center comes out clean. Cool for 20 minutes on rack, then punch 20-25 holes in the top with the handle of a wooden spoon. Microwave the hot fudge sauce for 20 seconds and then pour it into the holes. Microwave the caramel sauce and the condensed milk separately and add one at a time just like the hot fudge sauce. Frost with the whipped topping. Sprinkle the Heath Bars over the whipped topping. Refrigerate.

Cookie Dough Cheesecake
From The Great Chocolate Scam by Sally Berneathy (page 174)

I love cheesecake and chocolate chip cookies, so it seemed only natural to combine them. This recipe is included in *The Great Chocolate Scam*.

Cookie Dough:
3 Tbsp. butter, softened
1/2 c. brown sugar
1/2 egg (approximately 2 Tbsp.)
1/8 tsp. baking soda
Dash of salt
3/4 c. flour
1 tsp. vanilla

1/2 c. (rounded or heaped) miniature chocolate chips

Cream together butter and sugar. Stir in egg. Mix flour, salt and baking soda and add to mixture. Add vanilla. Stir in chocolate chips. Put mixture into refrigerator while mixing cheesecake.

Cheesecake:
4 (8-oz) packages cream cheese, softened
1-1/2 c. sugar
1/4 c. flour
Dash of salt
4-1/2 large eggs
2 c. sour cream
1/4 c. cream
2 teaspoon vanilla

Line the bottom of one standard spring-form pan with parchment paper.
Beat cream cheese until smooth. Add sugar and continue beating until well mixed. Add flour and salt and mix well. Add eggs, one at a time, beating continuously. Add sour cream and mix well. Add cream and vanilla and beat until smooth.

Pour approximately half inch of batter into pan. Dot with pieces of cookie dough. Add another half inch to cover, then dot with pieces of cookie dough again. Continue until you use all the cheesecake. Final layer should be cheesecake.

Bake at 350 degrees for 60 minutes. Turn off oven and open door slightly, leaving cheesecake in the oven for another hour.

Remove and cool half an hour, then remove from pan. Store covered in refrigerator for at least 8 hours to allow cheesecake to ripen.

Slice and serve. Drizzle with Chocolate Ganache or serve plain.

Chocolate Ganache:
9 ounces bittersweet chocolate, chopped
1 c. cream

Heat cream in sauce pan until it steams but doesn't boil. Add chocolate and stir until it dissolves. Remove from heat and cool.

Cozy Food

Cookies, Bars, and Brownies

Cookies

Where The Sand Meets The Sea Shortbread
From *The Day She Died* by Catriona McPherson (page 210)

Jessie Constable in *The Day She Died* gets hired to clean and prepare caravans (= US trailers) for vacation rentals at Sandsea. Part of her job is setting out the "warm Scottish welcome": a couple of teabags, some powdered creamer and a miniscule packet of store-bought shortbread.

Even bad shortbread is quite good. Fresh home-made shortbread, however, is sublime. And so easy!

9 oz of multi-purpose flour
6 oz of cold salted butter
3 oz of sugar

Extra butter for greasing the pan
Extra sugar for sprinkling

You will need a shallow baking pan at least 10x13 inches.

- Set the oven to 325F.
- Grease the baking pan with the butter paper or a little chip of butter.
- Mix the flour and sugar in a bowl.
- Cut the butter into small cubes.
- Rub the butter cubes into the flour/sugar with your fingertips until the mixture resembles breadcrumbs and there are no big lumps left.
- Knead the mixture until it forms a soft dough which holds together and divide the dough into two.
- Flatten each batch of dough and roll it out into a circle about ¼ inch in thickness (no need to be precise)
- Carefully lift each round onto the greased baking sheet by rolling it onto your rolling pin and then off again. (Don't worry if it breaks up a bit – it will rejoin while cooking)
- Score the rounds into eight wedges – known as petticoat tails – with a knife, and prick each wedge with a fork once or twice to stop the shortbread puffing up. You can also press patterns into the edges with the fork tines.
- Bake for 20 minutes, but keep an eye out if your oven is fierce.
- Remove when the shortbread is a pale golden colour, sprinkle with a little sugar and allow to cool on the tray. It is soft while hot but will crisp up as it cools.
- Leftovers – unlikely – can be stored in an airtight tin.

Whoopie Pies
From the Do It Yourself home renovation mysteries by Jennie Bentley (page 174), featuring textile-designer-turned-renovator, Avery Baker, and her boyfriend, handyman Derek Ellis, in Waterfield, Maine.

Whoopie pies are a Pennsylvania Amish tradition originally, although these days, they're considered more of a New England phenomenon. According to food historians, whoopie pies were originally made from leftover batter, and when the children would find them in their lunch boxes, they'd yell "Whoopie!" Hence the name.

Traditional whoopie pies are made with vegetable shortening, not butter (although the recipe will work with butter, too). The original and most common whoopie pie is chocolate with vanilla filling, although pumpkin whoopie pies are a favorite seasonal variation. They're Avery's favorite dessert, and in the prologue to Wall to Wall Dead, Derek proposes with a diamond ring as the crowning glory of a whoopie pie.

1 cup firmly packed brown sugar
1 egg
1 ½ cup solid vegetable shortening
4 cup cocoa
2 cups all-purpose flour
1 teaspoon baking powder
1 teaspoon baking soda
1 teaspoon salt
1 teaspoon vanilla extract
1 cup milk

Preheat oven to 350 degrees F. Lightly grease baking sheets.

In a large bowl, cream together shortening, sugar, and egg. In another bowl, combine cocoa, flour, baking powder, baking soda, and salt.

In a small bowl, stir the vanilla extract into the milk. Add the dry ingredients to the shortening mixture, alternating with the milk mixture; beating until smooth.

Drop batter by the 1/4 cup (to make 18 cakes) onto prepared baking sheets. With the back of a spoon spread batter into 4-inch circles, leaving approximately 2 inches between each cake.

Bake 15 minutes or until they are firm to the touch. Remove from oven and let cool completely on a wire rack.

Meanwhile, make the filling:

1 cup solid vegetable shortening
1 ½ cups powdered sugar
2 cups Marshmallow Fluff
1 ½ teaspoons vanilla extract

In a medium bowl, beat together shortening, sugar, and Marshmallow fluff; stir in vanilla extract until well blended. When the cakes are completely cool, spread the flat side (bottom) of one chocolate cake with a generous amount of filling. Top with another cake, pressing down gently to distribute the filling evenly. Repeat with all cookies to make 9 pies. Wrap whoopie pies individually in plastic wrap, or place them in a single layer on a platter (do not stack them, as they tend to stick). You can freeze them the same way, by wrapping each pie in plastic wrap and putting them in a freezer proof container. Thaw them again in the fridge.

And that, my friends, is how you make whoopee ... pies!

Amaretti Cookies
From the Angie Amalfi Mysteries by Joanne Pence (page 220)

Angie Amalfi wants two things in life—a good job, and marriage to San Francisco Homicide Inspector Paavo Smith. Angie experiences a new culinary-based career in almost every book, everything from writing a newspaper column about food, to being on TV and radio shows, to doing restaurant reviews on videotape. But nothing ever quite works out as she expects it will, however. Fortunately, she's having more success with Paavo.

Angie is part of a large Italian family. When times get tough, she finds comfort in a cup of coffee with some good Italian cookies, preferably those that should be "dunked" into the coffee before being eaten. Amaretti cookies fit that bill exactly. They are flavorful, hard on the outside with a slightly softer center. Here's Angie's favorite recipes for these cookies:

3 cups blanched almonds (it doesn't matter if they're cut or whole since they will be ground fine)
1 ½ cups white sugar
3 egg whites
1 teaspoon almond extract

Preheat oven to 300 degrees F. Coat baking sheets with non-stick spray or line them with parchment paper.

Using a food processor, grind the almonds into a very fine meal. Add the sugar and continue to process for another 10-20 seconds until sugar and almonds are mixed. Next, add egg whites and almond extract. Process the mixture until a smooth dough forms around the blade.

Form round spoonfuls of dough, about the size of a walnut, and place them on the prepared baking sheets. Keep the cookies about 2 inches apart. Bake in preheated oven for about 20 minutes. They will not brown very much at all, but just turn slightly golden. Since it's difficult to tell if they're done, you may wish to take one cookie off the baking sheet and cut it in half to be sure the middle is cooked before removing them from the oven. The longer the cookies bake, the harder the center will be. Allow cookies to cool completely before removing. Store in a dry place.

Cherry Date Balls
From Joyce Oroz (page 215)

I am a gluten intolerant mystery writer, so I love gluten-free recipes. I bake most of my sweet treats myself and pop them in the freezer for later. My protagonist, Josephine Stuart tends to follow suit, but she has little time to waste—with all the crime going on around her. She loves simple to make, but scrumptious baked items. The following recipe qualifies as a "keeper."

This is a recipe for Cherry Date Balls by Barbara Endersbe … gluten-free and fabulous! I eliminated the granulated sugar because the dates and cherries are so sweet—your choice.

2 eggs, well-beaten
1 cup sugar—optional
1 cup chopped nuts---I use pecans
1 cup chopped dates
½ cup flaked coconut---I use unsweetened
½ t. almond extract
½ t. vanilla
1/8 t. salt
Cooking spray
36 candied cherries
Powdered sugar

Preheat oven to 350 degrees. Combine eggs, sugar, nuts, dates, coconut, almond extract, vanilla and salt. Place in buttered 8-inch square pan. Bake 30 minutes, stirring mixture thoroughly every ten minutes. Remove from oven and stir well, then let cool.

Spray a little cooking oil on your hands, then shape the dough into balls around cherries. Roll in powdered sugar - or not.

Cool and serve; makes about 20 cookies

Cold Creek Killer Cookies
From *Murder at Cold Creek College* by Christa Nardi (page 213)

Cold Creek Killer Cookies are a favorite of Sheridan Hendley, the amateur sleuth in the new series set in Cold Creek, Virginia by Christa Nardi. Sheridan is a professor and psychologist at a private college in Virginia, where she is also in charge of dealing with crises on campus. In *Murder at Cold Creek College*, she gets pulled into the investigation when her colleague, Adam, is murdered. As Sheridan tries to connect all the people in Adam's life the suspect pool grows, as she identifies so many women with motives for killing him. Sheridan's curiosity and logical mind have her putting pieces together and the murderer is getting nervous. One of Sheridan's favorite comfort foods, these Cold Creek Killer Cookies are easy to make!

1 pkg. (12-15 oz) brownie mix (Fudge brownie mix works the best - one that includes chocolate chunks is okay, but not one that includes chocolate syrup packets)
½ cup flour
¼ cup oil
1 egg
2 tablespoons water
1 cup semi-sweet chocolate chips (even if mix includes chunks!)
½ cup chopped pecans (or ½ cup raisins)
Powdered sugar

Preheat oven to 350°. In large bowl, mix brownie mix and flour. Add flour, egg, water; mix well. Add chips and chopped pecans (or substitute raisins for chopped pecans for variety). Roll dough into 1½ inch balls. Roll in powdered sugar. Place 2 inches apart on greased baking sheet (or use parchment paper for quick clean up).
Bake at 350° for 12-15 minutes or until tops of cookies begin to crack. Do not overbake. Immediately remove to cooling rack. Cool before serving. Makes 2 ½ -3 dozen.

Lebkuchen to Die For
From the Carol Sabala Mystery series by Vinnie Hansen (page 194)

In the first mystery in my series, *Murder, Honey*, a chef collapses into a vat of lebkuchen. Carol Sabala, my protagonist, is the baker responsible for the seemingly deadly dough. Naturally, she has to investigate. She enjoys the process, and in later books trains as a private investigator.

Lebkuchen, traditionally made for the Christmas season, requires more effort than chocolate chip cookies, but the result is a delicious spice cookie.

Like my heroine Carol Sabala, I don't follow rules well. I started with a recipe to make these cookies, but I don't like things as sweet as recipes dictate, so I changed the amount of honey. I couldn't find citron, so I used dried orange peel. You get the idea. By the time I finished, I'd developed a new recipe. (The cookies were great!) However, if I were to bake them again, I'd try using orange or lemon zest rather than going through the bother of using dried orange peel.

Ingredients: (I use organic.)
3/8 cup honey
1/2 cup black strap molasses
3/4 cup brown sugar
1 egg
1 tsp. grated lemon peel
1 tbsp. lemon juice
2 ¾ cups all-purpose flour
1 tsp. each of cinnamon, cloves and nutmeg
1/2 tsp. soda
2 tbsp. dried orange peel, dampened ahead of time to render soft so you don't break anyone's tooth!
1/3 cup chopped walnuts

Optional icing: I used my mom's simple powder sugar/milk mix to create a thin icing to brush across the cookies. If you've never made this icing, start with 1/2 cup powdered sugar and add a tsp. of milk to it. Stir until all lumps are dissolved. Add miniscule amounts of milk until you have a thin glaze.

Combine the honey and molasses in a saucepan and bring to a boil. Cool. Stir in sugar, egg, lemon peel and juice. Mix in the other ingredients and chill for at least 8 hours.

Heat oven to 400. For one sheet of cookies, scoop about 1/3 of the dough onto a lightly floured board. Keep the remaining dough refrigerated. With a lightly floured rolling pin, roll the dough to 1/4 inch thick. Cut with a cookie cutter. Place 1 inch apart on a lightly buttered baking sheet. Bake 10 to 12 minutes.

Remove from baking sheet. Ice while warm. Cool and store in an airtight container with a slice of orange.

Makes 3-5 dozen depending on cookie size.

Seven O'Clock: Gobs
From *The Convict, the Rookie Card, and the Redemption of Gertie Thump* by Becky Lyn Rickman (page 224)

Psalms 82:4: <u>Deliver</u> the poor and needy: rid <u>them out</u> of the hand <u>of the wicked</u>.

Gertie Thump is the thorn in the otherwise idyllic town of Rosedale. She inflicts her standards on innocent people and pushes them to the brink of insanity by constantly belittling and correcting them. One day, she returns home to find 12 plates of homemade cookies with notes attached. On the notes are scripture passages that have had certain words highlighted to make them sound threatening. They may or not contain poison, but the words are toxic enough to put the fear of God into her. Following is a link to the chapter on my website containing the 12 types of cookies and their accompanying poison scripture.

The cookie link: http://beckytheauthor.weebly.com/another-sample-chapter-being-very-cryptic-and-containing-a-heinous-use-of-the-good-book.html

Gobs:
2 cups flour
½ cup cocoa powder
1 teaspoon baking soda
¼ teaspoon salt
½ cup shortening
1 cup sugar
1 egg + 1 yolk
1 teaspoon vanilla
1 cup buttermilk
1 cup hot water

Filling:
1 ½ cups marshmallow cream
1 ¼ cups shortening
1 cup powdered sugar
1 Tablespoon vanilla

Preheat oven to 450° F. Line cookie sheets with parchment paper. In medium bowl, blend the dry ingredients. Cream the shortening and sugar on medium speed until light and fluffy, about 3 minutes. Beat the egg and extra yolk and add with vanilla, to the mix and beat another couple of minutes until smooth. Turn mixer to low and alternately add 1/3 of the flour mixture, and hot water. Drop by spoonful (about 1½ Tablespoon of dough). Bake for 5-6 minutes until they spring back when you touch the tops. Allow to cool on the baking sheets for 5 minutes and then transfer to a rack or brown paper bag until completely cool.

To make the filling, cream together the shortening and marshmallow cream on medium speed until light and fluffy, about 3 minutes. Reduce speed and add the powdered sugar and vanilla. Mix until sugar is completely blended and then beat another 3-5 minutes on medium until light and fluffy. Put a glob of filling on a cooled cookie and top with another. Keep in airtight container up to 5 days. Yea, it's fun to pretend they would last that long.

Orange Coconut Cookies
From *Murder on the Cape Fear* by Ellen Elizabeth Hunter (page 196)

In Book 6, *Murder on the Cape Fear,* Ashley bakes a platter of Orange Coconut Cookies for a book signing at Two Sisters Bookery where she stumbles over a corpse in the book-cluttered storeroom.

Aunt Ruby took the plate of cookies from me and sniffed appreciatively. "I declare, Ashley, you're becoming a regular Paula Deen! These look scrumptious. And we surely do need them, this crowd is ravenous. You know what I always say: You have to feed folks if you want them to buy books."

Easy, delicious, and my stars! your house will smell heavenly.

One box of Duncan Hines Orange Supreme Cake Mix
4 eggs
1/2 cup white sugar
1 cup vegetable oil
1 cup sweetened coconut

In the bowl of your mixer, mix the eggs, oil, and sugar.
Add the dry cake mix. Mix well.
Mix in coconut.

Using a #70 cookie scoop (about 1 T), scoop dollops of the cookie mixture onto a cookie sheet lined with baking paper. (It may be necessary repeat this step depending on the number of cookie sheets available and the size of your oven.)

Bake each batch for 12 minutes at 365 degrees. Cool on wire rack. Makes about 3 ½ dozen cookies. Best served with sweet Southern iced tea.

ENJOY!

Gerry's Ginger Cookie Recipe
From The Miniature Mysteries by Margaret Grace, aka Camille Minichino (page 210)

My second series protagonist, Geraldine Porter, dollhouse and miniatures enthusiast, wouldn't be caught dead, so to speak, without a batch of her famous ginger cookies on hand. Like so many heroines of cozy crime novels, Gerry feeds her family and her guests, both expected and unexpected. She's even been known to serve her cookies to killers. Not that she knew that at the time. She is, after all, only an amateur sleuth!

I'm a big fan of dollhouse and miniatures shows so I can speak with authority when I saw the single biggest category of wares is miniature food. Recently I've bought a one-inch loaf of (clay) bread that you can slice with a real knife, and a half-inch wedge of cheese that can be grated! I wouldn't recommend eating either one, but they are amazing to look at.

Look in any dollhouse and what gives it that cozy, lived-in feeling is the coffee pot on the stove and the tray of cookies coming out of the oven. For a moment, polymer clay smells like fresh ginger and you feel like curling up on that one-twelfth-scale couch and reading a good mystery.

2 1/3 cups flour
1 cup sugar (Gerry doesn't skimp on sugar!)
3/4 cup butter, softened
1/4 cup molasses
1/4 tsp. nutmeg
1/4 cup chopped crystallized ginger
4 tsp. grated ginger root
2 tsp. baking soda
2 tsp. ground ginger
1/2 cup shortening
dash salt
1 egg
extra sugar for rolling

- Heat oven to 375°.
- Mix sugar, butter, crystallized ginger, nutmeg, molasses, and egg in large bowl.
- Stir in remaining ingredients, except extra sugar.
- Shape dough into small balls (approx. one inch); roll in extra sugar.
- Place a couple of inches apart on ungreased cookie sheet and flatten slightly.
- Bake 5 to 8 minutes or until edges are set.
- Remove from cookie sheet and cool on wire rack.
- Makes about 5 dozen cookies.

Double-Delight Peanut Butter Cookies
From *Dead Girls Don't Blog* by Pamela Frost Dennis (page 186)

In *Dead Girls Don't Blog,* Katy McKenna takes time out from attempting to stop the parole of the man who raped and murdered her high school friend sixteen years ago, to gorge on these addictive cookies.

This recipe was created by Carolyn Gurtz—the Pillsbury $1,000,000 2008 Bake-Off Winner. The original recipe says to flatten the cookie, but Katy likes a thicker, creamier center, so she leaves it in a ball to bake.

¼ cup dry roasted peanuts, finely chopped
¼ cup granulated sugar
½ teaspoon ground cinnamon
½ cup creamy peanut butter
½ cup powdered sugar

1 roll (16.5 oz) Pillsbury® refrigerated peanut butter cookies, <u>well chilled</u>

1. Heat oven to 375°F.
2. In a small bowl, mix chopped peanuts, granulated sugar and cinnamon; set aside.
3. In another small bowl, stir peanut butter and powdered sugar until completely blended. Shape mixture into 24 balls.
4. Cut roll of cookie dough into 12 slices. Cut each slice in half crosswise to make 24 pieces; flatten slightly.
5. Shape 1 cookie dough piece around 1 peanut butter ball, covering completely. Repeat with remaining dough and balls.
6. Roll each covered ball in peanut mixture; gently pat mixture completely onto balls.
7. On ungreased large cookie sheets, place balls 2 inches apart.
8. Sprinkle any remaining peanut mixture evenly on tops of cookies; gently press into dough.
9. Bake 7 to 12 minutes or until edges are golden brown. Cool 1 minute; remove from cookie sheets to cooling rack. Store tightly covered. Try not to eat them all!

Aunt Crystal's Almond Crescent Cookies
From *Murder on Parade* by Melanie Jackson (page 198)
It is hard to imagine Christmas without this family favorite.

Chloe Boston, Hope Falls greatest detective, likes to bake these when she can get away from solving crimes.

½ pound salted butter (use the real thing—this is no time to be health conscious)
4 T powdered sugar (make sure it is new and sift it for lumps)
1 tsp vanilla (again—use the good stuff)
1 C almonds (the fresher the better. You can substitute macadamia or pecans— both are great)
2 C flour (again, sift, it makes mixing easier)
1 T water

Cream butter and powdered sugar. Add water, vanilla, flour and nuts. Mix well. Refrigerate at least one hour. I usually make my next cookie dough while the first is firming. Preheat oven to 350 and shape dough into crescents. Bake for three minutes on bottom rack. Move to top rack and cook until golden (this will depend on your over. Mine is old and cantankerous so it takes almost ten minutes but yours may be faster. Watch closely!). Roll in powdered sugar (or cocoa powder if you feel reckless).

Grandpa Mac's Prettiest Sugar Cookies
From *Murder on Parade* by Melanie Jackson (page 198)
It is hard to imagine Christmas without this family favorite.

Chloe Boston, Hope Falls greatest detective, likes to bake these when she can get away from solving crimes.

1 C butter (don't make me repeat myself—use butter)
1 C sugar (the finest grain you can find)
1 C powdered sugar
1 C vegetable oil (not olive)
2 eggs
4 ¼ C flour
1 tsp salt

1 tsp cream of tarter
1 tsp baking soda
1 tsp vanilla

Cream butter, sugar and oil together in large bowl. Add eggs. Beat until smooth. Add flour, salt, cream of tarter, baking soda and vanilla. Mix well. Here you can do variations. I sometimes add lemon zest, powdered coffee, cinnamon or cocoa powder.

This dough needs to refrigerate overnight so it is not a spur of the moment dessert. Preheat oven to 375. Form dough into balls and place on greased cookie sheet (or use parchment paper. I love parchment because cleanup is super easy). Flatten cookies with the bottom of a glass dipped in 2 T sugar and 1 T nutmeg (if dough is plain— plain sugar if it is not). Bake at 375 for 8 minutes. Cool on rack (easy if you use parchment paper).

Macaroons
From the Daisy Dalrymple mysteries by Carola Dunn (page 189)

Macaroons are not what Americans think they are. The English kind are Daisy Dalrymple's favourite biscuit/cookie. She tries hard to resist temptation but these are irresistible. She'll never have the right figure for the 1920s no-bosom/no bottom look, as noted by Alec Fletcher, the policeman who enters her life in the first book in her mystery series, *Death at Wentwater Court*. "Not plump, but not the straight up and down boardlike figure young women strove for these days. Cuddlesome was the word that had sprung to his mind the moment she walked in."

1 1/4 cups ground almonds
2 eggs (only whites needed)
3/4 cup sugar
a few whole or sliced almonds

- Pre-heat the oven to 400F.
- Line a cookie sheet with parchment paper.
- Separate egg yolks from whites (carefully!). Beat the whites on Slow until foamy.
- Pulse ground almonds in a food processor for half a minute to make fine.
- Make a paste, adding a portion of egg whites, then sugar pulsing until combined after each addition.
- The mixture will be soft. Use a scoop, or let it sit for a few minutes to stiffen and work with your hands.
- Make balls about 1 1/2" round.
- Place the macaroons a few inches apart on your cookie sheet. (If you prefer a flatter biscuit, gently press.) Place a couple of almonds on top.
- Bake for 10–15 minutes, until lightly browned. Take care not to over-bake. They should be crispy outside and chewy inside.

Lady Locks
From the kitchen of Mollie Bryan (page 180)

The cookie crust of lady locks is flaky and holds a heavenly cream. When I was a child, I loved sucking the cream out first, then enjoying the flavorful crust. Makes about 4 dozen.

Cookies:

Cozy Food

3 cups all-purpose flour
2 sticks (8 ounces) unsalted butter, at room temperature
1/2 cup warmed, not hot, milk
1/8 teaspoon vanilla extract
1 .06-unce yeast cake or 1/4-ounce yeast packet
1 tablespoon sugar

Cream filling:
1 cup milk
1/2 teaspoon salt, or to taste
5 tablespoons all-purpose flour
1 cup sugar
1 cup solid shortening
1 teaspoon vanilla extract

Preheat oven to 350. Wrap wooden clothespins (the straight, simple ones – no metal or hinges) or dowels with aluminum foil.

Blend flour and butter by hand or in electric mixer until it gets crumbly, like pie dough. Add remaining ingredients and mix at low speed. Roll the dough to 1/4 inch-thick on a floured board and cut into half-inch strips. Wrap loosely around aluminum-foil covered clothespins or dowels. Let rise for 30 minutes.

Bake for 15 minutes, or until dough looks firm and have slightly darkened in color. Remove from oven, let cool enough so that you don't burn yourself when removing the lady locks carefully from dowels or clothespins.

While cookies are baking, make the cream filling. Combine the milk, salt, and flour in a saucepan and cook until thick, stirring constantly until mixture sticks to your spoon—about the consistency of pudding. Cool the mixture, then one at a time, slowly stir in the sugar, shortening and vanilla. The cream should be smooth and airy. Fill cookies with the cream by using a pastry bag, pastry tube, or a plastic bag with one corner cut off.

Ginger Cookies
From *Murder in the Gazebo* (2013) by Chloe Evans (page 190)

What in the world would Melanie eat when she's too grieved to even think of food? Her mother's ginger cookies, of course. The ginger is not just tasty; it's soothing to an upset stomach.

2 c sifted flour
¾ c shortening
1 T powdered ginger
1 egg, beaten
2 t baking soda
¼ C sorghum molasses
1 t cinnamon
½ c granulated sugar
½ t salt

Sift dry ingredients. Cream shortening and sugar until fluffy. Beat in egg and molasses. Combine with dry ingredients with creamed mixture and blend well. Roll teaspoons of dough in granulated sugar. Place 2 inches apart on ungreased cookie sheet. Bake at 350 degrees until crackly and lightly browned, about 12-15 minutes.

Grandma's Cookies
From the Bookmobile Cat Mysteries by Laurie Cass (page 181)

These are Minnie's favorite cookies. It was her grandmother's go-to recipe and Minnie's Aunt Frances makes them for special occasions. Minnie sometimes thinks that she needs to learn how to bake the cookies herself, but she hasn't done so. Next year. Or the year after, for sure.

2 cups brown sugar
1/2 cup margarine (softened)
1/2 butter (softened)
4 eggs
1/2 cup milk
1/8 teas. nutmeg
1/2 teas. salt
4-5 cups flour
1 teas. baking soda
4 teas. baking powder
2 teas. vanilla

Mix all ingredients. Roll out a large handful of dough on floured surface. Use cookie cutters to cut into shapes. (Eat the leftover dough – it's outstanding.) Place on greased cookie sheet and bake 6-8 minutes at 375 degrees. When cool, frost (see recipe below) and decorate with colored sugars.

Cookie Frosting:
1 lb. confectioner's sugar (approx. 3-3/4 cups)
1/2 c. butter or margarine, softened
3-4 T milk
1 teas. vanilla

Combine all ingredients in large bowl with mixer at low speed. Beat at medium speed 1-2 minutes until creamy. If desired, add more milk until frosting is of spreading consistency.

Chocolate Chip Cookies

Caprice's Choco Chunks and Chips Cookies
A special recipe developed by Karen Rose Smith (page 228) to accompany her Caprice De Luca Home Staging Mystery series

In addition to staging and redecorating clients' homes, Caprice De Luca loves everything retro. From a large Italian family, her relationships with her brother and sisters, parents and Nana Celia mean everything to her. Caprice and her sisters learned to cook from their mom and Nana. Cooking together is bonding time as are the De Luca family dinners once a month. In each

Cozy Food

Caprice De Luca home staging mystery, solve the murder with Caprice, cook along with her, watch her find homes for the stray animals she protects, be a part of the De Luca family.

1/2 cup salted butter softened
1/4 cup peanut butter
1 cup packed brown sugar
3/4 cup granulated sugar
2 large eggs
1/8 teaspoon cinnamon
3 teaspoons vanilla
1 1/2 teaspoons baking powder
1 teaspoon baking soda
3 cups flour
1 1/2 cups semi-sweet chocolate chips
6 oz. milk chocolate (I use two 3 oz. DOVE bars broken into small pieces or chunks. These bars break or cut up easily.)

Preheat oven to 375

In a mixer, cream softened butter and peanut butter. Mix in brown sugar and granulated sugar until creamed. Add eggs and mix well. Add cinnamon and vanilla. Add baking powder and baking soda. Blend well. Add 2 cups of flour, a quarter cup at a time with mixer on low speed, constantly scrapping bowl. Stir in the other cup of flour, a quarter cup at a time, by hand until completely blended. Stir in chocolate chips and chunks.

Roll into 1 1/2" balls, place on cookie sheet 2 inches apart and press down slightly with palm of hand. (I usually put 12 on one cookie sheet.)

Bake 11 – 12 minutes until golden brown and set. (The type of cookie sheet you use can affect the baking time. Darker cookie sheets bake faster.)

Remove from the oven and let the cookies sit a minute on a cool surface. Remove from pan. Recipe makes about 30-36 cookies. Let cool until the chocolate hardens. Unless you eat all of them gooey warm!

Ames's Family Oatmeal Peanut Butter Chunk Choco Chip Cookies
From *Organized for Murder* by Ritter Ames (page 170)

This is a recipe guaranteed to please Kate McKenzie in *Organized for Murder,* Book I in my Organized Mysteries series. The reason Kate would like the recipe is three-fold: 1) it's almost a complete organized meal in a cookie, loaded with fiber from the oatmeal, protein from the peanuts, dairy from the butter, healthy sugar from honey, and even antioxidants from the chocolate; 2) the cookies can be made ahead of time, and frozen into baking sized balls, so fresh cookies can always be just one pre-heated oven away at any time; 3) my whole family contributed their ideas to make these cookies the standout they are today—just like Kate feels every family should be involved in clean and de-clutter projects. We started with a simple oatmeal cookie recipe, then measured and substituted—and, of course, taste tested for recipe reliability—until we found exactly the mix of ingredients desired. This is the final version, and has become one of our family's staples. I know Kate McKenzie would approve. I hope you do, too.

¾ cup packed brown sugar

¾ cup honey (original we used 1 ¾ cup brown sugar instead—but I like the honey/brown sugar split, so that I get the sweet taste honey adds, while still getting the brown sugar kick)

1 cup crunchy peanut butter (you can use creamy, but my family is just nuts)

6 Tablespoons butter softened (if I use margarine I use "I Can't Believe It's Not Butter" in cube, not soft tub margarine)

3 eggs, slightly beaten

1 ¾ teaspoons baking soda

1 teaspoon vanilla extract

3 ¾ to 4 ½ cups quick oats (not instant, but cooks in a couple of minutes), I add oats until I get the consistency I want—usually it's around 4 cups because of the honey

1 bag of Nestlé's Chunks semi-sweet pieces. (I've tried other chocolate additions, but I think this size—even with the chocolate in chunks so there are less pieces—are better than more pieces that are smaller throughout the cookie.

Preheat oven to 350°F.

Beat sugar, peanut butter, and margarine until creamy. Add eggs, baking soda, and vanilla, mix well. Blend in oats and chocolate chunks.

Drop by tablespoons onto cookie sheet sprayed with cooking spray like Pam because the choco chunks will make it stick.

Bake 10 to 12 minutes. Let stand 5 minutes before removing to racks to cool. Makes 2 dozen 4-inch cookies.

Robin's Chocolate Chip Cookies with a Twist

From *Home Improvement* a free short story in the Pajaro Bay series by Barbara Cool Lee (page 202)

Welcome to Pajaro Bay, where mystery and romance mingle on the California coast. Readers praise the series for its "sweetness," its "excellent characterization," and say the books are "adorable, lively and like a warm hug."

Robin Brenham is the most popular real estate agent in Pajaro Bay. That may be because she's great at her job, but it's also because she makes the best gourmet coffee and cookies in town, and is happy to share them with all the other business owners in the downtown area.

Her chocolate chip cookies have a twist in them you might not expect—but it makes them healthier, and also makes them an unusual color. Give them a try and see what you think:

1/2 cup butter

1/2 cup mashed avocado

3/4 cup sugar

3/4 cup brown sugar

2 eggs

1 teaspoon salt

2 teaspoons vanilla

1 teaspoon baking soda

2 and 1/4 cups flour

1 cup milk chocolate chips

Mix butter, avocado, and both sugars with an electric mixer until smooth and creamy. Add eggs, vanilla, salt, and baking soda, and mix thoroughly. Gradually add the flour and mix in until well-blended. Stir in the chocolate chips.

Drop by rounded tablespoons onto an ungreased (or parchment-lined) baking sheet, and bake in a 375 degree oven for ten minutes (they will appear underdone). Take out and let sit on the pan for five minutes to set, then remove with spatula and let cool until you can't stand it anymore and you have to eat them. Don't burn your mouth on the melted chocolate.

Cashew Chocolate Chip Cookies
From the Subbing isn't for Sissies Mysteries by Carolyn J. Rose (page 224)

These cookies are a favorite of substitute teacher Barbara Reed. After a hard day of subbing at Captain Meriwether High School in Reckless River, Washington, Barb munches on these while sipping a frothy drink with her dog Cheese Puff, the world's most entitled mutt.

Cream:
1 stick (a quarter of a pound) of butter (the real stuff)
½ cup dark brown sugar
½ cup white sugar
1 egg
2 t. vanilla

Mix in:
½ t. salt
½ t. baking soda
1 cup oatmeal (old fashioned, not quick-cooking)
1 cup flour (or a little more or less)

Add:
1 cup cashew pieces (salted or plain)
1 ½ cups dark chocolate chips

Set oven to 360 degrees and bake a test pan to determine whether to thicken the batter with more flour for plump cookies or thin it with a little water for lacy, crunchy cookies.

Makes about 50 cookies, depending on how large you like them.

Remove from cookie tin as soon as they're done and cool on racks or paper towels. Store in the freezer for months—or until you eat them all.

Mysterious Chocolate Chip Cookies
From the Regan McHenry Real Estate Mysteries by Nancy Lynn Jarvis (page 199)

Regan keeps this cookie dough in her freezer ready to bake at open houses to make them seem homey and to bake and take to friends and clients accused of murder. The cookies are made with an unusual mystery ingredient. Don't worry, the chili oil doesn't make the cookies hot, it just enhances the chocolate experience.

Cream together until light and fluffy:
1 cup butter

3/4 cup light brown sugar
3/4 cup granulated sugar

Add:
2 eggs
1 1/2 t vanilla
1 t baking soda
1 t habanero chili oil (Regan uses Coeur D'Olives Habanero Oil)
1 t cinnamon
Mix well.

Add:
2 1/4 cups flour
Mix again until well blended.

Stir in:
18 ounces chocolate chips
2 cups rolled oats or oatmeal

Drop by generous spoonfuls onto an ungreased cookie sheet. Bake at 350° for between 12 and 15 minutes, depending on size of the cookies. Cool before removing from the cookie sheet. Makes 36 or more cookies.

SallyB's Chocolate Chip Cookies
From *Death by Chocolate* by Sally Berneathy (page 174)

My chocolate chip cookie recipe has evolved over the years to please my taste buds, but everyone else seems to love it too. This recipe is included in *Death by Chocolate.*

½ c. butter, softened
1½ c. dark brown sugar
1 egg
1 T. vanilla (yes, tablespoon, NOT teaspoon)
½ t. baking soda
dash of salt (bigger dash if you use unsalted butter)
1½ c. flour
¼ c. oat flour
½ c. hazelnut meal (optional)
½ c. semi-sweet chocolate chips
½ c. dark chocolate chips
½ c. white chocolate chips
½ to 1 c. chopped nuts

Cream butter with sugar. If butter is too hard to stir with a spoon, use a potato masher to soften. Add egg and vanilla and stir briskly until well mixed. Combine dry ingredients and add to butter mixture. Stir in chocolate chips and nuts. Dough should be very stiff and just a little sticky. Add more flour or butter as necessary to achieve this state.

Taste to see if it's perfect. Taste again if desired.

Form dough into balls larger than a jacks ball and smaller than a golf ball. Place on cookie sheet a couple of inches apart. Bake at 375° for 8 minutes. Cookies will be moist and chewy with a firm outer crust.

Makes 2 dozen cookies, more or less, depending on how many samples were tested before baking.

Bars

Cissy's Turtle Bars
From the Augusta Goodnight Mystery series by Mignon F. Ballard (page 171)

This recipe was introduced in the seventh and last of the Augusta Goodnight mysteries set during the Christmas season in Stone's Throw, South Carolina, when guardian angel/sleuth Augusta Goodnight comes to the aid of Lucy Nan Pilgrim and her friends as they discover a stranger's body while searching for the perfect Christmas tree. And all is not fa-la-la holiday happy when they come upon another in their own church sanctuary.

I have hoped in vain the quirky angel, a fabulous cook in her own right, might come for an extended visit with me. Not only does she produce heavenly meals, but a speck of dirt wouldn't dare to invade her tidy kitchen. This recipe, however, comes from Cissy, the choir director at Lucy Nan's church, who makes them to treat her choir members during the season's Lessons and Carols. I've served this rich bar cookie often at Christmas and other times and rarely have leftovers. Augusta gives them her stamp of approval, and so do I.

Crust:
2 cups all-purpose flour
1 cup firmly packed dark brown sugar
½ cup butter, softened
1 cup whole pecan halves

Caramel layer:
½ cup firmly packed dark brown sugar
2/3 cup butter
12 ounces milk chocolate chips

Preheat oven to 350 degrees

Combine the flour, brown sugar and butter for crust; mix well and pat firmly into an ungreased 9 x 12-inch pan. Sprinkle the pecans evenly over the unbaked crust. Prepare the caramel layer by combining the brown sugar and butter in a heavy saucepan. Cook over medium heat, stirring constantly, until mixture begins to boil. Boil ½ to 1 minute, stirring the whole time. Pour over pecans and crust. Bake for 18 - 22 minutes or until crust is light golden brown. Remove from oven and immediately sprinkle with chocolate chips. Allow them to melt, then swirl. Cool and cut into bars.

Makes 3 – 4 dozen

Snickerdoodle Blondie Bars
From Allison Cesario Paton (page 219)

2 2/3 cup all-purpose flour
2 teaspoons baking powder
1 teaspoon cinnamon
1/4 teaspoon ground nutmeg
1 teaspoon salt
2 cups packed brown sugar
1 cup butter or soy margarine, at room temperature
2 eggs, at room temperature
1 tablespoon vanilla extract
2 tablespoons granulated sugar
2 teaspoons cinnamon
pinch of nutmeg

Preheat oven to 350°. Grease a 13 x 9 inch baking dish. Combine the flour, baking powder, cinnamon, nutmeg and salt. Set aside. Now beat together the brown sugar and the butter. Add the eggs one at a time, followed by the vanilla. Stir in the flour mixture. Spread evenly into prepared pan. Combine the granulated sugar, cinnamon and nutmeg. Sprinkle over dough. Bake 25 to 30 minutes until toothpick inserted near center comes out clean. Don't over bake!! Let cool completely before cutting.

Oatmeal Fruit Bar
From Joyce Oroz (page 215)

Josephine likes to sleep late but doesn't like to be late for work so she has quick, make-ahead breakfasts like oatmeal fruit bars. Solow likes them too. So easy to make, Josephine keeps a stash of in the freezer. Freezer to microwave in 60 seconds.

3 ripe bananas
1/4 cup milk--Josephine uses rice milk
1/3 cup applesauce
1/2 cup yellow raisins or dried cranberries
1 cup chopped nuts--Josephine likes walnuts
1 T cinnamon
1/2 t sea salt
2 cups oats--Josephine uses gluten free oats

Fire up the oven to 350 and run some butter over an 8x8 baking pan. Mix ingredients, scoop into pan and bake a good 20 minutes or more until knife comes out clean. Eat um hot or cold or warm with whipped cream.

Chocolate Coconut Bars
From the Reigning Cats & Dogs mystery series by Cynthia Baxter (page 173)

Jessica Popper, the veterinarian who's the heroine of my Reigning Cats & Dogs mysteries, is a big fan of Ben & Jerry's ice cream. I also love ice cream, especially varieties like Ben & Jerry's that combine different flavors and textures. These 3-layer bars achieve that same effect: mixing together delectable flavors and textures that play off each other perfectly. The combination of dark chocolate and coconut in these bars is reminiscent of Mounds candy bars, with the addition of a layer of moist chocolate cake. It's best to freeze them before cutting into individual bars. And they can be kept frozen for weeks.

Makes 24 bars.

Chocolate Cake Layer:
2/3 cup chocolate chips (such as Nestle Toll House Morsels)
½ cup (1 stick) butter
1 cup sugar
2 eggs
1 ½ tsps vanilla
1 2/3 cups flour, divided
¾ tsp baking soda
1/8 tsp salt
1 cup water

Coconut Layer:
5 1/3 cups (14 ounces) flaked coconut (such as Baker's Angel Flake Coconut)
1 can (14 ounce) sweetened condensed milk

Chocolate Top Layer:
¾ cup heavy cream
2 Tbsps butter
1 2/3 cups chocolate chips

Preheat oven to 350 degrees. Grease and flour 13 x 9 inch cake pan.

To Make Chocolate Cake Layer:
Microwave 2/3 cups chocolate chips and ½ cup butter in large bowl until melted. Stir. Stir sugar into chocolate until well-mixed. Beat in eggs, one at a time, with electric mixer. Add vanilla. Beat in 1/3 cup of flour, baking soda, and salt. Beat in remaining flour alternately with water until smooth. Pour cake batter into cake pan. Bake 30 minutes or until toothpick comes out clean. Cool completely in pan on wire rack.

To Make Coconut Layer:
Mix coconut and sweetened condensed milk by hand until well blended. Spread on top of cake. (HINT: Freeze cake before spreading on this layer.)

To Make Chocolate Top Layer:
Microwave heavy cream and 2 Tbsps butter in large bowl, stopping to stir, until mixture boils. Add 1 2/3 cups chocolate chips and stir until they are melted and mixture is cool. Spread over coconut layer. Refrigerate or freeze until top layer of chocolate is firm enough to cut into bars.

Granola Bars
From The Dream Club Mysteries by Mary Kennedy (page 201)

Ali and Taylor Blake, the sisters who run Oldies But Goodies, a vintage candy store in The Dream Club Mysteries, always keep plenty of these on hand. Customers love them and Ali offers free samples to drum up business. She also serves them at Dream Club meetings where the group loves to discuss their dreams and eat home-baked goodies as they work at solving a murder or two.

2 cups rolled oats (the old fashioned ones, not the "quick" version)
1/2 cup wheat germ (you can find it in the cereal aisle.)
1 cups sliced almonds or walnuts
1/2 cup dried cranberries or cherries
1 can (14 oz) condensed milk (not evaporated milk)
1/2 cup chocolate chips

Mix all ingredients and bake in a 9 x 9 inch square pan lined with tinfoil. To make clean-up easier, place two sheets of tinfoil in a "cross pattern." Spray sheets with PAM. Leave ends long, so you can lift the whole thing out when it is cooked. No mess that way.

Bake for 30 minutes. Let cool, the lift out. These freeze very well. Serves 12.

Carrie's Oatmeal Bars
From *A Valley to Die For* by Radine Trees Nehring (page 214)

A Valley to Die For. In this novel Carrie McCrite tells us that her kitchen helper is more likely to be the Pillsbury Dough Boy than Julia Child. However, she does create a simple cookie for a special guest in her home.

Heat oven to 350 degrees
1 stick margarine
1/4 cup dark corn syrup
1/2 cup brown sugar
1 Tbsp molasses
2 1/2 cups oatmeal
pecan halves

Line 8 inch square pan with greased foil, spread mixture on the foil, top with pecans, bake for 35 minutes.
Cut into bars when cool.

Brownies & Fudge

Sinfully Sweet Chocolate Kahlua Brownies
From *Murder for the Halibut* by Liz Lipperman (page 203)

3/4 cup cocoa, unsweetened
1/2 teaspoon baking soda
2/3 cup melted butter, divided
1/4 cup boiling water
1/4 cup Kahlua
2 cups granulated sugar

2 eggs, lightly beaten
1 teaspoon vanilla extract
1 1/3 cups all-purpose flour
1/4 teaspoon salt
1/2 cup coarsely chopped walnuts or pecans
1 bag (12 ounces) semisweet chocolate chips

Preheat the oven to 350° F. In a large bowl, combine the cocoa and baking soda. Blend in 1/3 cup of melted butter. Add boiling water and Kahlua and stir until well blended. Stir in sugar, beaten eggs, vanilla, and the remaining 1/3 cup of butter, then the flour and salt. Add the nuts and chocolate chips and pour the batter into a greased 13x9x2-inch baking pan. Bake for 35-40 minutes or until chocolate brownies are firm and begin to pull away from sides of pan. Cool before cutting into squares.

Rocky Road Brownies

From *Brownies & Betrayal*, the first book in the Sweet Bites Bakery mysteries by Heather Justesen. (page 199)

Tess Crawford moves to Silver Springs, AZ to get away from her cheating ex and the high-pressure restaurant she's been working in, but before she can even get her grandmother's old restaurant renovated into a bakery, she becomes a murder suspect. Desperate to clear her name and find out who the real killer is, she and her childhood friend, Honey, search for the real killer. When she learns the truth, things become explosive. Murder, romance, and decadent desserts all roll together to make this a tasty story.

This recipe was one Tess and Honey developed together when they were in 4-H—it won all kinds of awards then, and is every bit as good now!

2 cups sugar
4 eggs
1 cup plus 3 Tbsp butter
1 tsp vanilla
2 cups melted unsweetened chocolate chips
½ cup plus 1 Tbsp cocoa
Mix, then add: 2 ½ cup flour
¼ tsp baking soda
1 tsp salt
1 cup pecan bits
1 cup semi-sweet chips
4 cups miniature marshmallows

Mix the sugar, eggs, butter, vanilla and cocoa until smooth. Melt the chocolate chips in the microwave, stirring every twenty seconds until smooth Cool and mix in the rest of it.

Add the baking soda and salt, then the flour, mixing between cups. Add the nuts and chocolate chips into the batter, mixing well, and pour into greased and floured 9x13 pan. I usually use a spray oil like Pam or Vegalene, then flour the pan to keep it from sticking. Bake at 350 degrees for 30-35 minutes, adding mini-marshmallows to the top of the pan for the final five minutes or until the marshallows on the edge just start to turn golden. *The marshmallows will cut better if you let the brownies cool most of the way first.*

Cookies, Bars, and Brownies

White Chocolate and Plum Brownies
From *Assault with a Deadly Glue Gun* by Lois Winston (page 237)

(In this excerpt from *Assault with a Deadly Glue Gun* by Lois Winston, Anastasia has once again missed lunch. Food editor and sometimes Watson to sleuth Anastasia Pollack, Cloris McWerther offers her a white chocolate and plum brownie.)

I hesitated. "How many calories per bite?"

"What the hell are another thousand calories or so in the greater scheme of life?"

Easy for her to say with her mach ten metabolism. I had a sneaking suspicion that Cloris exhaled calories and fat grams instead of carbon dioxide. On me, the calories and fat moved directly from my mouth to my hips, bypassing the entire digestive process.

But that didn't stop me from caving in and grabbing a brownie. My willpower never stands a chance against my salivating taste buds.

Prep Time: 15 min.
Cook Time: 30 min.
Yield: 16 – 2" squares

baking spray
8 oz. semisweet chocolate
1/4 cup vegetable oil
1/2 cup sugar
1/2 cup plum preserves
2 large eggs
1 tsp. vanilla extract
1/3 cup + 2 Tbsps. all-purpose flour
1/8 tsp. salt
1/2 cup white chocolate chips

Heat oven to 325°F. Coat the bottom of an 8" x 8" pan with baking spray. Melt chocolate with oil in microwave safe bowl in microwave. Whisk in sugar and plum preserves. Whisk in eggs and vanilla. Fold in flour and salt. Fold in white chocolate chips. Spread evenly in pan. Bake approximately 45 minutes or until knife inserted into center comes out clean. Cool on wire rack at least 10 minutes.

Sweet and chewy gluten-free brownies made with black beans
From Joyce Oroz (page 215)

I am a gluten intolerant mystery writer, so I love gluten-free recipes. I bake most of my sweet treats myself and pop them in the freezer for later. My protagonist, Josephine Stuart tends to follow suit, but she has little time to waste—with all the crime going on around her. She loves simple to make, but scrumptious baked items.

One of Josephine's favorites is this recipe for chocolate brownies made out of black beans. She loves the whole idea of eating beans that taste like chocolate. It's like eating dinner and dessert in the same bite, saves time too. She loves to bake them—so easy to make, and keeps a stash in

the freezer for chocolate emergencies. Check out more good stuff at
http://authorjoyceoroz.blogspot.com

Sweet and chewy gluten-free brownies made with black beans *(but you'd never know it from the taste)!* So simple and amazingly delicious! Yield: 16 squares

2 cups cooked black beans (or 1 can, rinsed and drained)
3 eggs
1/3 cup melted butter
1/4 cup cocoa powder
2 teaspoons vanilla extract
1 cup sugar (or 1/2 cup honey) Josephine uses honey
1/2 cup semi-sweet chocolate chips
1/2 cup finely chopped walnuts (optional)

1. Pre-heat oven to 350 degrees. In a food processor bowl or blender, combine the black beans, eggs, melted butter, cocoa powder, vanilla, and sugar. Pulse or blend until smooth (or as smooth as possible).
2. Grease an 8x8-inch glass baking dish. Pour the batter into the greased dish. Sprinkle chocolate chips and nuts (if using) over the top and use a spatula to push them down into the batter just a little (but not too much; they will sink some while the brownies bake).
3. Bake at 350 degrees for 40-50 minutes, until brownies are set in the middle. Watch the edges for excess browning if you're not sure they're done. (Mine seem to take a full 50 minutes or more, and are still chewy but not gooey.)
Cool and then chill before serving! Store in fridge.

Caramel Peanut butter Fudge
From the kitchen of Nancy J. Parra (page 219)

Bottom Layer:
1 cup milk chocolate chips
¼ cup butterscotch chips
¼ cup peanut butter

Filling:
1 cup butter, melted
1 cup peanut butter, melted
2 cups of powdered sugar (More if it seems too runny)
1 tsp vanilla

Caramel:
1 14 oz package of caramels unwrapped
¼ cup heavy cream
Top Layer:
1 cup milk chocolate chips
¼ cup butterscotch chips
¼ cup peanut butter

Lightly grease a 9x13 inch dish.

For the bottom layer: Combine 1 cup milk chocolate chips, 1/4 cup butterscotch chips and 1/4 cup creamy peanut butter in a small saucepan over low heat. Cook and stir until melted and smooth. Spread evenly in prepared pan. Refrigerate until set.

For the filling: In a heavy saucepan over medium-high heat, melt butter and peanut butter together. Remove from heat. Stir in powdered sugar until stiff add vanilla. Spread over bottom layer, score into pieces-return to refrigerator until set.

For the caramel: Combine caramels and cream in a medium saucepan over low heat. Cook and stir until melted and smooth. Spread over filling. Chill until set.

For the top layer: In a small saucepan over low heat, combine 1 cup milk chocolate chips, 1/4 cup butterscotch chips, and 1/4 cup peanut butter. Cook and stir until melted and smooth. Spread over caramel layer. Chill 1 hour before cutting into 1 inch squares.

Savannah's Famous Fudge
From the Savannah Reid Mysteries under the pseudonym G.A. McKevett by Sonja Massie (page 206)

Savannah: Hi, everybody. If you want to make an awesome, quick, inexpensive goodie for somebody (or yourself), this is it! You can give it away for birthday presents, holiday gifts, and even as bribes, when necessary.
It tastes like that wonderful fudge you ate as a kid and left out for Santa. And anybody can make it. It turns out great every single time.

It tastes best if eaten within the first 24 hours. This is usually NOT a problem. (Especially if you have a Dirk in your house.)

The Pledge
Before you look at this secret recipe, I have to ask you to take a pledge not to share it with anybody, ever. I mean it! I've been perfecting this for years, and it's got to stay just between you and me. We don't want anybody knowing how easy it is. That'll ruin it for all of us!

When you give some of this heavenly stuff to somebody, be sure to look like you're plum wrung out from all the work of making it. Throw some water on your face for sweat, sprinkle flour on your cleavage, mess up your hair, and smear your lipstick. Tell them it was a whole lot of hard, hot work - sigh - but THEY are worth it. Now if you're willing to abide by these rules, raise your right hand and make this pledge:

"If I ever share this recipe with anybody or let on to a soul that making it's as easy as getting a wet foot in a thunderstorm, every bite I eat of this divine concoction will go directly to my left buttock and stay there for the rest of my life!

Okay, here's the recipe....

1 12 oz. bag semi-sweet chocolate chips
I use Trader Joe's because they're cheap and wonderful, but any brand will do.
4 to 5 oz. of Hershey's Milk Chocolate bars, broken into squares.
This is three of the regular 1.55 oz bars. Or you could buy one of the big 7 oz. bars, eat part of it, and then use the rest. Don't worry about getting the exact amount. It's not a big deal.
1 can Eagle Brand Sweetened Condensed Milk

Cozy Food

Don't use evaporated milk! You'll have chocolate soup. Which can also be eaten in a pinch, but ...

Dash of salt
Teaspoon of vanilla
Or another flavor of extract if you'd rather, like mint, orange, coffee, whatever.

Put ingredients into a microwavable bowl. I use my big, four cup measuring cup. Zap it about 1 1/2 minutes. Take it out, stir it, put it back in for another 30 seconds. Take it out, stir. Keep doing this every 30 seconds until all of the chocolate has melted and the lumps are gone. Time will depend on your microwave. Mine takes 2 minutes and 30 seconds.

While the chocolate is melting, I line an 8x8 square pan with heavy duty foil and spray it <u>very</u> lightly with Pam. You can prepare the pan before you start if it's been a long day and multitasking might blow your fuse.

When the chocolate is all smooth, stir in the vanilla extract. That's it. It's all done. Spread it in the pan. Make pretty little swirly marks on top with your spoon. Set bowl and spoon aside to be licked later.

Refrigerate for one hour.

Take it out (foil and all). Peel back the foil from the sides and use a big butcher knife to cut it into 16 pieces. Put it back into the pan and stick it in the fridge for another hour. You can just wait two hours to cut it, if you want, but it's a bit more difficult to do when it's that firm. I find this way easier.

Take it out, put the squares into air tight plastic containers. If it's a Christmas gift, use the disposable ones, slap a bow on the top and an adhesive gift tag. Ho, ho, ho. You'll get a lot of love for five minutes of "work."

Variations:
If you want, you can have a lot of fun with this recipe. After the chocolate is melted, before you spread it in the pan, you may want to add something like nuts, (Georgia pecans are especially nice) or maraschino cherries. Just make very sure the cherries are cut in half, well drained and then blotted completely dry with paper towels. Otherwise the cherries will make it too moist, and you'll have to eat it with a spoon. (I assure you that this, too, can be done if push comes to shove.) Granny loves her cherry fudge. If I don't make it for her every Christmas, I hear about it till Valentine's Day - when I whip her up a double batch.

You can make a great chocolate/peanut butter version like this: Spread half of the melted chocolate into the pan. Quickly sprinkle on a layer of Reese's peanut butter chips (You'll find them in the store next to the chocolate chips.) Mash the chips down into the chocolate just a little with the backs of your fingers. Now gently but quickly spread on the other half of the chocolate. When you cut it, the peanut butter makes a pretty - and tasty - layer in the middle. This is Dirk's favorite.

Try doing the same with Andre's mint baking chips for an after-dinner-mint version. This is Ryan's and John's favorite.

If you make this and love it as much as I do, write me at my website and tell me. If for any weird reason that I can't imagine, you don't like it, then just keep it to yourself. I hear enough griping from Dirk.

Breakfast, Brunch, Lunch, and Teatime

Pear Almond Bread

From the Anastasia Raven mystery series by Joan H. Young (page 237)

Anastasia Raven is a recent divorcee who has moved to the Northwoods for some peace and quiet. But murders seem to follow her. Her friendships with the local gossip, Adele, and county historian provide information and laughs as they solve the puzzles. Ana often forgets to fill her refrigerator, and is always glad to receive leftovers from any function. However, she did get her act together in Bury the Hatchet in Dead Mule Swamp to gather pears and make some bread to take to Adele. She was hoping to keep the woman happily gossiping, and it worked!

1 c sugar
1/2 c vegetable oil
2 eggs
1/4 c sour cream or thick yogurt
1 t vanilla

1 t almond extract
2 c sifted flour
1 t baking soda
1/2 t salt
1/4 t cinnamon
1/4 t nutmeg
1 1/2 c chopped pears
1/2 c slivered almonds
1/2 t grated lemon peel (or more)

Combine the sugar and oil and mix till homogenous. Add eggs one at a time and beat well after each. Add the sour cream (or yogurt) and the extracts. Stir in fruit and nuts. Mix dry ingredients together and add to liquid all at once. Combine thoroughly and spoon into greased loaf pan. (Can be one large pan or will make three small foil pans)

Bake at 350 degrees F for about one hour (less for small loaves) until tester (toothpick or metal wire tester) comes out clean. Cool in pan for 15 minutes, turn out, and then let loaf cool before cutting for neat slices.

Zennia's Homemade Granola
From *Green Living Can Be Deadly*, Kensington, 2014, by Staci McLaughlin (page 209)

Dana Lewis, the marketing maven at the O'Connell Organic Farm and Spa, loves fast food and doesn't understand all the fuss about including vegetables in her diet. Zennia, the farm's cook, shudders when she sees double cheeseburgers with extra mayo and wishes everyone would eat only healthy foods. She created this granola mix as a compromise between her and Dana's tastes. It's great as a stand-alone snack or as a topping for yogurt.

Two cups rolled oats
One cup sliced almonds
One cup shredded coconut
2 Tbsp. brown sugar
¼ tsp. salt
1 ½ Tbsp. canola oil
3 Tbsp. honey

- Preheat oven to 350 degrees.
- In a large bowl, mix together the rolled oats, almonds, coconut, brown sugar, and salt.
- Drizzle in the oil and honey, and then toss to combine.
- Spread the mixture on a nonstick cookie sheet and bake on the center rack for ten minutes or until a golden brown.
- Let cool and store in an airtight container.
- Makes about 4 cups.

Aunt Madge's Apple-Cranberry Muffins
From the Jolie Gentil cozy mysteries by Elaine L. Orr (page 216)

In the Jolie Gentil cozy mysteries, Jolie's Aunt Madge is well known for her muffins, which she serves at the Cozy Corner B&B. Jolie's author, Elaine Orr, is equally well known for some cooking disasters. Elaine asked her friend, romance author Leigh Michaels, for a couple of her muffin recipes for the series' fifth book, *Trouble on the Doorstep*. Leigh is also the author of *Simply Good: Recipes for the Busy Cook*. She was pleased to permit Jolie to use these two recipes, which are presented at the end of *Trouble on the Doorstep*, and has granted permission for the recipes to be included in this book.

1 3/4 cups plus 2 tablespoons flour
1/2 cup sugar
1 1/2 teaspoons baking powder
1/2 teaspoon baking soda
1/2 teaspoon salt
1 egg
3/4 cup milk
3/4 cup sweetened applesauce
1/4 cup butter or margarine, melted
1 cup fresh or frozen cranberries, coarsely chopped
1/2 teaspoon ground cinnamon

In a medium bowl, combine flour, 1/4 cup sugar, baking powder, baking soda, and salt. Add cranberries (thawed if they were frozen), and toss to mix. In a small bowl, combine egg, milk, applesauce, and butter; mix well. Add egg mixture to flour mixture, stirring just until moistened. Spoon batter into muffin cups. Combine remaining sugar and cinnamon and sprinkle over batter. Bake in 400 degree oven 20 to 25 minutes. Makes 12 muffins.

Aunt Madge's Dried Fruit Muffins
From the Jolie Gentil cozy mysteries by Elaine L. Orr (page 216)

8 ounces dried fruit, coarsely chopped (pitted dates, apricots, prunes, raisins, cranberries, cherries, blueberries, pineapple)
3/4 cup boiling water
1/4 cup canola oil
1/2 teaspoon vanilla
1 cup flour
1/2 cup whole wheat flour
1/4 to 1/3 cup sugar (depending on how sweet the fruit is)
1/3 cup coarsely chopped walnuts or pecans, or 1/3 cup wheat germ
1/2 teaspoon baking soda
1 teaspoon cinnamon (optional)

In small bowl, combine fruit, water, oil and vanilla; stir to mix. In a large bowl, combine flours, sugar, nuts or wheat germ and baking soda. Add fruit mixture to dry ingredients, stirring just until moistened. Spoon 1/4 cup batter into each greased or paper-lined muffin cup. Bake at 375 degrees for 15 minutes. Makes 12 muffins.

Mister Rogers and Miss Piggy highly recommend the prune muffins.

Butternut Valley Ginger Stout Cake or Muffins
A Recipe for Those Who Hate Beer from Lesley A. Diehl (page 186)

So don't drink the beer, eat it instead!

With the recent popularity of craft beers, more individuals are trying beers locally brewed and finding them right tasty. As with wine, those who love to cook are looking for ways to incorporate beer into their dishes. Usually, we think about beer and the savory, but this recipe is for a sweet dish, muffins or cake. Stout is one of those beers that works well in both types of dishes, but is particularly suited for these spicy muffins. And it pairs well with chocolate, intensifying the taste of the chocolate much like adding coffee to a chocolate cake. If you like these muffins, you might want to try making a stout float with either vanilla or chocolate ice cream. Delicious!

Note: Hera Knightsbridge, my protagonist in *A Deadly Draught* and in *Poisoned Pairings*, the first and second books in the microbrewing series shines as a microbrewer, but is a terrible cook. Although the recipe never appeared in either of the books, this is the type of treat her friend, Sally, who runs a local bakery and tea room, would make in the autumn to offer to the patrons of her shop.

2 cups all-purpose flour
2 teaspoons ground ginger
1 ½ teaspoons baking powder
1 ½ teaspoons baking soda
¾ teaspoon ground cinnamon
½ teaspoon salt
¼ teaspoon ground cloves
½ cup (1 stick) butter, softened
1 tablespoon candied ginger (finely chopped) or 1 teaspoon ground ginger or 1 tablespoon grated fresh ginger
1 cup granulated sugar
½ cup packed light brown sugar
3 large eggs
12 ounces stout (Use your favorite stout from a local microbrewery. I do!)
½ cup molasses

1. Preheat oven to 350 degrees F. Grease muffin pans or 13 x 9 baking pan. Combine flour, ground ginger, baking powder, baking soda, cinnamon, salt, and cloves; set aside.
2. Beat butter and candied ginger with electric mixer on medium speed until combined. Add sugars; beat to combine. Add eggs, 1 at a time, beating well after each addition.
3. Mix stout and molasses to combine and add to wet ingredients. Alternately add dry ingredients in 3 additions, with the beer mixture; beating until combined and scraping down side of bowl as needed. Batter will be runny.
4. Pour into the muffin pans (do not overfill especially if making mini-muffins). Bake 12-18 minutes. Makes over 24 regular muffins or around 80 minis. If using a 9x12 cake pan, bake 45 minutes. In both cases, muffins or cake is done when toothpick inserted into the center comes out clean.
Note: Cake and muffins do not round up when baked.

Try with a dollop of ginger spiced whipped cream or top with a slice of crystallized ginger, or both.

Melanie's Poppy Sherry Muffins
From *Murder in the Gazebo* (2013) by Chloe Evans (page 190)

Ever wonder what the perfect accompaniment is to a chilled summer soup? Why not a slightly sweet muffin like Melanie's Poppy Sherry Muffins? Or you can just try them fresh from the oven for breakfast.

½ C butter
1 C sugar
2 extra large eggs
4 oz. cream sherry wine (cheapest is best)
1 t pure vanilla extract
2 ½ C flour
1 T baking powder
½ t salt
¾ C poppy seeds

Cream butter until soft, add sugar, and continue until smooth (about 1 min. on slow speed). Add eggs and mix until smooth. Add cream sherry and vanilla extract and mix until blended. In a separate bowl, stir the flour, salt and baking soda and poppy seeds together. Pour into the wet mixture and mix until blended. Don't over mix. Spoon into a greased, non-stick muffin pan and bake until a toothpick comes out clean (about 30 to 35 min.) Muffins should be lightly browned around the edges.

Makes one dozen large muffins.

Dump these lovelies out onto a rack. Serve warm with sweet butter, and fruit jam, or with cream cheese for a rich treat.

Whole Wheat Banana-Blueberry Muffins
From Quincy Mac, A Maid in LA Mystery series by Holly Jacobs (page 198)

Quincy Mac went to LA with stars in her eyes, but instead of fame and fortune she becomes a single mom and business owner. Mac'Cleaners is one of the premiere cleaning services in LA and life is good … until the day Quincy accidentally cleans a murder scene. She sets out to find the real murderer. Along the way she finds out who her true friends are, gains a new love interest and inspires a whole lot of laughter.

Quincy might be a maid, an amateur PI and an award winning scriptwriter, but first and foremost, she's a mom. She got the recipe for these healthy—but tastes like a treat—muffins from a good friend from Valley Ridge, NY, Mattie.

1 3/4 cup whole wheat flour
1 tsp. baking soda
1/2 tsp. salt
2 tsp. cinnamon
1/3 cup oil
1 cup brown sugar
2 eggs
1 cup mashed banana
1/4 cup hot water
1/2 cup walnuts (or pecans)
1 cup blueberries (frozen, fresh or dried)

Mix wet ingredients, add dry and mix. Add solids (nuts, berries).

Bake at 350 for about 15-20 minutes.

Cozy Food

Zucchini Muffins for Healthy Investigation
From *FURtive Investigation* by Joyce Ann Brown (page 180)

Klutzy landlady and sometimes sleuth, Beth Stockwell, tends her backyard garden and loves to feed her family and friends. In *FURtive Investigation*, she treats her kids and arranges outings for her friends—with the ulterior motive of investigating the murder of whoever became the skeleton in her duplex attic. Here is her favorite Zucchini Muffins recipe:

3 cups grated fresh zucchini (or 2 c. zucchini and 1 c. grated carrots)
2/3 cup melted unsalted butter (or 1 c. veg. oil, or 1 mashed banana + ¼ c. oil)
1 1/3 cup sugar (or 1 c. brown or raw sugar + 1/3 c. fruit)
2 eggs, beaten
2 teaspoons vanilla
2 teaspoons baking soda
Pinch salt
3 cups all-purpose flour (or whole wheat flour or 2 ½ c. any flour + ½ c. wheat germ, powdered milk, oatmeal flour, etc. combo)
2 teaspoons cinnamon
½ teaspoon nutmeg
1 cup walnuts (optional) (or any nuts you like)
1 cup raisins (or other dried fruit of your choice)

1. Preheat the oven to 350° F (175° C). In a large bowl, mix together the sugar, eggs, and vanilla. Mix in the grated zucchini (or combo) and then the melted butter or oil. Sprinkle baking soda and salt over the mixture and mix in. In a separate bowl, stir together the flour, cinnamon, and nutmeg. Add these dry ingredients to the zucchini mixture. Fold in the walnuts and dried fruit.

2. Coat each muffin cup in your muffin pan with vegetable oil spray. Fill the cups up completely with the dough. Bake on the middle rack until muffins are golden brown and the top of the muffins bounce back when you press on them, about 25-30 minutes. Set on wire rack to cool.

Note: This makes about 14 muffins with the muffin cups filled above the surface of the muffin cups. The muffins may take longer to bake if you use more fruit. I sometimes add blueberries, chopped pineapple, diced apple, or another fruit in place of the oil to make the muffins very moist. Enjoy these treats during the fall and winter and remember the summer's bounty!

Emma's Favorite Muffins
From *The Accidental Sleuth* by Helen Osterman (page 216)

In this book, the second in the Emma Winberry series, Emma finds herself mixed up with an anorexic teenager, a couple of hoodlums who thinks she is someone else, and a cadre of street people who refer to her as the muffin lady. This title gets her in trouble, but her guardian Angel is there to save the day.

2 ½ cups whole wheat flour
1 ½ cups white flour
1 cup sugar
4 tsp baking soda
4 tsp cinnamon

½ tsp nutmeg
5 cups apples with skins, finely chopped
1 cup fresh blueberries
2 cups nonfat yogurt
½ cup milk
4 tsp vanilla extract
4 whole eggs

Preheat oven to 350 degrees. Combine dry ingredients in large bowl. Shred apples in food processor. Add them to flour mixture.

Mix yogurt, milk, vanilla and eggs; add them to apple and flour mixture. Add blueberries.

Grease muffin tins.
Yield: 36 regular sized muffins. Bake for 25-30 minutes, cool, and remove from tins.

These may be frozen and eaten later. Delicious and healthy!

Devereaux's Dime Store Valentine Muffins
From Devereaux's Dime Store Mystery series by Denise Swanson (page 230)

Devereaux Sinclair, owner of Shadow Bend, Missouri's vintage dime store, had no intention of becoming the local amateur sleuth, but dead bodies keep turning up in her life. Her friends Poppy and Boone are happy to help her figure out whodunit, as long as she supplies the baked goods. Here's one of their favorite recipes.

3 cups all-purpose flour
1 teaspoon baking powder
½ teaspoon baking soda
½ teaspoon salt
½ cup softened butter
1½ cups sugar
4 eggs
2 teaspoons lemon extract
1 cup buttermilk
1½ cups macerated fresh strawberries
12 slices of fresh strawberry (should look like hearts)
Red granulated sugar

Preheat an oven to 350°F and place paper liners in cupcake pans. Mix the flour, baking powder, baking soda and salt together in a bowl and set aside.

Cream together the butter and 1½ cups sugar in a large bowl. Beat in eggs, one at a time. Add the lemon extract. Stir buttermilk. Fold in strawberries. Stir the butter mixture into the flour mixture until dry ingredients are just moistened. Pour about ¼ cup of batter into prepared muffin. Place a strawberry slice on top of each muffin and sprinkle with red sugar. Bake 25 to 30 minutes — until toothpick inserted in the middle comes out clean.

Makes 2 dozen.

145

Cozy Food

Green Eggs
From Maggie Bishop (page 175)

Doctor Oz has green shakes.
Doctor Seuss has green eggs and ham.
Mine beats both of those – green eggs – and lots of them.

In a skillet use a couple of handfuls of frozen greens or half a can of cooked greens, collard, turnip, spinach, mustard or mixed – makes no difference. If you use frozen, add a little stock or water to them and cook over medium heat for a couple of minutes until most of the "frozen" is thawed.

Push greens to sides and make a ring to free up the middle. Crack open two eggs and plop into the liquid in the center of the ring. Cook until half-done then flip the eggs and finish. If egg yolk breaks, do an emergency scramble with a shorter cook time.

Pour into a bowl and eat with a spoon so as to catch most of the liquid. Serve with unbuttered toast to sop up the last in the bowl. All this is for one person. I believe in a big breakfast.

Connie Shelton's (semi) Famous Breakfast Burritos
From the Charlie Parker Mystery series by Connie Shelton (page 227)

Charlie is one lucky girl, since her wonderful husband Drake often cooks the meals at their house. Here is one of their favorite breakfasts, which I often make for my husband and our friends at home. You'll notice that the green chile sauce is the same one used with Pedro's Chicken Enchiladas, found elsewhere in this book.

The quantities shown are for two burritos; to make more simply double or triple everything.

Burritos:
2 large flour tortillas
4 slices bacon, fried crisply and crumbled
1/2 c. packaged hash brown potatoes or French fries, fried crisply in the remaining bacon grease
3 large eggs, scrambled
1 recipe Green Chile Sauce, below
Shredded cheddar cheese

Cook the bacon and potatoes as described above and set aside. Scramble the eggs. Warm the tortillas for 30 seconds in the microwave. Lay a tortilla on each person's plate, then begin assembly. Place half the eggs down the center of each tortilla. Top the eggs with crumbled bacon, then with the fried potatoes, dividing each topping equally between the two tortillas. Spoon about a tablespoon of sauce over the toppings and add a sprinkle of cheddar cheese.

Roll the tortilla around the filling, setting it on the plate with the seam side down. Spoon more sauce over the entire burrito (we like ours 'smothered'), then sprinkle with cheddar cheese. Microwave each plate for 30 to 45 seconds, just long enough to melt the cheese. Serve and enjoy!

Green Chile Sauce:
1 T. shortening or vegetable oil
1/2 c. chopped onion

1 c. chopped green chile (canned is fine, any "hotness" that you like)
1 c. chicken broth
1/4 t. garlic powder
2 T. flour
1/2 t. salt (if chicken broth is salty, start with less and taste before adding the full amount)

Heat shortening in saucepan, sauté onions until glossy. Add green chile, garlic powder and chicken broth. Bring to a boil. Stir the flour into a small amount of cold water in a cup until smooth, then gradually stir the flour mixture into the boiling chile sauce. It will thicken pretty quickly. Taste, and add salt if desired.

(For an added touch, I usually add about 1/2 cup diced tomato. You can also add a little chopped leftover beef or pork.)

Simmer 15 to 20 minutes so the flavors will blend well, then serve over enchiladas, burritos or any Mexican dish that needs a sauce. Makes approximately 4 servings.

Baked Eggs
From the Amber Fox Mysteries by Sibel Hodge (page 195)

Amber Fox is an ex-cop turned insurance investigator who is culinary challenged! Luckily, she's better at solving crimes than cooking, and is surrounded by people who can whip up a storm in the kitchen. This recipe is one Amber's mum uses, which is perfect for breakfast, brunch, lunch, or dinner.

Tip: If you can, use organic or free range eggs, which not only taste better, but are kinder to chickens. This recipe is so yum when the egg yolks are still soft and ooze out into the rest of the sauce. If you can't get smoked paprika, you can use ordinary paprika and it won't spoil the fabulousness.

2 cloves of garlic – crushed and chopped
1 onion – diced
1 green pepper – diced
4 mushrooms – sliced
1 small leek – sliced thinly
1 400 gr can of chopped tomatoes and juice
1½ tablespoons of oregano
1 tablespoon of smoked paprika
¼ teaspoon of dried red chilli flakes (optional)
4 eggs
Mozzarella/cheddar – grated
1 – 2 tablespoons of olive oil for frying
¼ cup of flat leaf parsley – chopped
½ cup of hot water or vegetable stock
Salt and pepper to taste

- Fry the garlic, onion, pepper, leek, and mushrooms in a saucepan until soft.
- Add the tomatoes, water, herbs, salt, and stir well.
- Cover and simmer until the vegetables are cooked.
- Turn off the heat and mix in the flat leaf parsley.
- Transfer the sauce into two individual-sized oven dishes and press down flat.

Cozy Food

- Crack two eggs on the top of each dish and sprinkle with the cheese.
- Place under a hot grill until the egg is cooked and the cheese is golden and bubbling.

Serves 2.

* Gluten Free Option – Use gluten free stock

Custard French Toast

From *Hot Chocolate* a cozy mystery by Dawn Greenfield Ireland (page 197) and consumed by the Alcott family characters.

Lila Mae Alcott, the middle-aged chocolate heiress of Houston's River Oaks, turns sleuth to find out how her middle sister Dorothea could possibly be accused of murder. Amelia, Lila Mae's house manager and cook, prepares comfort food to sooth frayed nerves while the mystery is solved.

2 -3 eggs, beaten
1/4 cup milk
1/2 teaspoon pure vanilla extract (organic is tastier)
Liberal amount of cinnamon
Your favorite bread
Olive oil for cooking
Maple Syrup (the real stuff – not flavored)
Line a shallow baking pan with bread slices.

In a small bowl, beat eggs. Add milk, vanilla and cinnamon. Pour enough mixture over the bread until soaked. Use a fork or spatula to lift the bread to make sure the bottoms of each slice are soaked. Let sit for 30 seconds to1 minute.

Add oil to skillet or griddle and heat over medium heat. When a drop of water sizzles in the pan, add soaked bread. Cook until browned on the bottom, checking often; flip and cook the remaining side.

Repeat until all egg mixture is gone. Send someone to the store to buy more eggs, if necessary.

Make Ahead Carmel French "Toast"

From the Maternal Instincts Mystery series by Diana Orgain (page 215)

Sleep deprivation, diaper blowouts, and breastfeeding mishaps are status quo for new mom Kate Connolly. But when she decides to turn private investigator in order to work from home, her To-Do List expands exponentially (1. Buy diapers. 2. Get back in shape. 3. Order lock pick set…) Thank God, she can prepare a tasty breakfast recipe the night before!

Cooking Spray
1 cup light brown sugar
½ cup light-colored corn syrup
¼ cup butter
6-8 Croissants
2 cups milk
1 tbs flour

1 ½ tsp vanilla extract
¼ tsp salt
2 eggs
2 tbs sugar
1 tsp cinnamon

Spray 13 x 9-inch baking dish with cooking spray and arrange croissants in a single layer.

Combine brown sugar, corn syrup and butter in a small saucepan. Cook over medium heat 5 minutes or until mixture is bubbly, stirring constantly. Pour mixture evenly over the croissants.

Combine milk, flour, vanilla extract, salt and eggs in a large bowl, stirring with a whisk. Pour egg mixture over bread slices. Cover and refrigerate for 8 hours or overnight.

Next Morning: Preheat oven to 350°.

Combine sugar and cinnamon. Sprinkle evenly over bread then bake at 350° for 50 minutes or until golden. Let stand for 5 minutes before serving – wait for the smiles!

Peanut Butter and Jelly French Toast
From the Mrs. Frugalicious mystery series by Linda Joffe Hull (page 196)

To make ends meet after her TV financial guru hubby loses the nest egg in a Ponzi scheme, Maddie Michaels secretly starts bargain hunter's blog, Mrsfrugalicious.com. While Maddie is researching teen shopping deals for her 'Frugarmy', Eternally 21 store manager Laila DeSimone accuses her of shoplifting, then promptly drops dead. When evidence points to Maddie as the prime suspect, she must track down the real culprit before she is accused and her identity is revealed. Along the way however, she gives and gets bargain hunting tips. Once a well-heeled housewife, Maddie learns there's never a good reason to pay full price, no excuse not to use coupons, and no need to skimp where delicious dining is concerned.

Since Mrs. Frugalicious is all about using coupons and then storing and stockpiling the food for later use, she loves recipes you can pull together right from your pantry! Here's one of her faves:

2/3 cup reduced-fat milk
1 large egg, lightly beaten
1/2 teaspoon baking powder
1/2 teaspoon vanilla extract
1/8 teaspoon salt
8 Slices of Whole-wheat bread
1/2 cup strawberry jam
6 tablespoons peanut butter
1 tablespoon canola oil, divided
1 tablespoon powdered sugar

Combine first 5 ingredients stirring well with a whisk. Place bread slices on a flat surface. Spread 2 tablespoons strawberry jam over half of the bread slices, and spread 1 1/2 tablespoons peanut butter over each of the remaining 4 bread slices. Assemble sandwiches. Carefully dip 2 sandwiches in milk mixture, turning to coat.

Cozy Food

Heat a large skillet over medium-high heat. Add canola oil to pan; swirl to coat. Place coated sandwiches in pan; cook 2 minutes on each side or until toasted. Remove sandwiches from pan. Sprinkle powdered sugar evenly over sandwiches; cut each sandwich in half and serve!

Meme's Ham and Egg Pie
From Elaine Macko (page 205)

My recipe is called *Meme's Ham and Egg Pie*. Though traditionally eaten at Easter, this pie works all year round. You have to bake it, but you eat it cold. It's an old Italian recipe brought over from the Naples area by my grandmother and, as I base the character of Meme in my series on my own grandmother, I'm sure she'll be baking this at some point for Alex and the gang. Enjoy!

Crust:
Use your own best pie crust recipe, enough for two, and add a fair amount of coarse black pepper to the dough.

Filling:
1 pound of ham, cubed
½ pound of salami
½ pound of provolone cheese (use the good stuff!)
1 large container of ricotta cheese
More coarse black pepper (as much as you think you can handle)
4 eggs

Mix all ingredients together and then pour into pie shell. Place the other crust on top and trim the edges. I like to use a glass pie pan at least an inch deep. Bake in a 425 degree oven for at least an hour. You may want to start inserting a knife in the center after about 55 minutes. You want the knife to come out clean. Once it's fully baked, let it cool for several hours then put in the refrigerator overnight. The next morning it will be ready to have with your morning tea or coffee. I like to eat a piece later in the day with a nice salad.

World's Best (and easiest) Cheese Grits Souffle
From *Doing it at the Dixie Dew* by Ruth Moose (page 211)

The Dixie Dew is a bed and breakfast set in the mythical Southern town of Littleboro. If you stopped by, you could have this for breakfast, but since you can't, you can try it at home.

4 packages instant grits
2 cups water
4 eggs
1 cup milk
2 cups grated cheddar cheese

Heat water in a glass mixing bowl in microwave to boiling. Stir in grits. Stir in cheese until melted, then add milk. Beat in the eggs until well blended. Pour into a 9x12 greased casserole dish and bake uncovered at 350 degrees for 45 minutes until golden brown and puffy. Serves 6 to 8.

I have sometimes added 1 tsp red pepper flakes and some powdered garlic.

For extra color (and vitamins) stir in, just before baking, some thin ribbons of Kale. Not a lot, but bits just for color.

Kedgeree
From the Daisy Dalrymple mysteries by Carola Dunn (page 189)

In the 1920s, the time of the Daisy Dalrymple mysteries, country house parties usually had informal breakfast buffets. Ladies often breakfasted in bed—or at least in their rooms—but Daisy would never miss an opportunity to mingle with the other guests and possibly come across a Clue. Kedgeree was a staple of such buffets and is mentioned in *A Mourning Wedding* among other titles in the series. This recipe comes from my grandmother's cookbook, published in Edinburg in 1929.

1 cup or 4 oz cooked rice
1 cup or 4 oz fish filet, cooked and flaked (Finnan—smoked--haddock is a favourite)
[Here I'd better confess that my arithmetic skills are not up to this, even with Google's help. The recipe says "For each 4 oz of each:..."][PS Daisy's school believed female brains were too delicate to study math beyond household accounts, so she wouldn't have been able to figure it out either. When she and her friend Lucy lived together, they ate mostly cheese, eggs, and sardines.]
1 hard-boiled egg
1 oz butter
Salt, pepper (preferably white pepper)

Melt butter in saucepan till hot but not browning.
Add rice and fish, stirring with a fork till well mixed.
Season to taste with salt and pepper.
Heat through (again, don't let it brown!).
Turn into dish.
Chop or slice egg and use as garnish.

Killer Quiche Lorraine
From the kitchen of Eleanor Cassidy in the Someday Quilts Mysteries by Clare O'Donohue (page 215)

Eleanor has to run a business and keep an eye on her granddaughter - quilter and crime solver, Nell Fitzgerald. It's amazing she has time for anything else. But for Eleanor, taking care of people is second-nature, whether it's wrapping them in a warm quilt, or cooking them a hot meal. Besides, as Eleanor says, "No one solved a murder by going hungry."

Her recipe for a quick and filling quiche:

1 pre-made (or homemade) deep dish pie crust
4 eggs
1 ½ cups milk (2% or whole)
6 oz. Swiss Cheese
6 slices bacon
1 small onion
¼ tsp pepper
¼ tsp paprika

Pre-heat oven to 375. Cook the bacon until crisp. In a mixing bowl, combine eggs, milk, pepper & paprika. Set aside. Dice the onion and cheese. Put the pie crust into a pie plate and sprinkle the onion and cheese over the bottom. Crumble the bacon over the onion and cheese. Put the pie crust onto a baking sheet and pour the egg/ milk mixture into it until it reaches the very top. You may want to place the pie and baking sheet in the oven first as the mixture tends to spill when moved.

Cook the quiche for 45 minutes, or until it's set. Let cool for a few minutes then serve with muffins and fruit for a great breakfast, or salad for lunch.

Swap out the bacon for mushrooms and spinach for a vegetable quiche, or use ham instead.

Crepes & Lobster Crepes
From the Darby Farr Mysteries by Vicki Doudera (page 187)

Many of the Darby Farr Mysteries take place in Darby's hometown of Hurricane Harbor, a rocky island on the coast of Maine. It's a place where lobster is plentiful, hence this yummy dish. The recipe was originally published in a cookbook my husband I put together when we owned The Blackberry Inn in Camden, Maine. It's a perfect fit for a casual supper or an elegant brunch.

Crepes

1 ½ cups flour
¼ teaspoon salt
2 cups milk
3 eggs
2 Tablespoons melted butter
1 Tablespoon oil

It's worth investing in a good crepe pan to make these. I bought mine right after I spent a college year in Paris, France – so it's made more than its share of crepes over the years!

Combine flour, salt, milk, eggs and melted butter in a blender or mixer. Chill one hour if possible.

Rub the oil in a small nonstick skillet (a short-sided pan for crepes is best) over medium heat. Pour a scant ¼ cup of the batter in the center of pan, lifting and tilting to coat and cover the bottom of the skillet in a thin layer. Pour excess back into batter and return skillet to heat. Crepes should be quite thin. When crepe is dry on top and slightly golden on bottom, remove from skillet and place on drying rack. Makes one dozen.

Note: cooled crepes can be stacked between wax paper sheets and refrigerated for later use.

Lobster Crepes

12 crepes
1 lb. cooked lobster meat (crab can be substituted)
5 Tbs. butter
5 Tbs. flour
2 cups milk

½ tsp. salt
1/8 tsp. white pepper
1 1/3 cups grated Gruyere cheese
½ lb. small Maine shrimp, cooked
1 cup grated Cheddar cheese

Preheat oven to 350 degrees. Melt butter in saucepan over low heat and whisk in flour. Gradually add milk, stirring constantly. Cook and stir over medium heat until sauce thickens. Add salt and white pepper and remove from heat.

Reserve one half of sauce. To remaining sauce, stir in lobster and Gruyere. Place 4 tablespoons of lobster mixture on each crepe and roll. Arrange on a buttered 9 by 13 inch baking dish, rolled edge down.

To reserved cup of sauce, add cooked shrimp and Cheddar cheese, and warm until cheese just melts. Pour over middle of crepes. Bake for 25 minutes or until hot and bubbling.

Makes 12 lobster crepes.

Dutch Baby with Cardamom Honey Apples
From the kitchen of Tamar Myers (page 212)

Sometimes called a popover pancake, this audacious-looking flapjack is made in a large skillet. It puffs up, rising dramatically as it bakes in the oven. It is topped with sautéed apple slices laced with ground cardamom and sweetened with honey. Golden Delicious apples are best for this recipe because they keep their shape when cooked. The pancake takes 18 minutes to bake—just enough time to put together the apple topping.

Dutch Baby:
2 large eggs
¾ cup milk
¾ cup unbleached all-purpose flour
1 tablespoon sugar
2 tablespoons unsalted butter

Cardamom Honey Apples:
2 large apples (Golden Delicious)
1 tablespoon unsalted butter
½ teaspoon ground cardamom
½ cup honey
1 tablespoon fresh lemon juice

To make the Dutch Baby: Preheat the oven to 400 F. Place an 8-to-10 inch cast-iron skillet or other heavy skillet with a heatproof handle in the oven. Combine the eggs, milk, flour and sugar in a medium bowl and whisk until smooth. Using a pot holder, remove the skillet from the oven and add the butter; tilt the pan to melt the butter and coat the skillet. Add the batter all at once and immediately return the skillet to the oven. Bake until the pancake puffs up around the edges, 18 to 20 minutes.

Meanwhile, make the Cardamom Honey Apples: Peel, quarter and core the apples. Cut into thin wedges. Heat the butter in a medium skillet until sizzling. Add the apple wedges and cook, stirring gently, until lightly browned on both sides. Sprinkle with the cardamom and stir to coat. Add the honey and heat to boiling. Remove from the heat; stir in lemon juice.

To serve the pancake, slide it from the skillet onto a large platter. Pour the Cardamom Honey Apples into the center. Cut into wedges and serve, distributing the filling evenly.

Katy McKenna's To-Die-For Grilled Cheese Sandwich
From *Dead Girls Don't Blog* by Pamela Frost Dennis (page 186)

In *Dead Girls Don't Blog*, Katy McKenna remembers how she literally swooned when she saw the original Café Muse version of this recipe on the Oprah show. Over time she has lazified it, but the original printable recipe can be easily found online at her favorite website: http://www.beautybloomers.com/favorite-things/favorite-recipes/

2 slices Havarti cheese (or Cheddar)
Butter, softened
Honey
Fresh basil, chopped (two or three leaves)
2 slices tomato
2 slices bread (organic multigrain bread works best)
Sauté pan large enough for 2 slices of bread
Sea Salt

Place a slice of cheese on a slice of bread.
Top with chopped basil, sliced tomato.
Drizzle with honey a sprinkle of sea salt, and top with the other slice of cheese.
Liberally butter both sides of bread and place in a preheated pan (Katy always uses an old iron skillet) over medium-low heat.
Flip when golden brown. At this point, Katy puts a foil-wrapped brick on the sandwich until done.
Try it with an extra drizzle of honey over the top of the sandwich.

Bowling Alley Hamburgers
From the Cressa Carraway Musical Mystery series by Kaye George (page 192)

Cressa reluctantly accepts Mo Tombs' offer to take her out to lunch in tiny Alpha, IL, the rural place where she hoped to compose some music. She knows his mother put him up to it to take Cressa's mind off the fact that she came upon her Gram's dead body while swimming, her first night. But she's hungry and Mo *is* good looking. Her misgivings multiply as they approach a rickety table in the noisy bowling alley, as Mo eyes her cleavage, and as he invites a friend to join them. But the first bite convinces her. Mo knows hamburgers.

1 1/2 lb. ground chuck (or leaner meat if preferred)
1 slice bread, torn into small pieces
1 egg, slightly beaten
1/3 c. minced onion
1/3 c. chopped green bell peppers
2 t. Worcestershire sauce
1/2 t. chili powder
salt and pepper to taste

sesame seed or poppy seed buns
butter

Optional toppings:
sliced American cheese
lettuce leaves
tomato slices
raw onion slices

Combine first group of ingredients. It's best to use your hands, washing them thoroughly before mixing and after forming patties. Form round patties about 2 inches in diameter. Put them on a baking sheet or broiler pan and flatten slightly.

Broil 5-6 minutes, turn, broil another 5-6 minutes until brown. If cheese is desired, add at the last minute. While the hamburgers are broiling, brush the buns with butter and warm in a skillet on top of the stove. Serve on toasted buns with garnishes of choice. Makes 6-8 hamburgers.

Cates's Quick Mexican Lunch
From the Cate Kinkdaid Files mystery series by Lorena McCourtney (page 207)

Assistant private investigator Cate Kinkaid, busy chasing down killers in Lorena McCourtney's Cate Kinkaid Files mystery series (*Dying to Read, Dolled Up to Die, Death Takes a Ride)*, doesn't claim to be the greatest cook, but she can do this quick and easy Mexican Lunch. (And *Dying to Read* showed up on a New York Times bestseller list.)

10-inch flour tortilla
½ lb. ground beef
16 oz. can refried beans
1 ½ cups shredded cheddar cheese
Shredded lettuce, chopped tomatoes, chopped green onions.
Salsa, sour cream, guacamole

Cook the ground beef until done. Add the refried beans, mix, and heat until warmed through. Warm the tortilla in a large skillet, until lightly browned on one side. Turn over and spread with the meat and beans mixture. Sprinkle the cheese on top, cover, and cook a couple of minutes more until the cheese melts and the tortilla gets crispy. Slide the tortilla onto a large place. Pile on shredded lettuce, chopped tomatoes and chopped green onions. (However much looks right to you.) Cut into wedges and serve with salsa, sour cream and guacamole.

Serves two for a light lunch.

Cozy Food

Queen of Afternoon Tea's Raisin Scones with Mock Devonshire Cream
From the Jillian Bradley mystery series by Nancy Jill Thames (page 231)

Jillian Bradley is a garden columnist for the *San Francisco Enterprise* with a nose for solving homicides, along with her garden club friends and Yorkie companion, Teddy. The adventures of Jillian and Teddy begin at a conference in Half Moon Bay, where the nosy widow and her friends look for clues, pausing for afternoon tea along the way. When Jillian hosts at home, here are the recipes she uses.

Raisin Scones: Makes 6-8 large or 12 small scones

1 cup sugar
3 tsps. baking powder
½ tsp nutmeg
3 cups flour
1 tsp salt
½ cup shortening
¾ cup raisins, plumped in hot water
1 cup milk
Extra milk for brushing tops

Mix dry ingredients together, cut in shortening, add raisins, milk, and mix until dry ingredients are moist.

Turn dough onto floured board (do not knead), pat into a circle one-inch thick, cut into 6-8 wedges or into rounds, brush with milk, sprinkle with sugar and place on parchment or foil covered cookie sheet.

Bake at 425 degrees on the middle rack for 12-14 minutes or until scones are light brown on the bottom. Test for doneness. Serve with Mock Devonshire Cream, lemon curd, or strawberry jam.

Mock Devonshire Cream: Makes 1 ½ cups

½ cup heavy whipping cream
2 Tbsps. powdered sugar
¼ cup sour cream

Whip cream until soft peaks form, then add powdered sugar and whip to incorporate.

Add sour cream and continue beating just until fluffy and well-combined.

Quick, Easy, Quirky, Saucy, & Even Pet Treats

Ellery Adams Easy Dinner Egg cups
From Facebook March 27, 2014 by Ellery Adams (page 168)

Easy dinner alert: Egg cups. 4 eggs, 1 1/2 cups heavy cream, a few tablespoons grated cheese, and whatever meat or veg you want to add. Mix and pour into muffin pan. Cook at 400 for 35-40 minutes. Today mine are filled with hot sausage, paprika, S&P, and fresh parsley with a little Mexican cheese blend melted on top. Serve with salad and you're done. Because I don't know about you, folks, but I am sick of figuring out what's for dinner…

Cozy Food

Deviled Ham on Toast
From *A Bat in the Belfry* by Sarah Graves (page 193)

A Bat in the Belfry (Bantam, April 2014) stars Jacobia "Jake" Tiptree, an ex-Wall Street money-management professional who moved to the Maine coastal village of Eastport to fix up a 200-year-old house.

Jake wasn't much of a cook in her first book, *The Dead Cat Bounce*, nearly 20 years ago, and she hadn't gotten to be one by the time of the most recent series installment, either, but when she does cook she tends to do something simple, like this supper dish. It goes well with some fresh sliced tomatoes or a green salad. Since she's in Maine she drinks Moxie with it, but you can substitute the closest thing to Moxie, which of course is champagne.

This dish really is delicious even though it does not sound that way and even though it has the very unglamorous name of ... Deviled Ham on Toast.

One can of deviled ham
One can of Heinz baked beans
Four thickish slices of good white bread
Butter or margarine.
On the side: fresh sliced tomatoes or green salad, Moxie or champagne.

First, bake a loaf of good white bread. Let it cool and cut four slices. Heat the baked beans in a saucepan until hot and bubbling. Open the can of deviled ham. Toast and butter the bread, spread the deviled ham on it, dividing the ham equally among the pieces of toast. Cut the toast into eight pieces, divide the pieces between two plates, and pour the hot baked beans over the top.

Serve with tomatoes or salad and Moxie or champagne.
Serves 2.

A nice hot fudge sundae will go over well for dessert, Jake says. Or for tomorrow's breakfast, for that matter, especially in the unlikely event there is any of that champagne left, or (this is what she recommends) you could just think ahead and buy an extra bottle of champagne while you are out getting the hot fudge.

Perplexingly Palatable Peach Pie Shake
From the Working Stiff Mystery series by Kerri Nelson (page 214)

Mandy has a lot of bad days, but any day can easily be improved with a huge glass of Peach Pie Shake. Served up routinely at the Back Porch Café, this treat will fill you up with sugary southern goodness. If only you could get sixty-something former Vegas showgirl, Ms. Maimie to serve it up for you—then you'd feel right at home. Don't forget to top with a fresh peach slice or crust crumbs sprinkled on top!

2 cups vanilla ice cream or vanilla frozen yogurt
1 cup of milk
1 piece of peach pie or peach cobbler **(see my cobbler recipe (page 88)
Whipped cream, fresh peach slice garnish, crust crumbs for garnish

Combine the ice cream (or yogurt) and the milk in a blender and run on medium speed until almost smooth. Add the slice of pie (1 piece of pie or cobbler—a normal serving size) and continue to blend on medium speed until smooth. Pour into two glasses and top with whipped cream. Garnish with a sprinkling of crust crumbs and a slice of fresh peach. Serves 2.

**Make a fresh peach pie or buy one frozen and bake as directed or use the easy southern peach cobbler recipe on (page 88) (our favorite).

No Bake Mini "Hamburger" Cookies
From The Miniature Mysteries by Margaret Grace, aka Camille Minichino (page 210)

Gerry Porter and her 11-year-old granddaughter, Maddie, love all things mini. The two stars of Margaret Grace's Miniature Mysteries were playing around in the kitchen one Saturday, unable to choose between vanilla and chocolate cookies. They came up with a new recipe that combined the best of both. Using two soft vanilla cookies and one soft chocolate cookie, they created a mini hamburger. After their day of creative play, adding embellishments, here's the result!

Preparation time is about 15 minutes. The yield is 12 mini hamburgers.

1 box vanilla wafers
1 box soft chocolate cookies (SnackWells or the equivalent)
1 tube green frosting
1 tube red frosting
1 tube yellow frosting
1/8 cup sesame seeds (optional)

1. Arrange 12 vanilla wafers, flat side up, on a tray or platter. These are the bottoms of the "hamburger buns."
2. Using the green frosting tube, squirt a ring around the edge of each wafer. Using your finger or a toothpick, rough up the frosting so it resembles ragged lettuce.
3. Place 1 chocolate cookie (the meat!) on top of each green-ringed wafer.
4. Using the red frosting tube (ketchup!), squirt a ring around the flat edges of a dozen additional wafers (the tops of the "hamburger buns).
5. Using the yellow frosting tube (mustard!), squirt a yellow ring over the red ring of Step 4, allowing the two colors to mix in places.
6. Place each newly ringed wafer, flat side down (top of the bun!), on top of a chocolate cookie/wafer.

DONE! You now have 12 hamburgers, with lettuce, ketchup, and mustard.

7. (optional) Dot the top of each "burger" with egg white, and use as adhesive for a few sesame seeds.

Be creative: add a smooth ring of white frosting for an onion, a square of orange frosting for cheese, or smooth the red ring so it looks more like tomato.

Cozy Food

Chickapoo's Peanut Butter Treats
From the Spadena Street mysteries by Marian Allen (page 169)

Spadena Street is a two-block cul-de-sac of Storybook Style houses dating back to the late 1920s. It has a Neighborhood Watch group, because it might as well, since everybody is always in everybody else's business, anyway. Although two of them have an online cooking show and some consider themselves gourmets, others consider a microwave dinner a home-cooked meal. Chickapoo is a good, plain cook, but she likes these because they're quick and pretty. Besides, her husband, Bee-beep, likes them.

12 Ritz crackers
6 Tbsp peanut butter
melted white chocolate
sprinkles

Make "sandwiches" out of the crackers and peanut butter. Dip each one in white chocolate and put onto waxed paper to cool. While still warm, garnish with sprinkles.

Serves three to six guests, or Bee-beep.

Oven S'mores
From *Pistols & Pies*, Book 2 in the Sweet Bites Bakery mysteries by Heather Justesen (page 199)

Tess Crawford thought all that murder business was behind her when she opened her bakery, and for a while it seemed to be true. Then a city councilman is killed and his troubled step-son is the police's main suspect, but the victim's wife is convinced her son didn't have anything to do with the murder. Tess can't ignore the woman's impassioned plea, or the bevy of other suspects the police seem to be ignoring. Helped once more by her best friend Honey, and a few others, Tess is on the case. If only untangling her messy love life and mysteries were as simple as this recipe, which was made by Honey's eleven-year-old daughter, Madison.

1 cup chocolate chips
1-8oz container of marshmallow fluff
8-10 graham crackers, the large rectangular size. About 1 plastic-wrapped package from a box.

Crumble up crackers into nickel- to quarter-sized pieces and spread across the bottom of a 9x13 cake pan. Sprinkle the chocolate chips across the top and then slide it into a preheated oven of 350 degrees. Bake for 10-15 minutes or until the chocolate chips go all melty when you touch them with a knife. Remove the pan and spread the marshmallow fluff on top. Allow to cool enough to handle and serve. Beware, they're messy, but really good. You can do these in the microwave in a pinch, but you get best results in the oven.

Grilled Twinkies
From *Killer Surf* by Chris Forman (page 191)

This is a favorite of Ian Wallace, the kilt wearing food writer who keeps getting involved solving murders.

Grilled Twinkies, that's right, grilled not fried. Now the fried ones are amazing and have a unique flavor, but there is the whole deep fried aspect. Grilling is healthier (marginally anyway) and imparts a flavor that is a cross between toasted marshmallows and toasted sponge cake, with a hint of smoke.

First, unwrap the Twinkie (the plastic would melt into it otherwise) and spread some butter on the bottom. Get your grill fairly hot and place the Twinkie bottom down. They will be some quick flames as the butter burns and this adds to the flavor. Give it about a minute and a half on the bottom and a minute or so more on the other three sides. Be careful or the Twinkie will stick to the grill. Get it nice and brown, but be careful not to burn it.

Next, plate it and eat. You can add some ice cream, chocolate syrup, anything you like. It's your Twinkie.

1630. Devonshire Cream
From *Mrs. Beeton's Book of Household Management* (1861)
From *Cinnamon Girl: A Village Cooks Mystery* by Valerie Horowitz (page 195)

Filled with cooking and cookbook lore, *Cinnamon Girl* is the first in a series of Village Cooks mysteries. It includes recipes from treasured cookbooks. The following recipe is included in the book in honor of the Village Cooks store cat, Mrs. Beeton, named after the English author of *Mrs. Beeton's Book of Household Management*, one of the most famous cookbooks ever published. Mrs. Beeton was the Victorian era's Martha Stewart. Devonshire cream is served with jam on scones. Put the jam on first, then top it with a big heap of Devonshire Cream. Yum. Perfect with a cup of tea.

The milk should stand 24 hours in the winter, half that time when the weather is very warm. The milk pan is then set on a stove, and should there remain until the milk is quite hot; but it must not boil, or there will be a thick skin on the surface. When it is sufficiently done, the undulations on the surface look thick, and small rings appear. The time required for scalding cream depends on the size of the pan and the heat of the fire; but the slower it is done, the better. The pan should be placed in the dairy when the cream is sufficiently scalded, and skimmed the following day. This cream is so much esteemed that it is sent to the London markets in small square tins, and is exceedingly delicious eaten with fresh fruit. In Devonshire, butter is made from this cream, and is usually very firm.

A Michigan from New York (hot dog sauce)
From *Death Dangles a Participle* by E.E. Kennedy (page 200)

Northern New York natives may recognize the reference to Michigans in the Miss Prentice mysteries. Nobody knows why they're called Michigans, but both Americans and Canadians drive long distances to obtain this delicacy. Chez Prentice housekeeper Hester Swanson, who worked for many years at the local college cafeteria, came up with this version of the special hot dog sauce and dictated it to Amelia. She makes no claims of authenticity, but says, "It surely tastes like what I remember!"

3 lbs finely ground lean beef, sautéed and well-drained
10 tsp chili powder
14 oz. can tomato sauce (or less)
Scant ¼ cup Frank's or other good hot sauce, NOT Tabasco! (Even less if your kids will be eating it.)
3 tsp garlic powder
3 tsp onion powder

2 tsp black pepper
3 tsp ground cumin

Make sure the beef is cooked into tiny particles. (Hester uses a pastry cutter to achieve this, chopping the beef as she browns it.) Add the tomato sauce, but sparingly. The mixture should ultimately be just barely moistened. Blend all ingredients well before simmering for 2 hours, stirring frequently. Results are best if you use non-direct heat, such as a crock pot or double boiler.

This is best (in the opinion of Amelia's husband, Gil) if served over a good quality steamed hot dog in a bun, topped by a thin line of yellow mustard and sprinkled with coarsely chopped sweet onions.

There is some controversy about using tomato sauce. Some say there should no tomato in this sauce, but this recipe turns out a very authentic-tasting result. It makes enough to top a whole lot of hot dogs! (At least 25.)

Mel's Texas BBQ Mop Sauce
From the Pampered Pets mystery series by Sparkle Abbey (page 168)

Melinda Langston owns the high-end Bow Wow Boutique. She sells party dresses, crystal collars, designer pet carries, and dog "pawlish" to the elite in Laguna Beach. That is when she's not busy solving a murder. Though she loves southern California, she hails from the great state of Texas and shares her Lone Star heritage with her friends via her very own sweet and spicy Texas BBQ sauce. Here's Mel's recipe:

1/4 cup butter
2 cloves garlic, minced
1/4 cup minced onion
3 stalks of celery, chopped
1 cup water
1 beef bouillon cube
1 cup ketchup
1/2 cup cider vinegar
3 tablespoons Worcestershire sauce
2 tablespoons spicy mustard
2 tablespoons honey
1 tablespoon paprika
2 teaspoons chili powder

In a medium sauce pan melt the butter and then add the garlic, onion, and chopped celery. Sauté them until they are lightly browned. Next add the water and bouillon and stir until the cube is dissolved.

Add the rest of the ingredients and stir. Let simmer for at least 15 minutes. This makes about 3 ½ cups of sauce. The sauce can be used on beef brisket, pulled pork, or whatever you like. Mel mostly uses it as a mop sauce which means she brushes it on the surface of the meat like a basting sauce during cooking.

Quick, Easy, Quirky, Saucy, & Even Pet Treats

Raisin-Cider Sauce
From the Comfort Food series by Christine Wenger (page 235)

I don't know where I found this recipe, but it is truly delicious with any kind of meat. I gave it to Trixie Matkowski, and she serves it with her turkey special at her Silver Bullet Diner when she isn't sleuthing around!

This sauce is absolutely perfect with ham or pork-poultry, too. Makes about 1-1/2 cups sauce.

Mix thoroughly in a saucepan:

3 tablespoons brown sugar
1 tablespoon cornstarch
¼ teaspoon salt
¼ teaspoon cloves
1/8 teaspoon cinnamon
Few grains nutmeg

Stir in: 1 cup apple cider
½ cup seedless raisins

Put over high heat and bring rapidly to boiling. Stirring slowly and constantly, cook until mixture is thick and clear (about three minutes). Remove from heat and stir in one teaspoon of lemon juice.

Tiny Truman's All-day Onions
From *The Winter Ground*, Book 4 in the Dandy Gilver series, by Catriona McPherson (page 210)

In *The Winter Ground* Tiny Truman – a circus clown – makes this onion concoction on a little stove in his caravan. It's more realistic, these days, to suggest a crockpot. Although, if you have a woodstove …

All-day onions – sometimes called onion jam in fancy places – can be eaten as an appetiser with a chunk of good bread, served with steak, added to soups and stews for flavouring, spread on flatbreads, spooned straight out of the container while you stand in front of the open fridge …

2 lbs of onions
¼ lb butter
2 tablespoons olive oil (this stops the butter from burning)
Salt and pepper
Nutmeg

You will need a very heavy-bottomed frying pan large enough to fit all the raw onions, and a crockpot if you have one.

- Peel and very thinly slice the onions
- Melt the butter and oil over a low heat.
- Tip the onions in and turn them until they are coated in butter and oil.
- While the crockpot is warming, cover the pan with a lid or foil and bring the onions gently up to a bubble.

Cozy Food

- Either tip the warm onions into the crockpot and set to low or, using a wok stand to diffuse the heat, leave them to cook very gently on the stove.
- The mixture can be left to cook overnight or – you guessed it – all day.
- When the onions are soft and caramelised and their delicious fragrance is driving you crazy return them to the heavy-bottomed pan on a medium to high heat (or take its lid off and remove the wok stand).
- Let the onions boil and bubble away until the excess water has evaporated and you are left with a golden, glossy, relish-consistency gloop.
- Now season with salt and pepper and a scrape of nutmeg and, before you cool and store in the fridge, allow yourself a generous scoop for your troubles.

Summer Squash Refrigerator Pickles
From *The Pickled Piper* by Mary Ellen Hughes (page 196)

7 cups thinly sliced zucchini, summer squash, or both
1 cup thinly sliced onions
1 cup grated carrot
1 green pepper, chopped finely
1 cup cider vinegar
2 cups sugar
1 tablespoon pickling salt (non-iodized)
1 tablespoon dill seeds

Mix everything in a large bowl, then refrigerate for several hours or overnight.
Fill quart jars with the vegetables and cover with the brine and cap tightly. These pickles will keep well in the refrigerator for as long as 3 months.

Dried Mammoth Meat /Neanderthal Mammoth Jerky
(can also be used for Mastodons, Sabre-toothed Tigers, and Musk Ox)
From the People of the Wind Neanderthal Mystery series by Kaye George (page 192)

The wind howls over the edge of the nearby glacier, blasts into the settlement of the Hamapa tribe, and stirs Enga Dancing Flower's long, copper-colored hair. She draws her bearskin cape tighter over her shoulders, watching the dance of the flames in the community fire pit. Fear is growing every day in every heart. The herds of giant mammoth are leaving. Enga gnaws on a small bit of mammoth jerky. If they have a big kill soon, more strips of the delicious meat will dangle near the fire to feed them in the coming Dark Season. If not…Enga shudders.

Large slabs of mammoth meat, preferably from the loin or shoulder (can use mastodon or musk ox).

Put a slab on a flat stone. With a sharp stone or obsidian knife, cut the meat across the grain into thin strips. Hang the strips on a rack near the fire. Set guards to protect the meat from marauding animals. When it is dry, store it in bunches, either in deep storage pits or suspended from tall tree branches. Check it often to make sure it hasn't been stolen.
Feeds one tribe of 24-28.

Quick, Easy, Quirky, Saucy, & Even Pet Treats

Beef Jerky, adapted for Cro Magnons and Modern Humans
From the People of the Wind Neanderthal Mystery series by Kaye George (page 192)

Lean cut of meat, such as brisket, round steak or flank steak (turkey, caribou, bison can also be used)
Marinade (teriyaki, barbecue sauce, or marinade of choice)

Trim fat.

For best results, freeze the meat for 1-3 hours before. Slice thinly against the grain. Slicing with the grain will produce thicker, harder to chew jerky.

Marinate the meat overnight, or up to 24 hours.

The object is not to cook the meat, but to dehydrate it. A dehydrator can be used or an oven. Heat the oven to 165-180 degrees. The lower temperature will take longer, but may work better.

Lay the strips out directly on the oven rack, leaving room between slices. Since the marinade will drip, this can be done over the sink or over a pan.

Use a drip pan in the oven, or foil on the bottom. Put the racks high in the oven. Prop the door slightly open with a wooden spoon or crushed beer can.

The process will take 2-6 hours. After 2 hours, check periodically. If a piece of jerky will bend easily, it is not done yet. When you bend it and the fibers start to tear, it is nearly done. At this point, leave one strip out of the oven for 10-30 minutes and retest, or taste.

When done, remove from the oven and let air cool at least 24 hours. You can start eating it right away, but don't store it yet. Store in refrigerator or freezer. In an airtight container, it should last 2 to 3 months.

Note: Sun drying can lead to spoiling and insect infestation.

Feeds one family for a long time.

Caro's Good Dog Treats
From the Pampered Pets mystery series by Sparkle Abbey (page 168)

Carolina Lamont, animal lover and former Texas beauty queen, moved to California after a very nasty and public divorce. With eleven-thousand dogs – more dogs than kids – Laguna Beach seemed like the perfect spot to open a pet therapy business. And it had been, up until she had to catch a killer by the tail. Whether dealing with misbehaving canines or murder suspects, Caro always keeps a few of her homemade dog treats on hand. Here's Caro's recipe:

First, preheat your oven to 350° F.
In a big bowl, combine all the ingredients with just enough water to make it the consistency of cookie dough.

1/2 cup of creamy unsalted peanut butter
1 cup oat flour
1 cup brown rice flour (Caro uses organic)

1 egg
1 tablespoon of honey
1/2 cup finely grated carrot (Dogbert , Caro's dog, loves carrots)
Optional: You can also add cooked bacon, a bit of grated cheese, or other ingredients for flavor, but don't add too much or it will mess with the consistency of the dough, and cause your treats to fall apart.

Once you've got your treat dough all stirred up, put it between pieces of parchment paper and roll it out to about ¼ inch thickness. Then cut the dough with a cookie cutter. You can use whatever shape strikes your fancy. Caro often uses dog bone shapes of different sizes. Next, put them on a regular cookie sheet and bake them between fifteen and twenty minutes or until they're golden retriever brown.

Let them cool and then put them in an airtight container. You can store your Caro's Good Dog treats for about a week (or you can freeze them for later use) but keep an eye on them. There are no preservatives, so watch out for spoilage.
This makes a couple of dozen treats so there's plenty to go around. Please share them with your dog.

Kitty Cat Tuna Crackers
From the Pampered Pets mystery series by Sparkle Abbey (page 168)

Preheat oven to 350 degrees.
1 can of tuna
1 cup of cornmeal
1 cup of flour
1/3 cup of water

Mix everything together and then place on waxed paper or a non-stick surface and roll to 1/4 inch thick. Cut into bite-sized pieces. The nice thing is you can size these for your feline. Bake for 20 minutes or until they are lightly browned and then cool.

Catnip Burgers
From the Bookmobile Cat Mysteries by Laurie Cass (page 181)

Although Minnie's favorite recipe is a take-out menu, she does occasionally make a foray into the kitchen to cook up treats for Eddie. Catnip burgers are his favorite, not that he would ever say so to Minnie…

4 oz. sausage or ground beef
3 tablespoons oatmeal
2 tablespoons catnip, finely chopped
1 egg

Knead ingredients together thoroughly and shape into 4 flat patties.
Broil on high heat until the outside is crisp, 8-12 minutes. Turn often to make sure they crisp up evenly. Remove from heat and allow to cool. Cut cooled patties into cat bite-sized pieces and serve.

Cozy Author Biographies

Cozy Food

Sparkle Abbey

Sparkle Abbey is the pseudonym of mystery authors Mary Lee Woods and Anita Carter. They write the national bestselling pet mystery series which features two feuding cousins who solve whodunits set in the wacky world of pampered pets, precious pedigrees, and secrets. The two authors chose to use Sparkle Abbey as their pen name because it combines the names of their two rescue pets, Sparkle (Mary Lee's cat) and Abbey (Anita's dog).

Books in the series:
Bk 1: Desperate Housedogs
Bk 2: Get Fluffy
Bk 3: Kitty Kitty Bang Bang
Bk 4: Yip/Tuck.
Bk 5: Fifty Shades of Greyhound

Find Sparkle Abbey online:
Website: www.SparkleAbbey.com
Twitter: www.twitter.com/sparkleabbey
Facebook: www.facebook.com/sparkleabbey
Goodreads: www.goodreads.com/sparkleabbey
Pinterest: www.pinterest.com/sparkleabbey
YouTube: www.youtube.com/sparkleabbey

Our Blogs:
Paws to Read: http://www.sparkleabbey.com/category/blog/
Killer Characters: http://www.killercharacters.com/
The Stiletto Gang: http://thestilettogang.blogspot.com/

Recipes
165 Caro's Good Dog Treats
166 Kitty Cat Tuna Crackers
162 Mel's Texas BBQ Mop Sauce

Ellery Adams (aka J. B. Stanley and Jennifer Stanley)

Ellery Adams grew up on a beach near the Long Island Sound. Having spent her adult life in a series of landlocked towns, she cherishes her memories of open water, violent storms, and the smell of the sea. Ms. Adams has held many jobs including caterer, retail clerk, car salesperson, teacher, tutor, and tech writer, all the while penning poems, children's books, and novels. She now writes full-time from her home in Virginia.

Ellery Adams writes The Charmed Pie Shoppe Mysteries, The Books By The Bay Mysteries, and The Book Retreat Mysteries. She also writes as J.B Stanley (Supper Club Mysteries and Collectibles Mysteries} and Jennifer Stanley (Hope Street Church Mysteries).

Her website http://www.elleryadamsmysteries.com
Ellery blogs on the Cozy Chicks blog site http://www.cozychicksblog.com/
Her books are on Amazon http://www.amazon.com/Ellery-Adams/e/B003USIVX2
And Barnes & Noble http://www.barnesandnoble.com/c/ellery-adams

Recipes
157 Ellery Adams Easy Dinner Egg cups

Judy Alter

Judy Alter is the award-winning author of the Kelly O'Connell Mystery Series and the Blue Plate Café Mystery Series, both set in contemporary Texas. A lifelong reader of cozy mysteries, she began crafting mysteries after writing fiction about women of the American West for many years. Her western books won major awards and many are now available on the web.

There is a connection between her western work and her mysteries—the books all feature strong, adaptable women.

A single mother of four and the grandmother of seven, she is now retired as director of a small academic press. Judy lives in Fort Worth, Texas, with her Bordoodle (a deliberate cross of poodle and border collie), Sophie, who mixes affection with mischief and energy. Judy enjoys reading, cooking, exploring new restaurants, and spending time with family and friends when she's not writing. Most afternoons she can be found doing second-grade homework with the grandson who lives near her.

Do her children and grandchildren read her books? "Only some of them," she admits with a wry grin. "So far none of them want to write but that may change. I do know they're proud to have an author in the family."

Find all of Judy's books at her Amazon author page: http://tinyurl.com/n473nw6
You can also find Judy at http://www.judyalter.com or her two blogs, http://www.judys-stew.blogspot.com and http://potluckwithjudy.blogspot.com.

Recipes
104 Gram's Chocolate Bundt Cake
56 Keisha's Noodle Casserole

Marian Allen

Marian Allen writes science fiction, fantasy, mystery, romance, humor, and anything else that occurs to her. There's usually food in anything she writes; if there isn't food in the story, there was certainly food somewhere nearby. Allen has shamelessly turned her own born daughter into an author on the theory that, if you want to find a writer whose work you like, you can give birth to one. Allen has published novels and short stories in print and on line. She blogs daily at http://MarianAllen.com, where readers can find sample chapters, buy links, and free reads. Her Spadena Street characters have only appeared (so far) in short stories, but their novels are currently under construction.

Recipes
160 Chickapoo's Peanut Butter Treats
31 Buckskin Bread

Cozy Food

Ritter Ames

Ritter Ames is the author of two mystery series, the fast-paced, light suspense Bodies of Art mystery series, starting with *Counterfeit Conspiracies,* and the cozy-style Organized Mysteries series, beginning with *Organized for Murder.* Both series are published by Gemma Halliday Publishing and are available in print and all ebook formats.

Ritter tries to blog regularly at http://ritterames.wordpress.com/ and uses her Pinterest boards at http://www.pinterest.com/ritterames/ to capture great places and ideas she wants to use in both series. Follow her blog and boards to learn more about Ritter and her upcoming books.

You can find her on
Facebook at https://www.facebook.com/ritter.ames
Twitter https://twitter.com/RitterAmes

Recipes
126 Ames's Family Oatmeal Peanut Butter Chunk Choco Chip Cookies

Donna Andrews

Donna Andrews was born in Yorktown, Virginia and now lives in Reston, Virginia. In 2013, Minotaur published the 15th and 16th in books in her Meg Langslow series: *The Hen of the Baskervilles* and *Duck the Halls.* And 2014 will bring *The Good, the Bad, and the Emus* and *The Nightingale Before Christmas.* She has also written four books in the Turing Hopper series from Berkley Prime Crime. In her free time … um, what free time? Alas, she rarely cooks, but she does try to make THE Pumpkin Pie every Christmas.

Website: http://donnaandrews.com
Blog: http://femmesfatales.typepad.com/
Facebook: https://www.facebook.com/DonnaAndrewsBooks
Barnes & Noble: http://www.barnesandnoble.com/c/donna-andrews
Amazon: http://tinyurl.com/n3ydh9w

Recipes
97 THE Pumpkin Pie

Traci Andrighetti

Traci Andrighetti is the author of the Franki Amato Mysteries. In her previous life, she was an award-winning literary translator and a Lecturer of Italian at the University of Texas at Austin, where she earned a PhD in Applied Linguistics. But then she got wise and ditched that academic stuff for a life of crime—writing, that is.

In her debut novel, *Limoncello Yellow,* Traci introduces Francesca Amato. Franki, as she is known, is a tough-talking rookie cop in Austin, Texas—until an unfortunate 911 call involving her boyfriend, Vince, and a German female wrestler convinces her once and for all that she just isn't cut out for a life on the police force. So Franki makes the snap decision to move to New Orleans to work at her friend Veronica's detective agency, Private Chicks, Inc. But Franki's hopes for a more stable life are soon dashed when Private Chicks is hired by the prime suspect in a murder case to find out what really happened to a beautiful young boutique manager who was found strangled to death with a cheap yellow scarf. When she's not investigating, Franki is hoping to seduce handsome bank executive Bradley Hartmann, but most of her time is spent dodging date offers from a string of "good Italian boys"—make that not-so-good aging Italian men—that her meddlesome Sicilian grandma has recruited as marriage candidates. As Mardi Gras approaches and the mystery of the murdered shop girl gets more complicated, Franki must decipher the odd ramblings of a voodoo priestess to solve both the murder and the mystery of her own love life.

To learn more about Traci's books, go to her website http://traciandrighetti.com/, goodreads page http://bit.ly/Q4kvLi, or Amazon page http://amzn.to/1iIzQrU.

Recipes
20 Limoncello
90 Limoncello-Mint Sorbetto
108 Limoncello Cake with Limoncello Syrup and Lemon Glaze

Amy Beth Arkawy

Amy Beth Arkawy is the author of The Eliza Gordon Mystery series: *Killing Time* (Hen House Press) *Dead Silent* (Cozy Cat Press) and the coming *Murder Deferred*; and several plays including: *Psychic Chicken Soup (*McLaren Comedy Award nominee); *Full Moon, Saturday Night; Listening to Insomnia: Rage Amongst Yourselves; Crazy Vivian Doesn't Shop at Bloomie's Anymore, The Lost Mertz* and *The Postman Always Writes Twice.* Her work has been produced in New York City and across the country and featured in several anthologies. She is also a creativity coach/writing teacher, radio talk show host and freelance journalist. She is working the third Eliza Gordon Mystery.

Here's a link to my books and e-books on Amazon: http://tinyurl.com/mrmthjq

Recipes
23 Eliza's Don't Spill the Beans Soup
58 Eliza Gordon's 'Healthy' Killer Cajun Chicken Wraps

Mignon F. Ballard

Born close to Halloween, Mignon Ballard spent much of her childhood telling ghost stories under the eerie green glow of a neighborhood funeral home sign with her sister and friends. Usually last chosen for team sports (clumsy!) and inept at anything to do with numbers, she learned early-on a career in music was out of the question. Although her heart wants to dance, but her feet ask, "Say what?" And her piano teacher was forthright in announcing to her mother that she was wasting her money. Writing was IT, and has always been IT. At the age of 79, Mignon, along with her title character, Miss Dimple Kilpatrick, is still exploring what's around the next bend in the road in Elderberry, Georgia, during the 1940's.

A native of Calhoun, Georgia, Mignon Ballard earned a degree in journalism from the University of Georgia, and is the author of seven Augusta Goodnight mysteries and nine previous novels. The fourth in her latest mystery series, and her twentieth book, *Miss Dimple Picks a Peck of Trouble*, set during WWII and featuring longtime first grade teacher, Miss Dimple Kilpatrick, was published by St. Martin's Minotaur in February. An earlier stand-alone mystery, *How Still We See Thee Lie*, as well as *The Christmas Cottage*, an inspirational fantasy for "grownups who still believe in magic," are available from Bella Rosa Books. Many of her books are on Kindle and can be found on her website www.mignonballard.com or Amazon http://tinyurl.com/mseeu2k

Recipes
90 Lemon Mystery
130 Cissy's Turtle Bars

Sandra Balzo

Sandra Balzo is an award-winning author of crime fiction, including two mystery series from Severn House--the Wisconsin-based Maggy Thorsen Coffee Mysteries and Main Street Murders, set in the High Country of North Carolina and featuring journalist AnnaLise Griggs.

Garnering starred reviews from Kirkus and Booklist, Balzo's novels are recommended to readers of Janet Evanovich, Charlaine Harris, Joan Hess and Margaret Maron and have been optioned toward development as a television series or movie.

For more on Sandy and her books, go to www.SandraBalzo.com and www.amazon.com/author/sandrabalzo.

Hungry for more brand-name classics? Check out Mama's Pinterest board at http://bit.ly/1qPtNrB.

The Maggy Thorsen Mysteries:
Uncommon Grounds
Grounds for Murder
Bean There, Done That
Brewed, Crude and Tattooed
From the Grounds Up
A Cup of Jo
Triple Shot
Murder on the Orient Espresso

The Main Street Mysteries:
Running on Empty
Dead Ends
Hit and Run

Recipes
22 Murder on the Orient Espresso Martini
111 Bacardi Rum Cake

JoAnn Bassett

JoAnn grew up in Seattle but always preferred palm trees to pine trees so when she sold her firefighter training company (yeah, that's right, I worked with hunky men for over twenty years—tough duty but somebody's gotta do it) she and her husband bought a home in Honokawai, Maui. While in Maui, JoAnn noticed there were lots of steamy romances and scary "trouble in paradise" mysteries based in Hawaii, but not many cozy mysteries. So, she set out to write some. The result is the Islands of Aloha Mystery Series, a series of eight books (five finished so far) set on each of the major Hawaiian Islands. The books star Pali Moon, a no-nonsense wedding planner based on Maui who owns a shop called, "Let's Get Maui'd."

The Islands of Aloha Mystery Series includes the following titles (with more to come):

Maui Widow Waltz http://tinyurl.com/ld9aegf
Livin' Lahaina Loca http://tinyurl.com/kbmcrbr
Lana'i of the Tiger http://tinyurl.com/lqq5hjg
Kaua'i Me a River http://tinyurl.com/m9y8u4o
O'ahu Lonesome Tonight? http://tinyurl.com/mbedbsv

JoAnn's can be reached at her website: www.joannbassett.com

Recipes
17 Hawaiian Spam Musubi (Similar to sushi)
94 Hawaiian Chocolate and Coconut (Haupia) Pie

Cynthia Baxter (aka Cynthia Blair)

Cynthia Baxter's main goal in life has been to have a good time, which is reflected in the humor she incorporates into her writing. She is the author of two popular mystery series. One is the 9-book Reigning Cats & Dogs mystery series, which features Long Island veterinarian Jessica Popper and her dogs, cats, parrot, and chameleon. Books include *Dead Canaries Don't Sing*, *Putting On the Dog*, and *Crossing the Lion*.

Her other series is the 2-book Murder Packs a Suitcase mystery series, whose heroine is travel writer Mallory Marlowe. The books are *Murder Packs a Suitcase*, set in Orlando, Florida, and *Too Rich and Too Dead*, set in Aspen, Colorado.

Cynthia has been a full-time writer for more than 30 years, with more than 50 published novels. Most were written as Cynthia Blair. They include the popular Young Adult series about the identical Pratt twins: *The Banana Split Affair, The Hot Fudge Sunday Affair*, and 11 others. (Not surprisingly, Cynthia is a big fan of desserts. Also not surprisingly, the recipes she submitted for this cookbook are for four of her favorites!)

In addition to baking (and eating), Cynthia enjoys quilting, rug hooking, and many other crafts, as well as drawing and painting. She is passionate about traveling, and in the past few years has gone to South America, Iceland, Russia, and Lithuania, where her ancestors are from. She has worked as a travel writer, specializing in the Caribbean, as well as a journalist. She has also taught creative writing at universities and workshops.

For more information, visit http://www.cynthiabaxter.com/ and http://www.belgravehouse.com/

Recipes
110 Carrot Cake
110 Classic New York Cheesecake
84 Crème Brulée
131 Chocolate Coconut Bars

Cozy Food

Jenna Bennett (aka Jennie Bentley)

New York Times and USA Today bestselling author Jenna Bennett/Jennie Bentley writes the Do It Yourself home renovation mysteries for Berkley Prime Crime and the Cutthroat Business mysteries for her own gratification. She also writes a variety of romance for a change of pace. For more information, please visit her website http://www.jennabennett.com

Recipes
115 Whoopie Pies
98 Bûche de Noël, Yule Log

Sally Berneathy (aka Sally Carleen, Sally Steward, and Sara Garrett)

I grew up in a small rural town in southeastern Oklahoma where our favorite entertainment on summer evenings was to sit outside under the stars and tell stories. When I went to bed at night, instead of a lullaby, I got a story. That could be due to the fact that everybody in my family has a singing voice like a bullfrog with laryngitis, but they sure could tell stories—ghost stories, funny stories, happy stories, scary stories.

For as long as I can remember I've been a storyteller. Thank goodness for computers so I can write down my stories. It's hard to make listeners sit still for the length of a book! Like my family's tales, my stories are funny, scary, dramatic, romantic, paranormal, magic.

Besides writing, my interests are reading, eating chocolate and riding my Harley.

I have two ongoing mystery series, Death by Chocolate (*Death by Chocolate*; *Murder, Lies and Chocolate*; *The Great Chocolate Scam*, and *Chocolate Mousse Attack*) and Charley's Ghost (*The Ex Who Wouldn't Die* and *The Ex Who Glowed in the Dark*).

I also sold fifteen romance novels ranging from comedy to dark suspense under the names Sally Carleen, Sally Steward and Sara Garrett. For those novels, I won several awards including National Readers' Choice, Romantic Times Best Silhouette Romance and two Rita finalist slots. Most of the Silhouettes are available as e-books, and I have e-pubbed six of the out-of-print single titles.

Contact information is available on my website. I love to talk to readers! And writers. And riders. And computer programmers. And teachers. And gardeners. And dogs. And puppets and poets and pirates and pawns and kings. Okay, I just plain love to talk!
http://www.sallyberneathy.com
http://www.facebook.com/berneathy

Recipes
129 SallyB's Chocolate Chip Cookies
102 Triple Chocolate Mousse Cake
112 Cookie Dough Cheesecake

Cozy Author Biographies

Maggie Bishop

Maggie Bishop is the author of a mystery series, Appalachian Adventure Mysteries, and two romance novels set in the Mountains of North Carolina in the Boone area. "I started with romance and have turned to murder."

The Start: In *Murder at Blue Falls*, when her horse finds a body, CSI wannabe Jemma starts to investigate, Detective Tucker comes in and it twists and turns from there.

And Then: Since pay is low in the mountains, Jemma has more than one job and is also a carpenter. In *Perfect for Framing*, trouble's a-brewing in the Property Owners Association where greed and a lust for power lead to murder in a clash of personal versus public needs.

Now: The photography group meets at Blue Falls Guest Ranch and soon there is *One Shot Too Many* which features Detective Tucker. Yesterday's regret haunts, leading to today's deadly fix.

In the Appalachian Adventure Romance series, Award winning *Appalachian Paradise* takes place on a five-day backpacking trip in the spring amongst the bears, boars and girl scouts. With this book, you can take the hike without physically taking the hike.

Emeralds in the Snow involves downhill skiing at Sugar Mountain, an emerald mine, and a cold case mystery.

Maggie Bishop hikes, gardens, swims, explores and writes in the mountains of North Carolina where she settled in 1993 with her husband and cat. Every time they travel, they seek out other mountains but none are as exciting as the ancient Appalachians. When asked, "What do you do?" her answer is, "Entertain with word pictures."

She was awarded the honor of being one of "One Hundred Incredible East Carolina University Women" for literature and leadership. https://www.amazon.com/author/maggiebishop

Recipes
146 Green Eggs

Cindy Blackburn

Cindy Blackburn has a confession to make—she does not play pool. But that pesky detail didn't stop her from writing the Cue Ball Mysteries, starring Jessie Hewitt, pool shark extraordinaire. Four books and counting, Cindy loves giving Jessie trouble, both in and out of the pool room. A native Vermonter who hates cold weather, Cindy divides her time between south and north. During colder months you'll find her in South Carolina, but come summer she'll be on the porch of her lakeside shack in Vermont. When Cindy isn't writing she likes taking long walks with her cute hubby John (also not much of a pool player) or cuddling with her cute cat Betty (also not much of a pool player). Cindy's favorite travel destinations are all in Europe, her favorite TV show is NCIS, and her favorite color is orange. Cindy dislikes vacuuming, traffic, and lima beans. Oh! And Cindy's a pretty good cook!

The Cue Ball Mysteries are cozies with a lot of humor, a little romance, and far too much champagne. Murder meets menopause. Take a guess which wins. Or better yet, read the books!
Playing with Poison http://tinyurl.com/ljemgpd
Double Shot http://tinyurl.com/mq9xsev

Three Odd Balls http://tinyurl.com/lolec5y
Four Play http://tinyurl.com/lg4n9ru

Cindy has started a new series, The Cassie Baxter Mysteries: Small sleuth, tiny town, unfailing fun. It's *Unbelievable* (http://tinyurl.com/mm5hldm).

Learn more about Cindy Blackburn and her books at www.cbmysteries.com and on her Amazon Author page http://tinyurl.com/nxor789

Recipes
16 Pimento Cheese for Dummies
82 Bribe Your Best Buddy French Chocolate Mousse
38 Pop Open the Bubbly Champagne Vinaigrette

Juliet Blackwell

Juliet Blackwell is the New York Times bestselling author of the Witchcraft Mystery series, featuring a powerful witch with a vintage clothes store in San Francisco's Haight-Ashbury; and the Haunted Home Renovation Mystery series, about a failed anthropologist who reluctantly takes over her father's high-end construction company … and finds ghosts behind the walls. As Hailey Lind, Blackwell wrote the Agatha-nominated Art Lover's Mystery series, in which an ex-art forger attempts to go straight as a faux finisher.

Juliet spent several years in academia, where she studied different systems of medicine, health maintenance, and health care – both mental and physical —from around the world. She developed an avid interest in witchcraft, alternative belief systems, and botanical cures, and picked up two Masters degrees … but never quite finished that pesky PhD. In order to pay for school Juliet began to paint and eventually established a studio in her native California Bay Area, where she specialized in portraiture, decorative painting, and historic restoration. She has also worked as a waitress and a school social worker, published several non-fiction articles on immigration, translated Miguel Leon-Portilla's seminal work *Endangered Cultures*, and was a producer with the BBC for a documentary called *The Search*.

Juliet has worked in Mexico, Spain, Cuba, Italy, the Philippines, and France. She now divides her time between California and France, where she loves to paint, garden, hike, and dance. She raised a beautiful son, is foster mom to a great black cat, and volunteers in adult literacy and at the food bank. Juliet served two terms as president of Northern California Sisters in Crime, and is a former board member of MWA.

Visit Juliet at www.julietblackwell.net,
join her on Facebook (https://www.facebook.com/JulietBlackwellAuthor)
and on Twitter @JulietBlackwell

Amazon links:
The Witchcraft Mystery series (6 books) http://tinyurl.com/laqeqq7
The Haunted Home Mystery series (4 books) http://tinyurl.com/kgdjexg
The Art Lover's Mystery series (4 books) http://tinyurl.com/k2ud72o

Recipes
28 Gumbo's a-brewing

Susan Furlong Bolliger

Susan writes mysteries from the Midwest where she lives with her husband and four children. Just like her character, she loves to spend her free time scouring garage sales for killer deals. For more of her writing and a few peachy recipes too, watch for her new cozy mystery series, The Georgia Peach Mysteries (Berkley Prime Crime) or check out her website at: www.sfurlongbolliger.com

To find out more about Pippi O'Brien's quirky adventures, visit Amazon http://tinyurl.com/kfnpd2w where you can find links to *Murder for Bid* and *Murder on Consignment.*

Recipes
102 Pippi O'Brien's Chocolate "Dumpster" Cake (Chocolate Dump Cake)

Sheila Webster Boneham

Sheila Webster Boneham *can* cook, but she'd rather be outdoors or writing. Luckily, her husband, Roger, does most of the cooking at their house. Okay, all of it. Sheila has put her free time to good use writing the first three Animals in Focus mysteries, including *Drop Dead on Recall* (2012), *The Money Bird* (2013), and *Catwalk* (fall 2014), all based on Sheila's many years of experience showing, rescuing, breeding, training, writing about, and loving dogs and cats.

Drop Dead on Recall won the 2013 Maxwell Award for Fiction from the Dog Writers Association of America and was an NBC Petside Top Ten Dog Book of 2012.

Sheila has also published seventeen nonfiction books about dogs and cats, six of which have won major awards. She currently lives on the coast of North Carolina with Roger and Labrador Retriever Lily, and is at work on book four. Sheila has also written seventeen non-fiction books about dogs, cats, and animal rescue, several of which have won major awards.

Learn more online at the following sites:
Website and blog - http://www.sheilaboneham.com
Writers & Other Animals blog - http://www.writersandotheranimals.blogspot.com
Facebook - http://www.facebook.com/sheilawrites and
https://www.facebook.com/groups/writersandotheranimals/

Sheila's books are available from all the usual places in paperback, ebook, Audible, and large-print format. Sheila also works with her local independent bookstore to offer personally autographed copies of her books - find out more at
http://sheilaboneham.blogspot.com/p/autographed-books.html
Amazon - http://amazon.com/author/sheilaboneham
Barnes & Noble - http://www.barnesandnoble.com/c/sheila-webster-boneham

Recipes
34 Goldie's Bright Summer Salad
44 Tom's Quick & Fragrant Pasta Sauce

Cozy Food

Laura Bradford

While spending a rainy afternoon at a friend's house more than thirty years ago, Laura Bradford fell in love with writing over a stack of blank paper, a box of crayons, and a freshly sharpened number two pencil.

Those early attempts at the craft had her writing and illustrating stories for young children. Wise beyond her years, Laura saved her first writing attempt in a hand decorated shoe box (complete with sparkly stickers) and moved on to her next idea. Her second book—*O'Casey's Wish*—was so utterly brilliant, she sent it off to a well-known New York publishing house at the tender age of ten, confident she was on the verge of becoming the next Don Freeman (Corduroy) or Shel Silverstein (Giving Tree).

Months later, she received her first form letter rejection.

While she wasn't of the mindset to save that first crushing blow for posterity, Laura *did* save the original copy of this particular literary masterpiece in the event the letter was a mistake.

Desperate to prove her flexibility as a writer, Laura soon found herself dabbling in jokes (for her Girl Scout troop's newsletter), stories of angst (a somewhat autobiographical look at her teenage years), movie reviews (for the Xavier University Newswire), and countless news and feature articles (for newspapers in CT, SC, TN, and MO).

It wasn't until Laura was home raising children of her own though, that she was finally able to dust off that rainy day dream and bring it back to its original form—writing fiction. Today, she is a bestselling mystery author with Berkley Prime Crime (Penguin Publishing).

Her new Amish Mysteries, features English gift shop owner, Claire Weatherly, and Detective Jakob Fisher, a former member of the Amish community. The series takes place in Heavenly, a fictional town in Lancaster County, PA.

For a complete listing of all books in Laura's Amish Mysteries, visit her website: www.laurabradford.com.

To purchase the books in her series, visit Barnes & Noble: http://www.barnesandnoble.com/c/laura-bradford

Or Amazon: http://tinyurl.com/kd4w4xp

Recipes
92 Ruth Miller's Shoo Fly Pie
74 Schnitz und Knepp (Ham with Dried Apples and Dumplings)

Frances Brody

Frances Brody lives in Yorkshire in the North of England, the setting for her 1920s mystery series featuring Kate Shackleton. First World War widow turned detective, Kate Shackleton has been described as a young Miss Marple, a splendid heroine, and "who I imagine Nancy Drew growing up to be." Frances has obligingly provided her sleuth with a snazzy wardrobe, a smart motorcar, and a lovely little house that backs onto an enchanting wood. Kate is ably assisted by former policeman, Jim Sykes. She has the sterling support of her housekeeper, Mrs Sugden, who would love to become more involved in detection.

Of the six books in the Kate Shackleton Mystery series, three are published in the US and Canada: *Dying in the Wool*, *A Medal for Murder* and *Murder in the Afternoon*. More titles to follow.

Before turning to crime, Frances wrote for BBC radio and television, and for theatre. She penned several sagas, winning the HarperCollins Elizabeth Elgin award for the most regionally evocative debut saga of the millennium.

When not writing, Frances likes to walk in the Yorkshire Dales and on the moors – yes, think *Wuthering Heights*!

To find out more about Frances and her books, visit www.frances-brody.com Join her on Facebook: https://www.facebook.com/FrancesBrody?ref=hl or follow her tweets @francesbrody. She loves to hear from readers.

Her Amazon page is: http://tinyurl.com/n4clc4m

Recipes
79 Yorkshire Pudding
86 West Riding Pudding

Duffy Brown

Duffy Brown loves anything with a mystery. While others girls dreamed of dating Brad Pitt, Duffy longed to take Sherlock Holmes to the prom. She has two cats, Spooky and Dr. Watson, her license plate is Sherlok and she conjures up who-done-it stories of her very own for Berkley Prime Crime. Duffy's national bestselling Consignment Shop Mystery series is set in Savannah and the upcoming CyclePath Mysteries are set on Mackinac Island.

Berkley Prime Crime:
Consignment Shop Mysteries
Cyclepath Mysteries

Visit her website http://www.duffybrown.com

Happy eating.
Hugs, Duffy Brown

Recipes
93 Pecan Pie (yummy)
24 Easy-Peasy Mackinac Island soup

Cozy Food

Joyce Ann Brown

Joyce Ann Brown is a landlady, story teller, retired school Library Media Specialist, former classroom teacher, former Realtor, and now a freelance writer and published mystery author. Her pieces have appeared in *The Kansas City Star*, the *National Ski Club Newsletter*, the *Raytown Times*, and in *The Best Times*, a local Johnson County, Kansas newspaper where Joyce has been a regular contributor. Joyce writes for her blog followers and contributes as a guest blogger. She is a member of Sisters in Crime, Oklahoma Writers' Federation, and Kansas City Writers. Visit Joyce's Website at http://joyceannbrown.com , and friend her on Facebook.

The first book of her "Psycho Cat and the Landlady" cozy mystery series is the award-winning, *CATastrophic Connections*. Find the print and e-book versions at Amazon.com.

Catch a glimpse of her writing about all cozy subjects on her blog at:
http://retirementchoicescozymystery.wordpress.com

Recipes
14 Hummus for Celebrating
144 Zucchini Muffins for Healthy Investigation

Mollie Bryan

Mollie Cox Bryan is a cookbook author with a penchant for murder. She is also the author of the Cumberland Creek Mysteries: *Scrapbook Of Secrets* (nominated for an Agatha Award for Best First Novel of 2012), *Scrapped*, and the forthcoming *Death Of An Irish Diva*. She is also the author of *Mrs. Rowe's Little Book of Southern Pies* and *Mrs. Rowe's Restaurant Cookbook; A Lifetime of Recipes from The Shenandoah Valley*. She also is the author of a Kindle book *Honey, I'm Sorry I Killed your Aquasaurs (And Other Short Essays on the Parenting Life.)*

My books on Amazon http://tinyurl.com/kj422ul
Or Barnes & Noble http://www.barnesandnoble.com/c/mollie-bryan

Recipes
123 Lady Locks

B.B. Cantwell

B.B. Cantwell is the pen name for the wife/husband writing team of Barbara and Brian Cantwell, of Seattle. We lived 10 happy years in Portland, Ore., where our Portland Bookmobile Mysteries are set, but have always had family in Seattle, so we spent a lot of hours driving back and forth on I-5 -- perhaps the most boring three hours of freeway you'll find (on a cloudy day when the mountains aren't visible, which is most of the time). So after Barbara started writing a mystery novel, we got to talking out ideas and plot lines as we drove, trip after trip, and it became a joint effort. And it was, well, a hoot. Barbara worked on the bookmobile in Portland -- including a run into the scenic Columbia River Gorge -- and served as librarian to pretty much all the off-kilter characters you'll read about in *Murdermobile*. She's the big-idea half of the writing duo. Brian, a newspaper journalist, helps rein it in to reality (but not too far), helps fill out details and tends to the editing. Along the way, between the two of us, it's like we've created our own Imaginary Friends in protagonists Hester McGarrigle, the librarian on wheels, and Detective Nate Darrow, the OCD-ish, trail-running detective who drinks his coffee with way too much sugar. We're having great fun crafting cozy mysteries that are a little quirky, just like Portland. We hope you have fun with them, too, and we'd be honored if you'd submit a review.

Murdermobile and *Corpse of Discovery* are available on Kindle and in paper from Amazon at http://tinyurl.com/mhk7fkt

Visit our blog at http://murdermobile.weebly.com/

Recipes
85 Nana's Cream Puffs

Laurie Cass (aka Laura Alden)

Laurie Cass grew up in Michigan and graduated from college in the 80's with a (mostly unused) degree in geology. She turned to writing in the late nineties. After a number of years in management, she felt the need to move on and took a job with fewer responsibilities. A month later, she was dead bored and began to consider writing as a way to wake up her brain. She started reading a lot of books on writing and happened across a particular sentence: "What's it going to be, reasons or results?"

The phrase practically stuck her in the eye. She printed it out, framed it, and put it next to her computer. "Reasons or results?" At the end of her life, was she going to have a pile of reasons for not having done anything? Or was she going to sit down and write a book? Once she started looking at it that way, the decision was easy. A short 13 years later, her first book was published.

Currently, Laurie and her husband share their house with two cats, the inestimable Eddie, and the adorably cute Sinii. When Laurie isn't writing, she's working at her day job, reading, attempting to keep the flowerbeds free of weeds, or doing some variety of skiing. Laurie's debut novel written as Laura Alden, *Murder at the PTA* was an Agatha Award finalist for Best First Novel. Her fifth book in the series, *Poison at the PTA*, was released in February 2014.
The second book in Laurie's new series, Bookmobile Cat Mysteries, is soon to be released.

Laurie's books can be purchased at:
Barnes & Noble as Laurie Cass: http://www.barnesandnoble.com/c/laurie-cass
              as Laura Alden: http://www.barnesandnoble.com/c/laura-alden
Amazon as Laurie Cass: http://tinyurl.com/lhml5hr
         as Laura Alden: http://tinyurl.com/ls8m8ay
or requested at your favorite independent bookseller.

Recipes
125 Grandma's Cookies
166 Catnip Burgers

Cozy Food

Nancy J. Cohen

Nancy J. Cohen is the author of 20 published books, including the humorous Bad Hair Day mystery series featuring hairdresser Marla Vail. Several of these titles have made the Independent Mystery Booksellers Association bestseller list. Her latest title and 11th in the series is *Hanging By A Hair*. Coming next is *Peril by Ponytail*. Nancy is also the author of *Writing the Cozy Mystery*, a valuable instructional guide for writers on how to write a winning whodunit.

Her imaginative romances have proven popular with fans as well. Her titles in this genre have won the HOLT Medallion and Best Book in Romantic SciFi/Fantasy at *The Romance Reviews*. Coming next is *Warrior Lord*, #3 in the paranormal Drift Lords series from Wild Rose Press. A featured speaker at conferences, libraries, and community events, Nancy is listed in *Contemporary Authors, Poets & Writers*, and *Who's Who in U.S. Writers, Editors, & Poets.*

When not busy writing, she enjoys reading, fine dining, cruising and outlet shopping.

Website: http://nancyjcohen.com
Blog: http://nancyjcohen.wordpress.com
Facebook: https://www.facebook.com/pages/Nancy-J-Cohen/112101588804907
Twitter: http://www.twitter.com/nancyjcohen
Goodreads: http://www.goodreads.com/author/show/91508.Nancy_J_Cohen
Pinterest: http://pinterest.com/njcohen/
Linked In: http://www.linkedin.com/in/nancyjcohen
Google Plus: https://google.com/+NancyJCohen
YouTube: http://www.youtube.com/channel/UC6Yb2zOkXEQ6xmAeYv8Jp5w/

Recipes
72 Shepherd's Pie

Shelley Costa

Shelley Costa is the author of the Agatha Award-nominated *You Cannoli Die Once* (Simon and Schuster 2013), and its upcoming sequel, *Basil Instinct* (Simon and Schuster 2014). Her mystery stories have appeared in *Alfred Hitchcock Mystery Magazine, Blood on Their Hands, The World's Finest Mystery and Crime Stories,* and *Crimewave* (UK). In 2004 she was nominated for an Edgar Award for Best Short Story. Shelley teaches fiction writing at the Cleveland Institute of Art.

Find her at www.shelleycosta.com.

Recipes
16 Gorgonzola, Spiced Walnuts and Port Wine Syrup

Judith Cutler

Lina Townend, Fran Harman and JodieWelsh are all like me – hard-working, multi-tasking career women. Unlike me, they just happen to be fictional. Some have had stops and starts in their working lives, just as I have. For the first thirty years of my working life I was a college lecturer, working in a tough part of Birmingham, but privileged to teach a huge range of people of all ages. Alongside my job I was a mother and housewife. When I was in my late forties stuff happened that wasn't all good: my marriage ended, I moved house, I lost my job – but I did get my first novel published. And the next. You can meet my first heroine, Sophie Rivers, via eBooks. She was soon joined by another tough woman, a cop called Kate Power, whose tussles with crime also appear on eBooks.

Then by a miracle my life improved. I met a wonderful man called (among other things) Edward Marston, and this particular story has a happy ending: we're married and living in the glorious Cotswolds. I still cook and garden, and I've got new fictional women to inspire me. There's also, of course, a young man in my team of crime fighters, a nineteenth century clergyman called Tobias Campion. Tobias first appeared five or six years ago. He had one more adventure but I fancy he's been too busy in his parish to solve any more mysteries until now. However, he's just encountered a big problem and *Cheating the Hangman* will appear next year.

This is a guide to some books I hope you'll enjoy:
Sophie Rivers series – ten books mostly set in Birmingham
Kate Power series – six books mostly set in Birmingham
Fran Harman series – six books (and more to come) mostly set in Kent
Josie Welsh mini-series – two books set in Devon
Lina Townend and Griff Tripp series – six books (and more to come) mostly set in Kent
Jodie Welsh – so far just one (but more to come) set in Kent
Tobias Campion – two books (with another to come) set in Warwickshire

Check them all out on my website, www.judithcutler.com

Recipes
35 Warm Pea and Lentil Salad
33 Strawberry Surprise
36 Salmagundy

Rebecca (aka R.P.) Dahlke

My Dead Red Mystery Series: I sort of fell into the job of running a crop-dusting business when my dad decided he'd rather go on a cruise than take another season of lazy pilots, missing flaggers, testy farmers and horrific hours. After two years at the helm, I handed him back the keys and fled to a city without any of the above. And no, I was never a crop-duster.

I write about a tall, blond and beautiful ex-model turned crop-duster who, to quote Lalla Bains, says: "I've been married so many times they oughta revoke my license." I wanted to give readers a peek at the not so-perfect-life of a beautiful blond. Lalla Bains is no Danielle Steele character, she's not afraid of chipping her manicure. Scratch that, the girl doesn't have time for a manicure what with herding a bunch of recalcitrant pilots and juggling work orders just to keep her father's flagging business alive.

The books in my romantic suspense sailing trilogy are the result of my years sailing in Mexico with my husband aboard our cutter rigged Hylas 47 sailboat. Mexico is a culture that was, and still is, struggling to gain a foothold in the 21st Century. This trilogy, starting with *A Dangerous Harbor*, and continuing with *Hurricane Hole*, is about Americans who're here because they can't seem to outrun the problems they so desperately try to leave behind.

Cozy Food

Find out more about RP Dahlke: http://rpdahlke.com

Recipes
62 Chicken Cacciatore with Mushrooms and Olives
63 Emmy Winning Chicken entree

Kathi Daley

Kathi Daley lives with her husband, kids, grandkids, and Bernese mountain dogs in beautiful Lake Tahoe. When she isn't writing, she likes to read (preferably at the beach or by the fire), cook (preferably something with chocolate or cheese), and garden (planting and planning, not weeding). She also enjoys spending time on the water when she's not hiking, biking, or snowshoeing the miles of desolate trails surrounding her home.

Kathi uses the mountain setting in which she lives, along with the animals (wild and domestic) that share her home, as inspiration for her cozy mysteries. Each of her mystery series features memorable characters, animals, and romance.

For updates on her books, photos, recipes, blogs, and more check out the links below:

Facebook https://www.facebook.com/kathidaleybooks?ref=hl
Twitter https://twitter.com/kathidaley
Webpage http://www.kathidaley.com
Amazon Author Page http://tinyurl.com/k36k2zt

Books by Kathi Daley: Come for the murder stay for the romance.

Paradise Lake Series:
Pumpkins in Paradise
Snowmen in Paradise
Bikinis in Paradise

Zoe Donovan Mysteries:
Halloween Hijinks
The Trouble With Turkeys
Christmas Crazy
Cupid's Curse
Big Bunny Bump-off
Beach Blanket Barbie
Maui Madness
Derby Divas – July 2014

Road to Christmas Romance:
Road to Christmas Past

Recipes
13 Crab and Artichoke Dip
24 Timberland Shrimp Chowder

Cozy Author Biographies

Kathleen Delaney

Kathleen Delaney raised five children, which gave her a late start as an author, but she has five mystery novels in print and is working on the first in a new series. She has been a real estate broker on California's central coast, the setting for the Ellen McKenzie books. She has bred and shown Arabian and half Arabian horses, loves to cook, garden, travel and, of course, read. She currently resides in Georgia, where she lives with her 3 dogs and one cat and can see two of her grandchildren regularly.

Find out more about Kathleen Delaney and her books at her website: www.kathleendelaney.net or her Amazon page http://tinyurl.com/lyr9g7h

Recipes
40 Aunt Mary McGill's Wild Rice Salad with Apples

Diana Dempsey

Inspired by the Beauty Queen Mysteries featuring Ms America Happy Pennington and written by Diana Dempsey, who was never a beauty queen herself but who did work in TV news, which is almost the same thing.

Ms America Happy Pennington—the reigning title-holder in the nation's foremost pageant for married women—is extremely proud of her tiara, sash, and stilettos, but what she loves most is when people think she's smart. That's started to happen lately, thanks to Happy solving a mystery or two (or four).

The first was on Oahu, where Happy figured out who killed pageant rival Tiffany Amber when she tumbled dead out of the isolation booth during the pageant finale on national TV. (*Ms America and the Offing on Oahu*)

Since then, Happy has cracked the case in Sin City (*Ms America and the Villainy in Vegas*), South Beach (*Ms America and the Mayhem in Miami*), and snowy Minnesota (*Ms America and the Whoopsie in Winona*).

Happy's husband, NASCAR pit-crew stud Jason, is darn proud of his wife. Her teenaged daughter Rachel has started thinking her mom's investigative sideline is pretty cool. And hunky pageant emcee Mario Suave is downright dazzled—not just by the crime-solving but by the beauty-queen sleuth herself.

Find out why readers call the Beauty Queen Mysteries "super-fab fun" and "a giggle a minute" and have even wondered if Happy Pennington is "the next Stephanie Plum." Author Diana Dempsey would love that. ;-)

Diana was born and raised in Buffalo, New York, but has since traded the snow and ice for California's sun. She loves writing, reading, cooking, travel, her husband, and her Westie. (Actually, she's pretty keen on dogs of all types.)

To find out more about Diana and her books (her mysteries *and* her women's fiction), visit www.dianadempsey.com; join Diana on Facebook at http://www.facebook.com/DianaDempseyBooks; and follow Diana on Twitter at www.twitter.com/Diana_Dempsey.

Cozy Food

Pamela Frost Dennis

In my previous lives, I worked as: a street singer in San Francisco, a telephone operator, a lumberjack (kidding), a technical illustrator in the aerospace industry, a graphic artist, and an advertising director.

I married Mike during the aerospace phase and together we've lived in Nevada, Washington, Colorado, and Alaska.

These days we live on the California Central Coast and own two restaurants. I also run a website: beautybloomers.com—"the grown-up girls' guide to looking good and feeling great".

We have two incredible sons, two wonderful daughters-in-law, three brilliant grandkids, a few awesome nephews, and two canine-kids. And I'm blessed with some amazing gal pals!

Several years ago I was writing Y.A. (young adult) and just when I got a big publishing house interested in my work, our youngest son became disabled. Obviously, the only thing that mattered was my son's recovery—so my budding writing career came to a screeching halt. Eventually Spencer had back surgery and after a long recovery, played in the U.S. Amateur Golf Championship before turning pro.

My next foray into writing came when a friend in the film industry asked if I'd ever considered writing a screenplay. No. But I love a challenge, so I took classes, got a mentor, and finally wrote "Reality Check"—a family comedy. Unfortunately by the time I finished, my friend had gone on a sabbatical. Darn! I already had my Oscar acceptance speech written!

Recently, while nursing my husband through cancer, I realized life is short and it was time to start writing again. We got through the cancer and Mike is doing well—in fact, he's out playing golf as I write this. Life is good.
Dead Girls Don't Blog is the first in my new Murder Blog Mysteries series.

My Amazon author page: http://amazon.com/author/pamelafrostdennis

Lesley A. Diehl

Lesley retired from her life as a professor of psychology and reclaimed her country roots by moving to a small cottage in the Butternut River Valley in upstate New York. In the winter she migrates to old Florida—cowboys, scrub palmetto, and open fields of grazing cattle, a place where spurs still jingle in the post office, and gators make golf a contact sport. Back north, the shy ghost inhabiting the cottage serves as her writing muse. When not writing, she gardens, cooks and renovates the 1874 cottage with the help of her husband, two cats, and, of course, Fred the ghost, who gives artistic direction to their work.

She is author of several mystery series, all featuring country gals with attitude: the microbrewing mystery series set in the Butternut Valley of upstate New York—*A Deadly Draught* and *Poisoned Pairings;* the Big Lake Murder Mystery series—*Dumpster Dying* and *Grilled, Chilled and Killed*; and the Eve Appel Mysteries series (*A Secondhand Murder*). Untreed Reads publishes her short stories as well as a novel length mystery, *Angel Sleuth.* Her most recent mystery is *Murder is Academic.*

To learn more about Lesley and her books and stories go to her website http://www.lesleyadiehl.com and Amazon http://tinyurl.com/lbyz6mj

Recipes
141 Butternut Valley Ginger Stout Cake or Muffins

Leighann Dobbs

Leighann Dobbs has had a passion for reading since she was old enough to hold a book, but she didn't put pen to paper until much later in life. After a twenty year career as a software engineer with a few side trips into selling antiques and making jewelry, she realized you can't make a living reading books, so she tried her hand at writing them and discovered she had a passion for that too! She lives in New Hampshire with her husband Bruce, their trusty Chihuahua mix Mojo and beautiful rescue cat, Kitty.

My website: http://www.leighanndobbs.com, my author page at
Amazon http://www.amazon.com/Leighann-Dobbs/e/B008BH1VQQ, and my books at Barnes &Noble http://www.barnesandnoble.com/c/leighann-dobbs

Recipes
96 Cherry Cream Cheese Pie

Vicki Doudera

Vicki Doudera is a master at using the backdrop of high-stakes realty as a great setting for a murder mystery. Her latest release (and fifth in the Darby Farr series) is *Deal Killer*, set in Manhattan and featuring crime-solving, deal-making real estate agent Darby and her hunky investigative journalist pal Miles Porter. The duo encounter big trouble in the Big Apple, as the murder of a Russian billionaire pits them against New York's wealthiest -- and deadliest!

Vicki's suspenseful page-turners have twice been chosen by Suspense Magazine as top reads, with 2013's *Final Settlement* named a "Best Cozy" of the year, and she writes about what she truly knows. A broker with a busy Camden, Maine, firm and former Realtor of the Year, Vicki bicycled through California's wine country to research the setting for *Deadly Offer*, in which Darby risks her life to solve a murder at a magnificent vineyard estate. Her short spy thriller *A Neighbor's Story,* was chosen from hundreds of submissions for the Mystery Writer of America's anthology *ICE COLD: Tales of Intrigue and Suspense from the Cold War*, and is based on a true story.

Vicki is also the author of *Moving to Maine* from Down East Books, now available in a brand new third edition. She belongs to Mystery Writers of America, Sisters in Crime, and the

Cozy Food

National Association of Realtors. She's a cyclist, scuba diver, and hiker, and is writing a book about Maine's magnificent (and deadly) Mount Katahdin. Read more about Vicki at her official website, www.vickidoudera.com. Blogging on the Maine Crime Writers page: www.mainecrimewriters.com

My real estate sites, which also touch on my writing, are: www.vickidouderarealtor.com and http://www.camdenre.com/company/brokers/347

Buy her books on Amazon http://tinyurl.com/ky4y2sa
Or Barnes & Noble http://www.barnesandnoble.com/c/vicki-doudera

Recipes
152 Crepes & Lobster Crepes

Pamela DuMond

Pamela DuMond's originally from the Midwest, moved to L.A. for love, and when that tanked she stayed for the lovely weather. She discovered Erin Brockovich's life story, thought it would make a great movie and pitched it to 'Hollywood'. She writes romantic comedic mysteries, romantic YA time travel novels, and New Adult romance. Her book, *The Messenger (Mortal Beloved, #1)* will soon be shopped for a TV series.

She's addicted to *The Voice* and the show *Reign*. The movies *Love Actually* and *The Bourne* trilogy (with Matt Damon -- not that other actor guy) make her cry every time she watches them. (Like -- a thousand.)

She likes her cabernet hearty, her chocolate dark, her cats silly and she lives for a good giggle.

When she's not writing, Pamela's also a chiropractor and cat wrangler. She loves reading, the beach, working out, movies, TV, animals, her family and friends. She lives in Venice, California with her fur-babies.

Pamela's books include:
*Cupcakes, Lies, and Dead Guys (*A Romantic, Comedic Annie Graceland Mystery, #1)
Cupcakes, Sales, and Cocktails – A Novella (Annie #2)
Cupcakes, Pies, and Hot Guys (Annie #3)
Cupcakes, Paws, and Bad Santa Claus (Annie #4)
The Messenger (Mortal Beloved, #1)
The Story of You and Me (Driven, #1)

And the new Rom-Com coming soon… *Part-time Princess* (Ladies-in-Waiting, #1)

To sign up for Pamela's newsletter announcing upcoming books or bookish events visit her website at http://www.pameladumond.com. You can also check out her Amazon page at http://tinyurl.com/kw52vw8

Recipes
95 Mr. Appleton's Apple Pie
99 Gingerbread Cupcakes with Cinnamon Cream Cheese Frosting

Cozy Author Biographies

Carola Dunn

Carola Dunn is the author of over 50 historical novels, including 21 mysteries in the Daisy Dalrymple series (England 1920s), 3 Cornish Mysteries (around 1970), and 32 Regencies.

She was born and grew up in England, where she failed History (and Physics), so it's only natural that she's been writing historical fiction for 35 years. She switched from Regencies to cosy/traditional mysteries when her two Regency publishers both quit publishing Regencies within 6 months of each other. It was a strong hint that the time to move on had arrived.

After 20 years in Southern California, she now makes her home in Eugene, Oregon, with her lab/border collie Trillian. Her favourite occupations are reading, gardening, classical music, and bird-watching. She has two wonderful grandchildren.

http://www.CarolaDunn.weebly.com
https://www.amazon.com/author/caroladunn

Facebook: Carola Dunn, Carola Dunn Author, Daisy Dalrymple, Cornish Mysteries, Regencies by Carola Dunn

Some fun posts:
http://bloodredpencil.blogspot.com/2014/04/fun-times-with-editors.html
http://bloodredpencil.blogspot.com/2014/03/zeitgeist.html
http://bloodredpencil.blogspot.com/2014/02/cover-art-confusion.html
http://bloodredpencil.blogspot.com/2014/01/carola-dunn-on-regency-romance.html

Recipes
151 Kedgeree
123 Macaroons

Jean Erhardt

Jean Erhardt, a former private investigator, is the author of the Kim Claypoole mystery series which is largely set in and around the Great Smoky Mountains. Jean resides in Portland, Oregon, with her partner and their two Cairn Terriers, Hollis and Higgins.

You can find out more about Jean on
her website www.jeanerhardt.com,
or her Facebook page www.facebook.com/JeanErhardtAuthor/, and information about her books on Amazon http://tinyurl.com/n3b4u4n

Recipes
21 My Mother's Manhattan
65 Ted's Smoky Mountain Rosemary Trout

Cozy Food

Chloe Evans

Chloe Evans began composing fiction even before learning how to write. When asked what happened to the cookies her mother baked for a holiday celebration, she told the story of a Santa Claus who got lost while flying back to the North Pole, and because of the early onset of senility, could not control his reindeer, which ran amok in the kitchen and ate up all the cookies. Thus began Chloe's life-long interest in crime fiction and cooking. *Murder in the Gazebo* is her first novel. She cooks and writes in New York City.

Murder in the Gazebo on Amazon http://tinyurl.com/nkkusmj
and Barnes & Noble http://www.barnesandnoble.com/c/chloe-evans

Recipes
142 Melanie's Poppy Sherry Muffins
104 Deep in the Black Forest Cupcakes
20 Champagne Royale
19 Stimulating Decaf Coffee
124 Ginger Cookies
26 Dispatcho Gazpacho
59 Sichuan Chicken

Monica Ferris (aka Margaret Frazer, Mary Monica Pulver, and Mary Kuhfeld)

Before I was Monica Ferris, I wrote as Margaret Frazer, Mary Monica Pulver, Mary Kuhfeld, and Margaret of Shaftesbury. I sometimes joke that if I ever get arrested, I'll be assumed guilty because of all my aliases.

I began writing as Margaret of Shaftesbury, Abbess of Deer Abbey, in the Society for Creative Anachronism. My first professional sale was as Mary Monica Pulver, to *Alfred Hitchcock's Mystery Magazine*. My husband and I wrote a few stories together as Al and Mary Kuhfeld, most notably a little series of mystery shorts about Jack Hafner and Thor Nygaard, Minnesota police detectives.

Then I sold a novel — *Murder at the War* — to Saint Martin's Press. It was nominated for an Anthony as Best First Novel, and I went on to write four more in the Peter Brichter series.

Later a friend (the late Gail Frazer) and I joined forces as Margaret Frazer, writing the tales of a medieval nun at the priory of Saint Frideswide, in the days of Thomas Chaucer.

I was writing and selling short stories for anthologies when my agent called and asked, "Do you know anyone who might write a new mystery series about a middle-aged woman who lives in a small town and does needlework while solving crimes?" *Well,* I thought, *my mother does counted cross stitch, I have a good friend who does blackwork, and I have done embroidery.* "Sure," I replied. After all, how hard could it be?

"You'll need a new name," said my editor. "This is unlike anything you've done before. We don't want to confuse readers." So I took the name Monica – my middle name. And since the City of Excelsior (a real place, where my fictional character lives) once had a big amusement park I took the last name of Ferris, because I spin stories.

Monica's website: http://monica-ferris.com/
Her books on Amazon http://tinyurl.com/m7tjdog
Or Barnes & Noble http://www.barnesandnoble.com/c/monica-ferris

Recipes
54 Haute dish

Judy Fitzwater

Judy Fitzwater grew up an Air Force brat and has lived in nine states, including Maine and Hawaii. But her mother was from Georgia and she always felt like she carried a little bit of the South with her wherever she went, especially its wonderful food. Her first published mystery, *Dying to Get Published*, was plucked from a stack of unsolicited manuscripts at Ballantine Books. It was nominated for an Agatha Award for Best First Mystery. The subsequent seven-book series, The Jennifer Marsh Mysteries about a wannabe mystery writer desperate to get published, was a delight for her to write, especially the scenes with Jennifer's quirky writers' group. Judy is also the author of two suspense thrillers: *No Safe Place* and *Drowning in Air* and the very funny romantic comedy, *Vacationing with the Dead*, which is filled with ghosts and mayhem. All are available in Kindle, Nook, iTunes, Kobo, and Smashwords editions.
My website is www.judyfitzwater.com.
Amazon: http://tinyurl.com/n3hvnwy
Barnes & Noble: http://www.barnesandnoble.com/c/judy-fitzwater
Smashwords: http://www.smashwords.com/profile/view/judy+fitzwater

Recipes
80 Hot Rice
69 Vegetarian Meatballs

Chris Forman

Chris Forman is a high school teacher, writer and food photographer who lives in the Hudson Valley region of New York State with his lovely wife Teresa. They have four children, all grown now, and six grandchildren. His hobbies include eating, grilling, reading classic and cozy mystery novels and traveling to see his family. *Love in the Ashes* is Chris Forman's standalone entry in general fiction. Chris also has four books in the Maria Hart series centered in Chicago and two in the Port City Mystery series centered in Wilmington, NC. He is the author of a popular restaurant review blog. www.burgersandbrewsfoodreviews.blogspot.com
as well as www.chrisforman.blogspot.com

Buy his books on Amazon http://www.amazon.com/Chris-Forman/e/B002BMHLU2
Or Barnes & Noble http://www.barnesandnoble.com/c/chris-forman

Recipes
160 Grilled Twinkies
19 Escargots with wine
81 Roasted Red Peppers

Cozy Food

Kaye George

Kaye George is a short story writer and novelist who has been nominated for three Agatha awards and has been a finalist for the Silver Falchion. She is the author of four mystery series: the Imogene Duckworthy humorous Texas series (*Choke, Smoke*, and *Broke*), the Cressa Carraway musical mystery series (*Eine Kleine Murder*), the Fat Cat cozy series (*Fat Cat at Large* coming in 2014), and The People of the Wind Neanderthal series (*Death in the Time of Ice*).

Her short stories can be found in her collection, *A Patchwork of Stories*, as well as in several anthologies, various online and print magazines. She reviews for *Suspense Magazine*, writes for several newsletters and blogs, and gives workshops on short story writing and promotion. Kaye lives in Knoxville, TN.

Her webpage is http://kayegeorge.com/.
Links to her five novels are on the novel page at http://kayegeorge.com/novels.html.
Links to short stories are on http://kayegeorge.com/shorts.html

She would love to see you at her blogs: http://travelswithkaye.blogspot.com/ and http://makeminemystery.blogspot.com/.

Other links are on the webpage.

Recipes
154 Bowling Alley Hamburgers
80 Cheddar Green Onion Biscuits
32 Cornbread croutons
164 Dried Mammoth Meat/Neanderthal Mammoth Jerky
165 Beef Jerky, adapted for Cro Magnons and Modern Humans

Sally Goldenbaum

Sally Goldenbaum is the author of three dozen novels, most recently the Seaside Knitters Mystery series set in the fictional town of Sea Harbor, Massachusetts.

Sally was born in Manitowoc, Wisconsin, and now lives in Prairie Village, Kansas, with her husband, Don and a terrific Aussie, Sophie.

In addition to writing mysteries, Sally has taught philosophy, Latin, and creative writing, edited bioethics and veterinary healthcare journals, and worked in public television at WQED-Pittsburgh (then home to Mr. Rogers and his Neighborhood).

Sally's family includes her husband, Don, three wonderful adult children, their fine spouses, and six amazing grandchildren.

My most recent mystery is *Murder in Merino*, the eighth book in the Seaside Knitters Mystery series. You'll find great food packed in between red herrings and possible murderers. Please check it out at any of the online sites or bookstores near you.

My personal website is http://www.sallygoldenbaum.com.
See my books on Amazon http://tinyurl.com/lk3dlaa

and Barnes & Noble http://barnesandnoble.com/c/sally-goldenbaum
Please visit me on Facebook https://www.facebook.com/authorsallygoldenbaum?ref=hl

Recipes
52 Linguini with Roasted Vegetables & Shrimp

Barbara Graham

Barbara Graham began making up stories in the third grade and immediately quit learning to multiply and divide. Her motto is "every story needs a dead body and every bed needs a quilt." She writes because she cannot "not write." Barbara continues to be intrigued by the problems and situations her imaginary friends manage to get themselves into. She refuses to accept any blame for their misfortunes and actions.

Her Quilted Mystery series is set in an imaginary county in East Tennessee. It's great fun owning a county and her characters tend to take over and tell her what is "really going on". Who knew? The series follows Sheriff Tony Abernathy and his quiltmaker wife, Theo. Between the two of them; they know every person in the county. People will tell the shop owner and other friends all kinds of things they don't want to bother the sheriff with. Tony is both irritated and grateful for the information. Theo is busy running her shop, designing quilts and raising their children. As an "extra something" for quilters, each book contains a mystery quilt pattern. Barbara is quick to point out; it has nothing to do with the solution to the mystery.

A prize winning quilter herself, Barbara enjoys combining her fabric addiction with her predilection for telling tall tales. Married to a man who can do math in his head (very useful for a math challenged quilter), she has two perfect sons, two perfect grandchildren and "is not the worst mother-in-law in history." Visit her at www.bgmysteries.com. Available in print and ebooks, the titles in order are: *Murder by Serpents, Murder by Artifact, Murder by Music, Murder by Vegetable* and *Murder by Sunlight*

Recipes
49 Theo's Pasta Slaw
15 Theo's Bean Dip

Sarah Graves

Hi! I'm Sarah Graves, I live in Eastport, Maine, and I write two mystery series. The first is the northern-Maine based crime series whose opening salvo, *Winter at the Door* (Bantam, January 2015), stars Aroostook County Sheriff's Deputy Lizzie Snow. And the second is the cozier Home Repair is Homicide series whose newest book, *A Bat in the Belfry* (Bantam, April 2014), stars Jacobia "Jake" Tiptree, an ex-Wall Street money-management professional who moved to the Maine coastal village of Eastport to fix up a 200-year-old house.

Jake wasn't much of a cook in her first book, *The Dead Cat Bounce*, nearly 20 years ago, and she hadn't gotten to be one by the time of the most recent series installment, either, but when she does cook she tends to do something simple, like my recipe for Deviled Ham on Toast. It goes well with some fresh sliced tomatoes or a green salad. Since she's in Maine she drinks Moxie with it, but you can substitute the closest thing to Moxie, which of course is champagne.

Sarah's website is www.sarahgraves.net

Cozy Food

Twitter: @sarahgraves2011
Facebook: SarahGraves2011
Sarah's email: SarahGraves2011@hotmail.com

Recipes
158 Deviled Ham on Toast

Carolyn Haines (aka R. B. Chesterton)

Carolyn Haines is the author of the Sarah Booth Delaney Mississippi Delta Mystery series, and as R.B. Chesterton, she exercises her dark side with gothic chillers such as *The Darkling* and *The Seeker.*

Please see my website www.carolynhaines.com
and www.goodfortunefarmrefuge.org

Recipes
60 Chicken with Green Olives and Cranberries

Vinnie Hansen

Vinnie Hansen is the author of the Carol Sabala mystery series: *Murder, Honey*; *One Tough Cookie*; *Rotten Dates*; *Tang Is Not Juice*; *Death with Dessert;* and *Art, Wine and Bullets.* She was a Claymore Award finalist for her upcoming Carol Sabala mystery, *Black Beans and Venom.* Watch for her short story in the third Guppy anthology, *Fish or Cut Bait*, due from Wildside Press in 2015. Vinnie lives in Santa Cruz, California, with her husband, abstract artist Daniel S. Friedman.

Please visit her website at http://vinniehansen.com. She's also on
Facebook https://www.facebook.com/vinnie.hansen.583?fref=browse_search
Goodreads https://www.goodreads.com/author/show/769812.Vinnie_Hansen
and, of course,Misteriopress http://misteriopress.com/

Recipes
118 Lebkuchen to Die For

Traci Hilton

When not writing I Facebook too much, knit socks, and accompany my mandolin loving husband on the spoons. See https://www.youtube.com/watch?v=LdlwhgQ1JK0

I'm also the author of The Mitzy Neuhaus Mystery series, The Plain Jane Mystery series, and one of the authors in The Tangle Saga series of science fiction novellas. I was the Mystery/Suspense Category winner for the 2012 Christian Writers of the West Phoenix Rattler Contest, a finalist for Speculative Fiction in the same contest, and have a Drammy from the Portland Civic Theatre Guild. I currently serve as the Vice President of the Portland chapter of the American Christian Fiction Writers Association.

I have a degree in History from Portland State University and still live in the rainiest part of the Pacific Northwest with my goofy family and two small dogs.

More of Traci's work can be found at http://www.tracihilton.com
Her books on Amazon http://tinyurl.com/kdjjrze
Or Barnes & Noble http://www.barnesandnoble.com/c/traci-hilton

Recipes
53 Gnocchi a la Traci

Sibel Hodge

Sibel Hodge is an International Bestselling Author. She has 8 cats and 1 husband. In her spare time, she's Wonder Woman! When she's not out saving the world from dastardly demons she writes an eclectic mix of romantic comedies, mysteries, thrillers, children's books, and non-fiction.
Her work has been shortlisted for the Harry Bowling Prize 2008, Highly Commended by the Yeovil Literary Prize 2009, Runner Up in the Chapter One Promotions Novel Comp 2009, nominated Best Novel with Romantic Elements in 2010 by The Romance Reviews, Runner Up in the Best Indie Books of 2012 by Indie Book Bargains, and Winner of Best Children's Book by eFestival of Words 2013. Her novella Trafficked: The Diary of a Sex Slave has been listed as one of the Top 40 Books About Human Rights by Accredited Online Colleges.

To find out more about Sibel Hodge, check out her website: http://www.sibelhodge.com/

Recipes
147 Baked Eggs
27 Chilli Bean Soup

Valerie Horowitz

A life-long cookbook lover, Valerie Horowitz has always worked with books. She has sold out-of-print and rare books, was manager of a bookstore in New York's Greenwich Village and held various marketing and editorial positions at trade and professional publishers. Currently she is the managing editor of a scholarly publishing company. She is an associate member of the Antiquarian Booksellers Association of America, and belongs to Mystery Writers of America and Sisters in Crime. She lives in a house built in the 1750s with her husband, son, and cat in the bucolic northwestern New Jersey farm and horse country where *Cinnamon Girl* takes place.

Her books are available in paperback on Amazon; and on Kindle, Nook and iTunes.

You can find her online at her Facebook author page:
https://www.facebook.com/ValerieHorowitzAuthorPage and at
http://www.annabelpublishing.com/

Watch for *Tangled Up in Bleu*, the second in the Village Cooks series, in fall 2014.

Recipes
161 1630. Devonshire Cream

Cozy Food

Mary Ellen Hughes

Mary Ellen Hughes has started her new Pickled and Preserved mystery series with *The Pickled Piper*. She is also the author of the Craft Corner mystery series – *Wreath of Deception*, *String of Lies*, and *Paper-Thin Alibi*, as well as the Maggie Olenski mysteries – *Resort to Murder* and *A Taste of Death*, along with several short stories.

Mary Ellen lives in Maryland and is a member of Mystery Writers of America and Sisters in Crime.

Visit her website at: http://www.maryellenhughes.com
Buy The Pickled Piper: http://tinyurl.com/l5arle2

My protagonist in The Pickled Piper, *Piper Lamb, is an expert at making all kinds of pickles, most of them going through the canning process. Once in a while she likes to make it a little easier for herself. Nothing's easier—or tastier— than these refrigerator pickles.* – Mary Ellen Hughes

Recipes
164 Summer Squash Refrigerator Pickles

Linda Joffe Hull

Linda Joffe Hull is the author of *The Big Bang* (Tyrus Books) and *Eternally 21* (Midnight Ink) the first in the Mrs. Frugalicious mystery series. She is a native of St. Louis, Missouri and a graduate of UCLA. She currently lives in Denver, Colorado with her husband and children. Linda is a longtime member of Rocky Mountain Fiction Writers, currently serves on the national board of Mystery Writers of America, and is the 2013 RMFW Writer of the Year. Her next Mrs. Frugalicious mystery, *Black Thursday*, will be released in fall 2014.

To watch a recent interview with Linda please go to:
http://www.youtube.com/watch?v=GVtTrDmB4xA
or visit her website: www.lindajoffehull.com.
or her Amazon author page: http://tinyurl.com/n6ltuot

Recipes
149 Peanut Butter and Jelly French Toast

Ellen Elizabeth Hunter

Ellen Elizabeth Hunter lives in Historic Wilmington on the beautiful North Carolina Coast, a setting that inspires her mystery series. In 2001 she created Magnolia Mysteries with the first novel *Murder on the Ghost Walk*. There are now ten books in the series with the eleventh in progress.

Ellen studied American Literature and Creative Writing at New York University. She enjoys researching local historical events as the backdrop for her plots.

Ellen is dedicated to helping others, and frequently uses book sales to raise funds for worthy causes. For descriptions of her novels and a list of booksellers, visit: www.ellenhunter.com.

Magnolia Mystery series

"If you like sultry Southern nights, dining al fresco under the stars with views of spanking white yachts, and centuries-old live oak trees dripping with Spanish moss, then you'll love my Magnolia Mysteries: ten cozy mysteries set in the beautiful, historic, coastal city of Wilmington NC and adjoining, charming Wrightsville Beach. Book eleven is in progress." Ellen Elizabeth Hunter

Available on Amazon for Kindle: http://tinyurl.com/kvwpelj

Recipes
120 Orange Coconut Cookies

Dawn Greenfield Ireland

Dawn Ireland is the CEO of Artistic Origins Inc., a 100% woman-owned publishing and technical writing service company that has been doing business since 1995. She's an award winning independent publisher and author of *The Puppy Baby Book*, *Mastering Your Money*, and Amazon Best Seller *Hot Chocolate* (the first in the series, and her fifth novel). The *Hot Chocolate* audio book was awarded the AudioFile Earphones Award on Valentine's Day 2014.

Her family feature film screenplay *A Girl and Her Dog* was awarded a Kids First! Endorsement by the Coalition for Quality Children's Media in October 2012 and optioned by Shadow Cave Productions in February 2013.

Originally from Feeding Hills, MA, Dawn migrated to San Antonio in 1968, then when her first son was one year old, her family moved to Houston where work was more plentiful. After 40+ years of heat and humidity, she has her sights on the Pacific NW.

Dawn is the co-author of the animated screenplay *Memoirs of a Dog* which won the Spirit Award of the Moondance Film Festival (children's category) September 2011. Her dark comedy *Plan B* was a finalist in the Table Read My Screenplay script competition in 2010 and years before that, *Standing Dead* won the Women in Film and Television (Houston Chapter) screenplay award.

Stay tuned for *Bitter Chocolate*, book 2 in the *Hot Chocolate* Alcott Family Adventures (6/2014) *The Last Dog* (futuristic/sci-fi 2015), and *Spicy Chocolate* (2016 – book 3).

www.dawnireland-writer.com
www.artistic-origins.com
The Puppy Baby Book on Dawn's website
http://www.thepuppybabybook.com/
Hot Chocolate on Amazon
http://www.amazon.com/Hot-Chocolate-ebook/dp/B005XQYP5C/
Hot Chocolate on Dawn's website
http://www.dawnireland-writer.com/Hot-Chocolate.html

Cozy Food

"Never tell me the sky's the limit when there are footprints on the moon" - Unknown
"Never miss a good chance to shut up" - Will Rogers (1879 - 1935)
"As long as you are going to think anyway, think big" - Donald Trump
"If you stop chasing your dream, you're already dead" - Steve Mazan

Recipes
148 Custard French Toast
75 Sweet Potato Casserole with Pecan Topping

Melanie Jackson

Melanie has been writing since she was seven. One of her fondest childhood memories is receiving an IBM Selectric typewriter. She wrote romance novels for New York publisher Dorchester Publishing from 1999 to 2010. Then she switched to cozy mysteries. She has since released the Chloe Boston, Butterscotch Jones, Wendover House, Kenneth Mayhew and Miss Henry Mystery series.

Melanie Jackson is the award-winning author of more than ninety novels, novellas and poems published in various languages. She lives with her husband and bossy cat in the Sonoma wine country. Besides gardening, she is involved with animal charities. You can find out about her books or reach her at www.melaniejackson.com.

Recipes:
122 Aunt Crystal's Almond Crescent Cookies
122 Grandpa Mac's Prettiest Sugar Cookies

Holly Jacobs

Holly Jacobs leads a life full of romance and adventure. From skydiving to jet-setting around Europe, from snorkeling in coral reefs to writing while wearing beautiful silk peignoir sets and popping chocolate bonbons, Holly Jacobs leads a life that is the epitome of romance … Well, my fictional life sounds more interesting, but not better than my real life. Really, I'm the happily married mother of four. I cook a lot, garden and weave baskets! I write for Montlake Romance and Harlequin. My books range from lighthearted comedies to more serious dramas and now even mysteries … but at heart, they're all stories of love.

You can visit me at http://www.HollyJacobs.com.

Recipes
143 Whole Wheat Banana-Blueberry Muffins

Miranda James (aka Dean James)

Miranda James is the *New York Times*-bestselling author of the Cat in the Stacks series. These books feature widowed librarian Charlie Harris and his sidekick, Diesel, a Maine Coon cat. The series is set in fictional Athena, Mississippi, Charlie's hometown. "Miranda" is a pseudonym for Dean James, an award-winning writer of mystery non-fiction and the author of over twenty books. A seventh-generation Mississippian, Dean has lived in Houston, Texas, for thirty-two years. He holds master's degrees in history and library science, as well as a Ph.D. in medieval history from Rice University. He spent eighteen years in the Texas Medical Center as a medical librarian, and he found working in a medical library useful to his career as a mystery writer. He is an avid reader and book collector with an estimated seven to eight thousand books crowding the shelves in his house. He has two cats, Pippa and Toby, neither of whom is a Maine Coon.

There is a website that offers more information on the *Cat in the Stacks* series, along with the other books Dean has published in the past twenty-two years. The link is www.catinthestacks.com. He also blogs with two different groups, the "Killer Characters" at www.killercharacters.com and the "Femmes Fatales" at http://femmesfatales.typepad.com/ (where he is a "frère fatale). You can also find his author page on Facebook at www.facebook.com/mirandajamesauthor.

Recipes
29 Lazy Man's Vegetable Meatball Soup

Nancy Lynn Jarvis

Nancy Lynn Jarvis likes trying new things so it's not surprising that after earning a degree in behavioral science she worked in the advertising department of the San Jose Mercury News, was a librarian, and later the business manager for Shakespeare Santa Cruz at UCSC before becoming a Realtor.

After four mysteries — *The Death Contingency, Backyard Bones, Buying Murder* and *The Widow's Walk League* — she took a time out to write *Mags and the AARP Gang*, a comedy about a group of renegade octogenarian bank robbers. But she missed Regan and Tom, her husband-and-wife Realtor/amateur sleuth team and their friend Dave, a former police officer who has been forced into a semi-retired position as Santa Cruz Police Ombudsman after losing an eye in a shoot-out, so much that she came back to mystery writing for *The Murder House* and is working on the sixth book in the series.

Her husband Craig — her-go-to guy for everything computer, her initial editor (whether he wants to be or not) co-editor of *Cozy Food*, (though he doesn't want credit for it) and chief hand holder, gave her a great idea for another series about two old guys who have a handyman service that puts them in the midst of mystery and murder. Look for a Geezers With Tools series in the future.

Recipes
128 Mysterious Chocolate Chip Cookies
78 Roasted Vegetables
51 Whole Wheat Penne With Good Stuff
73 Pork Tangine

Heather Justesen

Heather Justesen remembers making her first scratch cake when she was about thirteen. Thankfully, her baking skills have improved dramatically from the lopsided, but tasty, mess she made that day. When she's not writing or developing recipes, she works on the board of her community garden, decorates cakes for friends and neighbors, plays with her dog, cat, and chickens, or just relaxes with her husband. She has published more than a dozen novels, and is working on her fourth Sweet Bites Bakery mystery for release summer of 2014.

Learn more about her at her website at http://heatherjustesen.com/ or her blog at http://heatherjustesen.blogspot.com/ or follow her Facebook fan page http://www.facebook.com/pages/Heather-Justesen/273141090197.

Recipes
134 Rocky Road Brownies
160 Oven S'mores

Pamela Kelley

Pamela M. Kelley lives in the historic seaside town of Plymouth, MA near Cape Cod and just south of Boston. She has always been a book worm and still reads often and widely, romance, mysteries, thrillers and cook books. She writes cozy mysteries and romances and you'll probably see food featured along with a recipe or two. She is owned by a cute little Maine Coon Cat, Kelley.

Here's a link to my mystery, *Trust*, on Amazon http://amzn.to/1bJ84re
My website is www.pamelakelley.com

Recipes
56 Lazy Lobster Casserole

E.E. Kennedy

E.E. Kennedy began writing the Miss Prentice Cozy Mystery Series when she ran out of Agatha Christies to read. She lives in NC with her husband, surrounded by five rambunctious grandchildren whose adorableness cuts dangerously into her writing time.

High school English teacher Amelia Prentice lives in the Adirondack region of northern NY State, surrounded by colorful regional characters, including an eccentric professor intent on finding the fabled Lake Champlain monster. Her snarky best friend Lily lives in the house behind hers and is always ready to provide hot gossip. Her childhood home has been converted into a B&B, run by a French-Canadian millionaire and his wife.

Beginning with *Irregardless of Murder*, where she stumbles over the corpse of a former student in the public library, the books cover Amelia's efforts to retain her dignity, promote good grammar and help get her friends out of trouble. Sometimes she succeeds.

Death Dangles a Participle begins as a pair of Amelia's teenaged students decide to cross a frozen lake in their vintage VW. What could possibly go wrong? When they're accused of a brutally murdering a man and leaving him to freeze into the ice, their teacher is the only one who believes in their innocence.

In *Murder in the Past Tense*, (September, 2014) Amelia and husband Gil explore their memories of one summer many years ago, when they were teenagers working in summer stock theater and an ingénue went missing. Was she the victim of a mob hit? Could it have anything to do with the recent murder of a handsome actor?

Cozy Author Biographies

Check out the opening chapters of all the books at the Miss Prentice website:
www.missprenticecozymystery.com and follow E.E. on twitter: @eekmystery

Recipes
161 A Michigan from New York (hot dog sauce)
37 Amelia's Fruit Salad with Sour Cream Sauce

Mary Kennedy

Mary Kennedy is a licensed clinical psychologist and the author of the Dream Club Mysteries for Penguin-Random House. The first release, *Nightmares Can Be Murder* will be released September 2014. Business consultant Taylor Blake has returned to Savannah, Georgia, to help her sister Allison turn her dream of running an old-fashioned candy store into a reality. Allison is also interested in dream interpretation and invites Taylor to her Friday night Dream Club, where members meet once a week to share and analyze their dreams. When a murder happens right across the street from the candy store, the Dream Club springs into action to solve the crime.

Nightmares can be Murder on Amazon http://tinyurl.com/ovhxz2x

Mary has written *Dream Interpretation, a psychologist's guide*, if you would like to learn more about dreams and their meaning. http://tinyurl.com/p7hfns9

Mary has written a fun cozy series set in south Florida called The Talk Radio Mysteries. She is also re-printing three of her Penguin young adult novels with new titles. *Golden Girl, Movie Star,* and *Secrets.* Be sure to visit her website for details. http://www.marykennedy.net/ Mary blogs every Saturday on The Cozy Chicks, a group of seven mystery writers. http://www.cozychicks.com/.

You can find her on FB and become her friend. https://www.facebook.com/mary.kennedy.948 and she's on LinkedIn and Twitter.

Recipes
94 Key Lime Pie
132 Granola Bars

Josi S. Kilpack

Josi grew up in Salt Lake City, graduated from Olympus High School in 1992, and was married not quite a year later to her high-school sweetheart. She began her first novel in 1998 and hasn't stopped. Her novel *Sheep's Clothing* won the Whitney Award 2007 for Mystery/Suspense and she was the Best In State winner for fiction in 2012. Book eleven in the Sadie Hoffmiller Culinary Mystery series, Fortune Cookie, was released in spring 2014 with the final book in that series, Wedding Cake, to be released in Fall 2014 along with a cook book containing all the recipes featured in the series. Josi also writes women's fiction and romance. She currently lives in Willard Utah with her husband Lee and three of their four children—the fourth lives on campus at the University of Utah. For more information visit her website. http://www.josiskilpack.com/

Recipes
105 Devils' Food Cake

Cozy Food

Kelly Klepfer (aka Michelle Griep and Ellie Marks)

Michelle Griep hears voices. Loud. Incessant. And very real. Which basically gives her two options: choke back massive amounts of Prozac or write fiction. She chose the latter. Way cheaper. She's been writing since she discovered blank wall space and Crayolas. Check out Michelle's books here.
(http://writeofftheleash.blogspot.com please link to Michelle's Blog)

Kelly Klepfer (aka Ellie Marks) dabbles in her kitchen as a self-taught foodie and loves to live life out loud. Creating characters that are multidimensional and placing them in crazy situations might be one of her favorite things to do. Setting up a difficult scenario for Michelle to follow is over the top fun. Kelly concocts here. (http://kellyklepfer.blogspot.com please link to Kelly's blog)

Coming soon, *Out of the Frying Pan*, a cozy mystery co-authored by Michelle Griep writing as Ellie Marks and Kelly Klepfer.

Out of the Frying Pan is a zany mystery with a dash of romance and pinch of danger. When Fern and Zula discover the body of their cook at Sunset Paradise Retirement Village, they realize that things might not be all sunshine and roses. Enter Detective Flynn, the police officer assigned to investigate the murder and, as Fern and Zula believe, the future husband of their niece, KC. Unfortunately, KC has sworn off men forever.

The humorous antics of Zula and Fern will have readers laughing, while the mystery will keep them turning pages. *Out of the Frying Pan* is full of food, cranky-pant moments and Fifi the wonder-dog.

Recipes
41 Cold Quinoa Muffuletta Salad
81 Spicey Dicey Onion Rings

Barbara Cool Lee

Barbara Cool Lee is the author of the Pajaro Bay mystery romance series, as well as the Deeds of the Ariane fantasy series. Her books have won many awards, but she thinks the biggest prize is hearing from readers who enjoy her stories. She lives in a cottage by the sea on the California coast, where she's busy writing her next novel. If you would like to be first to find out when Barb's next book is released, join the mailing list at her website at http://BarbaraCoolLee.com

Pajaro Bay mystery romance series:
The Honeymoon Cottage http://amzn.to/10wObWo
Home Improvement http://amzn.to/10wObWo

Recipes
25 Mel's Famous Artery-Clogging Clam Chowder
127 Robin's Chocolate Chip Cookies with a Twist

Cozy Author Biographies

Marilyn Levinson

A former Spanish teacher, Marilyn Levinson writes mysteries, romantic suspense, and books for kids.

Her latest mystery, *Murder a la Christie*, is out with Oak Tree Press. Untreed Reads has brought out a new e-edition of her first Twin Lakes mystery, *A Murderer Among Us*--a Suspense Magazine Best Indie--and will bring out a new e-edition of the sequel, *Murder in the Air*, in April. Her ghost mystery, *Giving Up the Ghost*, and her romantic suspense, *Dangerous Relations*, are out with Uncial Press. All of her mysteries take place on Long Island, where she lives.

Her books for young readers include *No Boys Allowed*; *Rufus and Magic Run Amok*, which was awarded a Children's Choice; *Getting Back to Normal*, & *And Don't Bring Jeremy*.

Marilyn loves traveling, reading, knitting, doing Sudoku, and visiting with her granddaughter, Olivia, on FaceTime. She is co-founder and past president of the Long Island chapter of Sisters in Crime.

My website: www.marilynlevinson.com
My Amazon page: http://amzn.to/K6Md1O
Murder a la Christie: http://amzn.to/1c1byHd and http://amzn.to/1ly1NJ9

Recipes
78 Sweet Potato Casserole

Liz Lipperman

Liz Lipperman started writing many years ago, even before she retired from the medical field. Although she wrote romances, her stories always had pesky villains and mysterious deaths. She finally gave up and decided since she read mysteries and obviously wrote them, why fight it? Although she signed her first contract with Berkley to write a cozy mystery series, she likes to call her genre Romantic Mysteries since you will find a heavy dose of boy meets girl and a happily "at least for now" in every story.

The first book of her Clueless Cook Mystery series, *Liver Let Die*, debuted in October, 2011 followed by *Beef Stolen-Off* in July 2012, *Murder for the Halibut* in January 2013, and *Chicken Cacchia-Killer* in December of 2014. *Heard it through the Grapevine*, the first book of A Dead Sister Talking Mystery series from Midnight Ink, written as Lizbeth Lipperman, released in May of 2013 with book 2, *Jailhouse Glock*, coming in May of 2014. *Mortal Deception and Shattered*, two romantic thrillers also written as Lizbeth Lipperman are available as well. In December *Sweepers: A Kiss to Die For*, a prequel to her new Romantic Suspense series out next year debuted in a compilation of short stories titled *My Bloody Valentine*. In May, *Can't Buy Me Love*, a short story from Amazon StoryFront released. Look for *Smothered, Covered, and Dead*, A Clueless cook novella coming in November 2014 and *Mission to Kill*, book 3 of A Dead Sister Talking series in May of 2015.

My website: http://lizlipperman.com/ and my Amazon Author page: http://tinyurl.com/latopz3

My Buy Links:
Ginny's Chicken Cacciatore from *Chicken Caccia-Killer* http://tinyurl.com/lb48qxs

Cozy Food

Myrtle's Better than Sex Cake from *Beef Stolen-off* http://tinyurl.com/mxdbq4m
Chocolate Kahlua Brownies from *Murder for the Halibut* http://tinyurl.com/m34wza9

Recipes
50 Ginny's Chicken Cacciatore
112 Myrtle's Better than Sex Cake
133 Sinfully Sweet Chocolate Kahlua Brownies

Gail Lukasik

Gail Lukasik began her writing career as a poet and earned a Ph.D. in English with a specialization in poetry from the University of Illinois at Chicago. Lisel Mueller described her book of poems, *Landscape Toward a Proper Silence*, as a "splendid collection." In 2002 she was awarded an Illinois Arts Council award for her poem, "In Country."

After spending a year interviewing homeless mothers living in Chicago area shelters, she wrote *Homeless, In My Own Words: True Stories of Homeless Mothers*. The poetic monologues tell the gut-wrenching stories of each woman's descent into homelessness in the women's own words.

She switched to writing mystery novels at the suggestion of her son who said, "Mom, you're always reading mysteries, why don't you try writing one." Her Leigh Girard seasonal mystery series is set in the resort community of Door County, Wisconsin and features local reporter and transplanted Chicagoan Leigh Girard. Lukasik says of Leigh, "She says and does things I would never say or do."

In *Destroying Angels*, the first book in the series, Leigh Girard finds that life in a small town can be fatal when an amateur naturalist dies of mushroom poisoning, a day later the local librarian commits suicide, then the buried bones of an infant are discovered.

Taking a break between *Death's Door* and *Peak Season for Murder*, Lukasik wrote her first stand-alone mystery, *The Lost Artist*, which involves the quest for one of the greatest lost art treasures of sixteenth-century America.

The 2014 Love Is Murder mystery conference awarded *Peak Season for Murder*, a Lovey Award for Best Traditional Amateur Sleuth.

Prior to writing books, she was a ballerina with the Cleveland Civic Ballet Company. She's worked as a choreographer, freelance writer, and college lecturer. She was certified as a canoe instructor and has led canoeing trips on the Des Plaines River. When she isn't writing, she likes to hike the beautiful forest preserves near her house.

Her website can be found at www.gaillukasik.com

Print books and e-books are available on her Amazon author page: http://tinyurl.com/ms3j3my

Recipes
70 Stabbed Kabobs

Cozy Author Biographies

Elaine Macko

I'm the author of the Alex Harris mystery series. I grew up in Connecticut and also lived in Europe for many years. I try to combine my love of both places in my stories by inserting a European connection.

They say write what you know and my career working as an office manager, executive assistant and a report editor gave me the impetus for centering the series around the Always Prepared temporary employment agency.

Alex Harris, my protagonist, is a Winston Churchill-quoting, M&M's-addicted woman with a mind of her own who discovers she really has a gift for finding dead bodies, much to the chagrin of a certain police detective.

In addition to Alex and her sister and partner Sam, the books include their parents, a couple of retirees who love playing board games; a bingo-playing, loan-sharking grandmother and her gang of goofy eighty-somethings; and Alex's adorable nephew, Henry, who talks in percentages.

I really enjoy writing and do my darnedest to bring you a great story, intriguing plot, lovely setting, and engaging characters—oh, yes, and lots of chocolate, tea, and plenty of bodies!

I currently have six books in the Alex Harris mystery series—*Armed, Poisoned, Flossed, Mahjonged, Smoked,* and *Pickled,* and I'm always on the outlook for a cool way to murder someone and welcome fun suggestions at elainemackobooks@hotmail.com.
I hope you enjoy my recipe and take a look at my Web site at www.ElaineMackoBooks.com. You just might find a fun new series to keep you company along with a link to buy the books! All books are available at Amazon in both e-book and hard copy.

...The writing reminds me of a cross between Mary Higgins Clark and Janet Evanovich.

Recipes
150 Meme's Ham and Egg Pie

Sylvia Massara

Sylvia Massara is a multi-genre novelist, based in Sydney, Australia, who dabbles in wacky love affairs, drama and murder (or all three) over coffee. Sylvia has been writing since her early teens and her work consists of novels and screenplays.

As with most authors, Sylvia draws on her varied experience in the sometimes-puzzling tapestry of life. These days, however, Sylvia has resigned from the human race, and she lives both in the animal kingdom, with her kitty cat, Mia, (a much better place to be), and vicariously, through the many characters in her head.

Sylvia has a soft spot for older female protagonists with an attitude who are on the cusp of 40 years and beyond. This is seen in her wacky, romantic comedies, and most recently, in her mystery novels.

An avid fan of classic black and white Hollywood movies of the 40s including film noir, Sylvia has placed her protagonist, Mia Ferrari, in a contemporary mystery series with a bit of a "film noir" flavour. Mia Ferrari is an older, spunky, smartarse female who works in the international world of hotels. The theme is comedic, sexy, and peppered with that film-noir-hero type of attitude. The stories are fast-paced and set in the modern day world.

On a more serious note, Sylvia's work in literary fiction brings forth *The Soul Bearers*, an inspirational story filled with hope, overcoming fear, loss, betrayal, and discovering the healing power of unconditional love.

Sylvia's novels to date:

Mia Ferrari Mysteries:
Playing With The Bad Boys
The Gay Mardi Gras Murders
The South Pacific Murders

Other fiction:
The Soul Bearers [literary fiction]
The Other Boyfriend [chick lit, romance]
Like Casablanca [chick lit, romance]

For more information please visit Massara's website at: http://www.sylviamassara.com.

Recipes
47 Tagliatelle with Hazelnut Pesto

Sonja Massie (aka G. A. McKevett)

Since publication of her first novel in 1986, Sonja Massie has authored more than 60 published works, including the highly popular and critically acclaimed Savannah Reid Mysteries under the pseudonym G.A. McKevett. Sonja's novels range from Irish historicals to contemporary thrillers. Her earthy humor and fast-paced plots delight her fans, while critics applaud her offbeat characterizations and incisive observations on human nature.

Irish by ancestry, Sonja has authored two non-fiction books on the history of Ireland: *The Complete Idiot's Guide to Irish History and Culture* and *Irish Pride: 101 Reasons to be Proud You're Irish*. Both books impart detailed knowledge of the complex and controversial Irish story with a light hand and plenty of humor. She also wrote the best seller *Far and Away,* a novel based on Ron Howard's movie, starring Tom Cruise and Nicole Kidman.

On national tours, Sonja lectures to published and "pre-published" authors in her workshop, "The Novel Approach." The seminar covers such topics as: story structure, characterization, plotting, pacing, and marketing. She has taught numerous courses at university and adult continuing education facilities including: general fiction, historical research, and mystery writing. She was managing editor of "Single Living" magazine and has functioned as a manuscript doctor for major publishers. Earlier in her career, she was a prolific ghostwriter for celebrities and professionals.

Having lived in Los Angeles, Toronto, and County Kerry, Ireland, she now resides in New York with her husband.

Her hobbies include: making jewelry, origami, Irish folk music, Celtic beading and needlework, and playing with her "grandangels."

Her personal websites: http://sonjamassie.com/ and http://gamckevett.com/
Find her on Amazon at: http://tinyurl.com/m2j25vh

Recipes
137 Savannah's Famous Fudge

Edith Maxwell (aka Tace Baker)

Massachusetts author Edith Maxwell's Local Foods Mystery series (Kensington Publishing) lets her relive her days as an organic farmer in Massachusetts, although murder in the greenhouse is new. *A Tine to Live, a Tine to Die* came out to critical acclaim in May, 2013. The second book in the series, *'Til Dirt Do Us Part* (2014), chronicles the murder of a CSA member after geek-turned-organic-farmer Cam Flaherty's Farm-to-Table dinner.

A fourth-generation Californian, Maxwell has published short stories of murderous revenge, most recently in *Best New England Crime Stories 2014: Stone Cold* (Level Best Books, 2013) and *Fish Nets* (Wildside Press, 2013). The *Stone Cold* story, "Breaking the Silence," won an Honorable Mention in the Al Blanchard Short Crime Fiction contest.

Edith Maxwell also authors *Speaking of Murder* and *Bluffing is Murder* (2014) under the pseudonym Tace Baker, which feature Quaker linguistics professor Lauren Rousseau and small-town intrigue (Barking Rain Press). Edith holds a long-unused doctorate in linguistics, is a long-time member of Amesbury Friends Meeting, and is currently writing a historical mystery set in 1888 Amesbury featuring Quaker midwife Rose Carroll, as well as John Greenleaf Whittier.

A mother, world traveler, and former technical writer, Edith lives in an antique house with her beau and three cats. She blogs every weekday with the rest of the Wicked Cozy Authors (http://wickedcozyauthors.com/). You can also find her at http://www.edithmaxwell.com/, at @edithmaxwell, and on Facebook, www.facebook.com/EdithMaxwellAuthor

Recipes
40 Tomato-Bean Salad with Eggs
15 Baba Ganoush

Lorena McCourtney

Lorena McCourtney began writing early in life, usually stories about horses, but she didn't intend to *be* a writer. Raising cattle and horses on a big ranch was what she had in mind. But time and life have a way of changing plans, and a writer is what she became. She wrote numerous short stories before turning to romance fiction, then Christian romances, and now feels she has found her real home in Christian romantic suspense.
She's published some 45 novels altogether. The most recent are the three books in the Cate Kinkaid Files, a lighthearted mystery series about a woman who becomes an assistant private investigator mostly because she's desperate for a job. She's supposed to have an easy first assignment, but instead finds herself up to her elbows in killers.

Lorena says she's had fun with this series, as well as with the lighthearted Andi McConnell Mysteries featuring an older woman and her limousine. But her favorite character will probably always be the aged-into-invisibility Ivy Malone. Probably because the invisibility part of the character came from her personal experience! An experience apparently shared by a number of readers, many of them considerably younger than Ivy.

Lorena and her husband live in southern Oregon – without cattle or horses. Their lone "livestock" now is one eccentric cat.

Three Secrets - a romance novella, is available now on Kindle, Nook and Kobo.
Dying to Read and *Dolled up to Die* (The Cate Kinkaid Files) are available in print and e-book now.

The Ivy Malone Mysteries, The Andi McConnell Mysteries, and The Julesburg Mysteries are available on Kindle, Nook and Kobo.

For more information about Lorena and her books, visit her on her website:
http://www.lorenamccourtney.com
Her Amazon author page: http://tinyurl.com/n7mxugx
Her Nook author page: http://www.barnesandnoble.com/c/lorena-mccourtney

Recipes
155 Cates's Quick Mexican Lunch
57 Ivy's Lazy-Day Casserole

Marja McGraw

Marja McGraw, born and raised in Southern California, is a true Californian. Her family traces back to the 1850's in Los Angeles. She worked in both criminal and civil law enforcement for several years before relocating to Northern Nevada, where she worked for the Department of Transportation. She also lived in Oregon where she worked for the Jackson County Sheriff's Office and owned her own business, a Tea Room/Antique Store. Her next stop was Wasilla, Alaska. The draw to Northern Nevada was strong, and she eventually returned.

Marja wrote a weekly column for a small newspaper in No. Nevada . She's also appeared on the morning news in Reno, Nevada, and on KLBC-TV in Laughlin, Nevada. She's also been a guest on several radio and Internet radio shows.

Starting with *Mysteries of Holt House - A Mystery,* Marja followed up with *A Well-Kept Family Secret - A Sandi Webster Mystery* and the beginning of a series. Most recently, she began a new series beginning with *Bogey Nights – A Bogey Man Mystery.*

She says that each of her mysteries contains *a little humor, a little romance and A Little Murder!* and that her books concentrate on the characters and solving the crime rather than the crime itself.

She and her husband currently live in northern Arizona where life is good!
To explore more of Marja's books, go to her website at www.marjamcgraw.com or to her Amazon page at http://tinyurl.com/mwem66s

Recipes
106 Self-Frosted Cake
59 Cashew Chicken

Eileen Haavik McIntire

Eileen Haavik McIntire writes the 90s Club series of cozy mysteries featuring 90-year-old Nancy Dickenson and her friends at Whisperwood Retirement Village. The inspiration for the series springs from meeting a slim, attractive woman swimming laps at a pool party, and she was 91 years old. Eileen now collects articles about people in their 90s and 100s who are active, alert, and able, some even hold down jobs. Her series changes the paradigm for people in their 90s.

Eileen's books receive excellent reviews and include *The 90s Club & the Hidden Staircase, The 90s Club & the Whispering Statue*, and *Shadow of the Rock*, an historical adventure. She travels widely, often using exotic settings in her novels. She has ridden a camel in the Moroccan Sahara, fished for piranhas on the Amazon, sailed in a felucca on the Nile, and lived three years on a boat, exploring the coast from Annapolis to Key West.

Eileen has many years experience writing, editing and designing all manner of publications for nonprofits and professional associations. She is now co-owner of Summit Crossroads Press, which publishes books for parents, and its fiction imprint, Amanita Books. She is a member and strong advocate of the Maryland Writers' Association, the Independent Book Publishers Association, the MidAtlantic Book Publishers Association, and Sisters in Crime and its Chesapeake Chapter.

Visit her website at http://www.ehmcintire.com/, her blog at http://eileenmcintire.com/, and like her on Facebook at https://www.facebook.com/EileenHaavikMcIntireAuthor.

Recipes
67 Tilapia Baked with Shrimp Sauce

Staci McLaughlin

Staci McLaughlin is the author of the Blossom Valley Mysteries, which includes *Going Organic Can Kill You, All Natural Murder*, and *Green Living Can Be Deadly*. For many years, she was a technical writer for computer software companies, but once she had her first child, she traded in her cubicle and coworkers for field trip chaperoning and carpool duty. In her spare time, she enjoys hiking, playing games with her family, and visiting amusement parks, especially those with teeth-rattling, stomach-clenching roller coasters.

You can find out more about her books and her writing at www.stacimclaughlin.com and at the LadyKillers blog, where a group of fellow mystery and crime writers post their thoughts on writing, reading, and life in general at http://www.theladykillers.typepad.com/. She lives with her husband, two kids, and various pets in the San Francisco Bay Area.

Recipes
140 Zennia's Homemade Granola

Cozy Food

Catriona McPherson

Catriona McPherson is the Agatha, Macavity and Lefty winning author of the Dandy Gilver series (Minotaur), set in her native Scotland in the 1920s and featuring a gently-born sleuth who has never so much as boiled an egg in her entire life. She has other talents though; *The Guardian* (UK) called her "brisk, baffled, heroic, kindly, scandalised and – above all – very funny."

Catriona also writes a series of stand-alone suspense (Midnight Ink) of which the first – *As She Left It* – was shortlisted for a 2014 Left Coast Crime award at Monterey. The follow-up – *The Day She Died* – was called "a tour de force, a creepy psychological thriller that will leave you breathless" in a *Kirkus* starred review.

Born in Scotland – a country whose heritage is rich with dipping things in batter and deep-frying them - Catriona was brought up on big pots of thick soup and a lot of home-baking and uses many of her mother's and grandmothers' recipes to this day. After moving to California in 2010, however, she has added more avocado-lore than the typical Scot possesses and now even knows her way around an okra.

Her book launch parties are nothing more than an excuse to bake and eat cakes and her top three USA tourist recommendations are: NYC for cheesecake; Amish country in Ohio for drive-thru mashed potato; and Yosemite for blackberry pie.

A visit to Catriona's website at www.catrionamcpherson.com will confirm her deep love of good food and hardly less deep love of just any food. You can also click to buy books from there.

Recipes
114 Where The Sand Meets The Sea Shortbread
45 The tastiest Mac you ever did Cheese
163 Tiny Truman's All-day Onions
87 (Don't Let Lady Macbeth Near The)Lemon Posset

Camille Minichino (aka Margaret Grace and Ada Madison)

Camille Minichino is a retired physicist turning every aspect of her life into novels. She's the author of more than 20 mysteries in three series: 8 books in The Periodic Table Mysteries; 8 books in The Miniature Mysteries (as Margaret Grace); 4 books in the Professor Sophie Knowles Mysteries (as Ada Madison); plus a stand-alone historical. She's working on a fourth mystery series and a collection of short stories. Descriptions, ordering information, and links to her blogs are available at http://www.minichino.com.

Camille teaches writing and science workshops around the Bay Area, and tries to stay outside only long enough to get from one building to another.

Recipes
159 No Bake Mini "Hamburger" Cookies
120 Gerry's Ginger Cookie Recipe

Cozy Author Biographies

Marie Moore

Author of The Sidney Marsh Murder Mystery series:
Shore Excursion, (2012) Camel Press
Game Drive, (2013) Camel Press
Side Trip to Kathmandu, (March 15, 2014) Camel Press

Shore Excursion was Marie Moore's first novel, but not her first writing experience, and like her protagonist Sidney Marsh, she is a native Mississippian. Marie graduated from Ole Miss, married a lawyer in her hometown, taught junior high science, raised a family, and worked for a small weekly newspaper, first as a writer and later as Managing Editor.

In 1985, Marie left the newspaper to open a retail travel agency. She completed agency and airline computer training, managed her agency, sold travel, escorted group tours, sailed on 19 cruises, and visited over 60 countries. Much of the background of her travel mystery series comes from that experience.

Marie and her mystery novels have been featured in *Click! Magazine, At Home Memphis and MidSouth Magazine, Southern Writer's Magazine, and Portico Magazine.* She has been a guest on WREG's *Live at 9, BookTalk, and The Earle Farrell Show* and was a featured author at *Bookstock!* 2012 and 2013. Marie has given 30 minute presentations: *Whodunnit? Crafting the Mystery Novel* and *Finding A New Career in Mid-life* to numerous civic groups, senior citizens groups, libraries, and from *The Balancing Act* Stage as part of the program of *The Southern Women's Show.* She has served as a program panelist for Malice Domestic Mystery Conference (Bethesda, MD, 2012 and 2013) and Killer Nashville Mystery Conference (2013).

Marie's travel mysteries were specially chosen in 2013 for inclusion in the onboard libraries of all ships in the Holland America and Seabourn Cruise Lines.

Game Drive, Marie's second novel, was named Finalist for Foreword Review's 2014 Mystery Book of the Year Awards. Marie is a member of Sisters in Crime.

See more about Marie on her website http://www.mariemooremysteries.com
Follow Marie on Twitter! MarieMoore@mariemmysteries
Like Marie on Facebook! http://www.facebook.com/mariemooremysteries

Her book Shore Excursion on Amazon http://tinyurl.com/kcevzpa
Her book Game Drive on Amazon http://tinyurl.com/krxo6ky

Recipes
43 Sidney Marsh's Oh-SO-Easy Killer Coleslaw

Ruth Moose

Doing it at the Dixie Dew is Ruth Moose's first novel though she has published 3 books of short stories and 6 collections of poetry. She lives in North Carolina and taught for 15 years on the creative writing faculty at UNC. The Dixie Dew is a bed and breakfast set in the mythical Southern town of Littleboro.

Ruth's website: http://ruthmoose.com/Ruth_Moose/Ruth_Moose_Home.html
See her books on Amazon: http://tinyurl.com/k47ucfa

Cozy Food

Amy Myers

Auguste Didier who shares in the recipe below was my first series detective. I was newlywed (to American James Myers), living partly in London and partly in Paris and I was full of enthusiasm for cooking. So I spent a happy few years exploring old Victorian cookbooks not to mention a lot of French markets, while I was writing about Auguste's cases. He was a Victorian master chef who had trained under Escoffier, had been born in Cannes to an English mother and French father and was now a chef to the very best stately homes, clubs and restaurants in England.

Auguste still lets me write about his cases in short story form, and they appear in *Ellery Queen Mystery Magazine.* He apologises for no longer being able to recount cases that demand full length novels, but nine of my novels about him are obtainable as ebooks on Amazon in America http://tinyurl.com/ny3vvqf and Amazon in the UK http://tinyurl.com/mh5v23z

I live now in Kent, England, with my husband Jim who being a classic car buff helps me with my current series of books starring Jack Colby, who runs a car restoration garage and falls in love with cars and women while still finding time to solve murder cases. I also write a series about wheelchair-bound ex-cop Peter Marsh and his daughter Georgia, who solve cold cases (even going back as far as one featuring Jane Austen in Kent). Add my Tom Wasp, Victorian London chimney sweep, to the list and invite Georgian rural Parson Pennywick along and you can see that I don't have much time left to explore those French markets any longer.

Details of my books can be found on my website www.amymyers.net and if you're interested in classic cars then visit www.jackcolby.co.uk Meanwhile enjoy the recipe that Auguste introduced me to.

Tamar Myers

Tamar Myers was born and raised in the Belgian Congo (now just the Congo). Her parents were missionaries to a tribe which, at that time, were known as headhunters and used human skulls for drinking cups. Hers was the first white family ever to peacefully coexist with the tribe, and Tamar grew up fluent in the local trade language. Because of her pale blue eyes, Tamar's nickname was Ugly Eyes.

Tamar grew up eating elephant, hippopotamus and even monkey. She attended a boarding school that was two days away by truck, and sometimes it was necessary to wade through crocodile infested waters to reach it. Other dangers she encountered as a child were cobras, deadly green mambas, and the voracious armies of driver ants that ate every animal (and human) that didn't get out of their way.

In 1960 the Congo, which had been a Belgian colony, became an independent nation. There followed a period of retribution in which many Whites were killed. Tamar and her family fled the Congo, but returned a year later. By then a number of civil wars were raging, and the family's residence was often in the line of fire. In 1964, after living through three years of war, the family returned to the United States permanently.

Tamar was sixteen when her family settled in America, and she immediately underwent severe culture shock. She didn't know how to dial a telephone, cross a street at a stoplight, or use a vending machine. She lucked out, however, by meeting her husband, Jeffrey, on her first day in an American high school. They literally bumped heads while he was leaving, and she entering, the Civics classroom.

Tamar now calls Charlotte, NC home. She lives with her husband, plus a Basenji dog named Pagan, a Bengal cat named Nkashama, and an orange tabby rescue cat named Dumpster Boy. She and her husband are of the Jewish faith, the animals are not.

Tamar enjoys gardening (she is a Master Gardner), bonsai, travel, painting and, of course, reading. She loves Thai and Indian food, and antique jewelry. She plans to visit Machu Pichu in the near future.

Her website is http://tamarmyers.com/
Buy her books on Amazon http://tinyurl.com/m79h9nb
Or Barnes & Noble http://www.barnesandnoble.com/c/tamar-myers

Recipes
153 Dutch Baby with Cardamom Honey Apples

Christa Nardi

Christa Nardi (pen name) has always been an avid reader. Her favorite authors have shifted from Carolyn Keene and Earl Stanley Gardner to more contemporary mystery/crime authors over time, but mystery/crime along with romance are her preferred choices for leisure reading. Writing has always been part of her life, from poetry and short stories in grade school to technical, research, and nonfiction in her professional life. Like Sheridan, Christa is a professor/psychologist. With *Murder at Cold Creek College*, Christa joins other reader/writers in writing in the genre she enjoys reading – the cozy mystery – with a bit of romance. The second in the Cold Creek series, *Murder in the Arboretum*, will be released late in 2014.

Keep up with Christa on Facebook at https://www.facebook.com/christa.nardi.5 or follow her blog, Christa Reads and Writes, at http://christanardi.blogspot.com/

Murder at Cold Creek College is available in print or as an eBook through Amazon http://tinyurl.com/lxe8dax

Recipes
117 Cold Creek Killer Cookies

Cozy Food

Radine Trees Nehring

Like Carrie McCrite, the female protagonist in my *To Die For* mystery series, I am rarely a "by the book" cook, so--what do the Nehrings eat?

These days, and after so many years of preparing meals, I pretty much know what goes well with what else, and often invent, or modify, new recipes. I also continue to prepare versions of ones we've enjoyed for years. In addition, convenience foods are now so far advanced in taste appeal, not to mention ease of preparation, that I frequently rely on those as well. The great thing about this is that it gives me more time for writing and book promotion.

Creative invention is part of every writer's life, and certainly that's what happens whether I'm cooking, or creating one of my series novels. (I'm now working on number eight.) How did it all begin? After my non-fiction book of essays (*Dear Earth*) was published, I decided to try writing a mystery, since cozy mysteries were my favorite choice for reading. I began *A Valley to Die For*, and, as I wrote, ideas came along just when I needed them. By the time *Valley* sold to a publisher, I'd also completed novel number two, *Music to Die For*. My publisher loved the series and I loved writing it, so I kept going! What a fun job I have.

I enjoy doing book research at my chosen locations in the Ozarks, and certainly enjoy writing about Carrie and Henry's adventures there. Also, (since readers consistently asked for recipes that soon became part of the story in each novel) I love creating what Carrie cooks, and include recipes from the story at the end of each adventure.

The *To Die For* series includes (in order) *A Valley to Die For, Music to Die For, A Treasure to Die For, A Wedding to Die For, A River to Die For, Journey to Die For,* and *A Fair to Die For*. Each novel features a special tourist destination in Arkansas as it is today. Area history often impels the plot, and is always accurately represented. All novels are available through brick and mortar bookstores, and at on line book sellers in e-book or print versions. (Amazon.com, B&N.com, and more.) See links on my website http://www.RadinesBooks.com http://radine.wordpress.com

Radine Trees Nehring, 2011 Inductee: Arkansas Writers' Hall of Fame
Sharing the magic of the Arkansas Ozarks in "To Die For" novels
including *A Fair to Die For* from Oak Tree Press.

Recipes
133 Carrie's Oatmeal Bars
60 Carrie's Chicken Pie

Kerri Nelson

Kerri Nelson survived a fifteen year career in the legal field and then took her passion for crime solving to the page. But her journey to become a mystery author took a decade long detour into the world of romance where she penned twenty two novels and novellas in various sub-genres.

Born and raised a true southern belle, Kerri holds many useful secrets: how to bake a killer peach cobbler; how to charm suspects with proper batting of the eyelashes; and how to turn your parasol into a handy weapon.

Kerri is an active member of Sisters in Crime and Romance Writers of America which includes various volunteer positions such as Board Member at Large and Daphne Published Contest Category Coordinator of Kiss of Death RWA (Chapter for Romantic Suspense Authors).

Learn more about Kerri and her new Working Stiff Mystery series, at her website: www.KerriNelson.com
Follow her on Twitter: www.twitter.com/kerribookwriter

Recipes
72 Suspenseful Camp Stew
158 Perplexingly Palatable Peach Pie Shake
88 Easy as a Peach Cobbler

Clare O'Donohue

Clare O'Donohue is the author of two critically acclaimed novels in the Kate Conway Mysteries, as well as five Someday Quilts Mysteries and two e-novellas. She is the current Mystery Writers of America Midwest chapter president. Clare also works as a TV producer and writer, and lives near Chicago, IL.

Clare's website: www.clareodonohue.com

Recipes
151 Killer Quiche Lorraine

Diana Orgain

Diana Orgain is the bestselling author of the Maternal Instincts Mystery series: *Bundle of Trouble, Motherhood is Murder*, Formula for Murder, and *Nursing a Grudge*. She is the co-author with NY Times Bestselling author Laura Childs of *Gilt Trip*. Diana's *For Love Or Money* the first in her new Reality TV Mystery series will be published by Penguin in Spring 2015. She lives in San Francisco with her husband and three children. Visit her at www.dianaorgain.com.

See her books on Amazon http://tinyurl.com/n8m4c9k
And Barnes & Noble http://www.barnesandnoble.com/c/diana-orgain

Recipes
148 Make Ahead Carmel French "Toast"

Joyce Oroz

Author Joyce Oroz has written five novels in her Josephine Stuart Mystery series: *Secure the Ranch, Read My Lipstick, Shaking in Her Flip Flops, Cuckoo Clock Caper*, and *Beetles in the Boxcar*—all available from Amazon. Ms. Oroz brings her experience as a muralist and commercial artist to her stories. Her protagonist, Josephine, is also an artist-muralist—part time sleuth who inconveniently happens onto murders while painting murals.
http://authorjoyceoroz.blogspot.com

Recipes
117 Cherry Date Balls
135 Sweet and chewy gluten-free brownies made with black beans
131 Oatmeal Fruit Bar

Elaine L. Orr

Elaine L. Orr writes fiction and nonfiction and introduced the Jolie Gentil cozy mystery series in 2011. The seven books and a prequel take Jolie from high school to her early thirties, but she's not always one to act maturely. Elaine created a setting she likes (an east coast beach town) and a profession that would let Jolie meet a lot of people and have an opportunity to get into regular trouble (real estate appraising). And friends, lots of friends. Elaine enjoys smart-mouth humor and her Jolie Gentil mysteries have a lot of it. On top of finding the occasional body, Jolie has reluctantly agreed to chair the town's food pantry committee. The zany fundraisers can be as much trouble as figuring out who wants her to leave murderers to their own devices. In addition to the series and several stand-alone mysteries, Elaine writes local and family histories and articles for Yahoo Voices. Elaine can be found at conferences such as the Midwest Writers Workshop and Magna Cum Murder, and does presentations on electronic publishing and other writing-related topics. She grew up in Maryland and moved to the Midwest in the mid-1990s.

Aunt Madge's recipes are the real-life creations of author Leigh Michaels. These and other recipes are in her book, *Simply Good: Recipes for the Busy Cook*, available at retailers such as Amazon: http://tinyurl.com/mw8true. In addition to her two cookbooks, Leigh Michaels has written more than one-hundred traditional and Regency romances.

Jolie Gentil Translates to Trouble on Amazon http://tinyurl.com/kn924kk

Elaine's website www.elaineorr.com

Recipes
140 Aunt Madge's Apple-Cranberry Muffins
141 Aunt Madge's Dried Fruit Muffins

Helen Osterman

Helen Osterman lives in Homer Glen, a suburb of Chicago. She has five children, nine grandchildren and one great grandson.

She received a Bachelor of Science Nursing degree from Mercy Hospital-St. Xavier College and later earned a Master's Degree from Northern Illinois University. Throughout her forty-five year nursing career, she wrote articles for both nursing and medical journals.

She is the author of the Emma Winberry Mystery series:

The Accidental Sleuth, 2007
The Stranger in the Opera House, 2009
The Elusive Relation, 2011
Emma Winberry and the Evil Eye, 2012
Locked Within, 1213

Notes in a Mirror, a paranormal/historical, 2009
Song of the Rails, a love story, 2011
Maker's Mark, a cozy mystery, 2012
Danger by Design, a cozy mystery, is scheduled for release in Sept. 2014.

She is a member of American Association of University Women, Mystery Writers of America, and Sisters in Crime and The Authors' Guild.
Website: www.helenosterman.com

Recipes
144 Emma's Favorite Muffins

Gail Oust

"Imagination is more important than knowledge" is one of my favorite quotes. Another one should be, "Ignorance is bliss." I never started out to be a writer. My goal was to become a registered nurse. Having that black band added to my nurses' cap was literally a crowning achievement. While my education excelled in the nursing arts, it sadly lacked the liberal arts. The only thing remotely close was once doing a research paper on the Sitz bath.

I was a stay-at-home mom while our children were small. Somewhere between the vacuum cleaner and the ironing board, my imagination shifted into high gear. I had stories inside my head that just wouldn't leave me alone. I'm talking plots, dialogue, characters, and costume, the whole ball of wax. During nap times, I'd take out my old portable typewriter and attempt to put it all down on paper. Well, was I in for a shock! I learned my very first lesson on becoming a writer. I quickly discovered writing—even bad writing--is hard work.

But ultimately my persistence paid off. It wasn't until I returned to work full-time as a nurse/technologist for a vascular lab that I made my first sale, *Sweet Possession*, a historical romance under the pseudonym of Elizabeth Turner. Eight more historical romances followed while juggling a family and a job as vascular technologist. It was a busy but rewarding time in my life.

I've been happily married for more years than I care to count to my husband, Bob, and have two grown children. In the course of our marriage, we've lived in Chicago, upstate New York, and suburban Detroit. A few years ago, my husband and I relocated to another small town, this time one in South Carolina with a community very much like the one inhabited by Kate McCall, the protagonist in my new Bunco Babe Mystery series. Along with a change in locale, I decided to change genres. I've been a mystery fan ever since devouring Nancy Drew novels as a girl so the transition from historical romance to cozy mysteries was as fun as it was painless. As my son reminded me, life's an adventure. I'm enjoying the ride.

Gail's website http://www.gailoust.com/
Amazon http://tinyurl.com/koyaayw
Or Barnes & Noble http://www.barnesandnoble.com/c/gail-oust

Recipes
31 Stuffed Pepper Soup

Cozy Food

K.B. Owen

K.B. Owen has a doctorate in 19th century British literature and taught literature and writing for nearly two decades at universities in Connecticut and Washington, DC.

Her favorite kind of mysteries are those written in the cozy style, with a dash of humor and intellect: Christie, Sayers, Gilman, and Cannell, among others. K.B. finally succumbed to the siren-call of writing her own, drawing upon her teaching experiences to create her amateur sleuth, Professor Concordia Wells. Of course, the intrepid Miss Wells does not think of herself as a detective, an unseemly endeavor for a lady professor at an 1890's New England women's college. But eavesdropping in alcoves, climbing out of windows, and setting traps for murderers (without a chaperone!) are rather unseemly behaviors, too. Sometimes these things cannot be helped.

There are currently two books in the series: *Dangerous and Unseemly,* and *Unseemly Pursuits.* A third book, *Unseemly Secrets,* will be released later in 2014.

Want to learn more about the series? Check out K.B. Owen's site:
http://kbowenmysteries.com/books/

On a more personal note, Kathy lives in Virginia with her wonderful husband and three boys. In her spare time she enjoys gardening, backyard bird-watching, crafting, and of course baking!

Recipes
91 Charlotte Russe
84 Pumpkin Crème Brulee

Sharon Pape

I guess my writing career could be divided into two stages. Back in the dark ages, before computers were in every household, I had three paranormal books published, the first of which was also condensed in Redbook Magazine. (I've recently rewritten and updated that book and will be re-releasing it in the near future.) Then life brought me an unexpected challenge by the name of breast cancer. Fortunately the problem was discovered early, but after treatment I didn't immediately return to writing. Wanting to help other women (and men) diagnosed with the disease, I became a volunteer for the American Cancer Society's Reach to Recovery Program. A number of years later, with the help of my surgical oncologist and two other survivors, we started our own non-profit organization to provide information and peer support to newly diagnosed breast cancer patients. It took a while to get off the ground, but once it was running smoothly and didn't require as much of my time, I returned to my first love - writing. I began this next phase of my career with cozy mysteries that have a little paranormal twist and I've been having a lot of fun with them.

Here's a list of those books:

Portrait of Crime Mystery series:
Sketch Me if You Can
To Sketch a Thief
Sketch a Falling Star
Sketcher in the Rye

Crystal Shop Mystery series:
Alibis and Amethysts

To learn more about me and my books, please visit my website:
http://sharonpape.com or my Amazon page: http://goo.gl/vKb3cZ

Recipes
30 Sierra's Pasta Ceci Soup
68 Rory's Spinach and Mushroom Quiche

Nancy J. Parra (aka Nancy J. Coco)

I currently have 12 books published - two made the top ten list and a total of five were given starred reviews by ALA's Booklist. Praise from readers and booksellers made *All Fudged Up* - by pen name Nancy Coco a 2013 National Bestseller. Thank you! I'm very excited to bring you three books in 2014 and 2015 as the three series heat up.

Nancy J. Parra's discovered she had a severe gluten allergy and had to give up her second favorite pastime, baking. Six months into her forced new diet, she was back in the kitchen figuring out how to make her own gluten-free baked goods and soon posted delicious pictures on the web. When a good friend suggested she mix her two loves-baking and writing, she wrote her first cozy mystery, *Gluten for Punishment*, Berkley Prime Crime May 7, 2013.

On a happy roll, she soon sold a Mackinac Island Fudge Shop mystery series, *All Fudged Up*.

With an MA in Writing Popular Fiction, Ms. Parra has written articles on writing, and has given workshops on writing techniques to various library and writers groups. She has a blog on the art and craft of writing, www.nancyjparra.blogspot.com.

Visit her website at www.nancyjparra.com for more information, a list of her books and full reviews. She can also be found at www.facebook.com/nancyjparraauthor and would love to add you as her friend.

Buy her books on Amazon http://www.amazon.com/Nancy-J.-Parra/e/B001KHQ8BW
Or as Nancy Coco on Amazon http://tinyurl.com/kfwvlrg

Or Barnes & Noble http://www.barnesandnoble.com/c/nancy-j-parra
Or as Nancy Coco http://www.barnesandnoble.com/c/nancy-coco

Recipes
92 Gluten-free Pumpkin Cheesecake with Caramel Sauce
136 Caramel Peanut butter Fudge

Allison Cesario Paton

Allison Cesario Paton is the author of five Vermont cozy mysteries: The Mrs. Bundle Mystery series, featuring a woman of a mature age and her refined cat Cracker), and Artist, showcasing the Original "close to nature" Limited Edition Watercolor Print series, which features characters and scenes from North Pillson Corners and beyond.

Cozy Food

Mix and Match Books and Paintings: One-Stop Shopping for all your Mrs. Bundle needs. Jeesum Crowbars---enjoy!

The Bundle Marketplace Link where fans get all the books and the paintings is https://squareup.com/market/bundle-publishing

Visit Allison's website https://www.facebook.com/pages/Mrs-Bundle-Mystery-Series/334559971736

The Case of the Springfield Shock Jock on Amazon: http://tinyurl.com/mjs44ab

In this fifth mystery, Mrs. Bundle's efforts are focused on solving a mystery in Springfield, Vermont. As usual, Cracker is at her side to offer assistance and unwavering loyalty at all costs. There's a loose cannon named "Hambone" causing a lot of trouble in this little burg, and Mrs. Bundle is right in the thick of it. Meanwhile, it seems there are a number of men of a mature age---all available---getting in her way. 282 pages, published 2011

Recipes
76 Perfectly Pleasing Popovers
64 Turkey Meatloaf
26 She Crab Soup/Bisque
131 Snickerdoodle Blondie Bars

Joanne Pence

Joanne Pence is an award-winning USA Today best-selling author of twenty-five novels and novellas. Her culinary mystery series, The Angie Amalfi mysteries, has been in print for over twenty years, and includes 15 books, a novella, and several short stories. Joanne's second series, the Rebecca Mayfield Mysteries, is new, and consists of two novels and a novella. Joanne has been honored with a Romantic Times Book Club Career Achievement award, and her mysteries have won or been nominated for RWA's Rita and Golden Heart Awards, the Independent Bookseller Association's Golden Quill Award, and a Daphne du Maurier Award.

Joanne has also written thrillers, romantic suspense, and contemporary and historical romances. *Dance with a Gunfighter* was a Willa Cather Literary Award finalist in best historical fiction, and *Ancient Echoes* was given a Top Idaho Fiction Book Award.

Joanne was born and raised in San Francisco (the setting of her two mystery series) and now makes her home on several acres in the foothills north of Boise, Idaho. She is married, with two sons, three grandchildren, and a plethora of pets including a peahen (female peacock) who showed up one summer evening and refuses to leave.

Visit Joanne's web page at: www.joannepence.com and find her books on Amazon at www.amazon.com/author/joannepence

Recipes
116 Amaretti Cookies
48 Carbonara

Cozy Author Biographies

Maggie Pill

Maggie Pill writes the Sleuth Sisters mysteries, one of which is published and another on the way. She has always loved reading cozies and was inspired to begin this series by her sister, who reads even more books than she does. Maggie lives in Michigan with her husband, two dogs, and three cats. She's pretty sure where the husband came from—the rest, who knows?

We all know sisters have a bond that's hard to break, even when one of them (two, in this case) would like to bonk another sister on the head most of the time. *The Sleuth Sisters* takes place in Michigan's "Up North" somewhere between Bay City and the Mackinac Bridge. Faye is about to be unemployed. Barbara is bored with the early retirement she took from practicing law. They decide to start a detective agency but agree their bossy, manipulative sister Retta will NOT be part of it.

When they finally get a case, however, Faye and Barb realize they need Retta. In fact, if they're going to find a man accused of murdering his wife and brother-in-law, bring him back home, prove he's innocent of the crime, and stay alive, they're going to need all the help they can get.

You can read Maggie's blog at http://maggiepill.wordpress.com and buy or sample Book #1, *The Sleuth Sisters*, at Amazon: http://tinyurl.com/q65cv39

Recipes
55 Crescent Casserole
94 Yum-Yum Pie

Ann Purser

Ann Purser lives in the East Midlands, in a small and attractive village which still has a village shop, a garage, pub and church. Here she finds her inspiration for her novels about country life. She has only to do her daily shopping down the High Street to listen to the real life of the village going on around her.

Before turning to fiction, she had a number of different careers, including journalism and art gallery proprietor. Running her own gallery in a 400-year-old barn behind the house, she gained fascinating insights into the characters and relationships of customers wandering around.

Working in a village school added more grist to the mill, as does singing in the church choir and membership of the Women's Guild. She reminds herself humbly that Virginia Woolf was President of her local WI…

Six years hard study won her an Open University degree. During this period, she wrote two non-fiction books, one for parents of handicapped children (she has a daughter with cerebral palsy) and the other a lighthearted book for schools, on the explosion of popular entertainment in the first forty years of the twentieth century.

Ten years of running the gallery proved to be enough, and while it was very successful she decided to sell. Time to start writing novels.

Round Ringford became Ann's village in a series of six novels, each with a separate story, but featuring the same cast of characters with a few newcomers each time. The list of books gives details of each story, and each features an issue common to all villages in our rural countryside. "Just like our village!" is a frequent comment from Ann's readers.

Next: the Lois Meade Mysteries, each title reflecting a day of the week. Ann has always loved detective fiction, and determined to make it her next series. So *Murder on Monday* was born, followed by *Terror on Tuesday*, and *Weeping on Wednesday*. The rest of the week follows!

Mornings are set aside for writing, and the rest of the day Ann spends walking the dog, retrieving bantams' eggs from around the garden, gossiping and taking part in the life of the village. She is never bored!

My website: http://www.annpurser.com/
My Author page
on Amazon: http://tinyurl.com/kgddycn
on Amazon.UK: http://tinyurl.com/km7n9nq
on Barnes & Noble: http://www.barnesandnoble.com/c/ann-purser

Recipes
76 Ivy's Parsnip Pie

Melissa Bourbon Ramirez (aka Melissa Bourbon)

Melissa Bourbon, who sometimes answers to her Latina-by-marriage name Misa Ramirez, is the marketing director at Entangled Publishing and is the author of the Lola Cruz mystery series: Living the Vida Lola and Hasta la Vista, Lola! from Thomas Dunne Books / St. Martin's Minotaur, Bare-Naked Lola form Entangled Publishing (April 2012), and A Dressmaker's Mystery series for NAL (Pleating for Mercy, 2011, A Fitting End, 2012, Deadly Patterns, 2012), A Custom-Fit Crime (2013), and A Killing Notion (2014). She also has written two romantic suspense novels, a light paranormal romance, and is the co-author of The Tricked-out Toolbox, a practical marketing guide for authors.

A former middle and high school teacher, this blonde-haired, green-eyed, proud to be *Latina-by-Marriage* girl loves following Lola and Harlow on their many adventures. Whether it's contemplating belly button piercings, visiting nudist resorts, or hanging out with seamstresses, she's always up for the challenge. Melissa has two middle grade series for girls in development, is published in Woman's World Magazine and Romance Writers Report, and GLOW Magazine, and has a children's book published. She fantasizes about spending summers writing in quaint, cozy locales, has a love/hate relationship with yoga and chocolate, is devoted to her family, and can't believe she's lucky enough to be living the life of her dreams.

Melissa's website www.melissabourbon.com
Buy her books on Amazon http://tinyurl.com/l4ycvfe
Or Barnes & Noble http://www.barnesandnoble.com/c/melissa-bourbon

Recipes
71 Tacos Buenos

Nanci Rathbun

Nanci Rathbun is a lifelong reader of mysteries – historical, contemporary, futuristic, paranormal, hard-boiled, cozy … you can find them all on her bookshelves. She brings logic and planning to her writing from a background as an IT project manager, and attention to characters and dialog from her second career as a Congregationalist minister. Her first novel, *Truth Kills*: An Angelina Bonaparte Mystery, is out in both paperback and ebook formats. The first chapter is available free on her web site and on her Goodreads page. *Cash Kills* is the second book in the series. Number three has a working title of *Deception Kills*, with plans to publish in 2015.

Nanci is a longtime Wisconsin resident who relocated to Tennessee to be closer to her granddaughters – oh, and their parents – and is planning an upcoming move to the West Coast for the same reason. No matter where she lives, she will always be a Packers fan.

Visit her web page: http://nancirathbun.com
She loves to hear from readers. Contact her at:
Facebook: Author Nanci Rathbun Twitter: @nancirathbun Email: contact@nancirathbun.com

Recipes
47 Not-Your-Sicilian Bolognese Sauce

Rosalee Richland

Rosalee Richland writes the Darla King series of mysteries. Rosalee Richland is actually not one person, but two. It is the pen name of two square dancers and writers, Cyndi Riccio and Rhonda Brinkmann. When not writing, the two co-authors enjoy reading, traveling, meeting readers and fans, networking with other authors, and – of course – square dancing. Currently they are working on Darla's next mystery and the twists and turns it will take. Like the first two, the title is a square dance call – *Follow Your Neighbor*.

In the first book of the Darla King series, *Right and Left Grand*, an assault on a square dancer leads to a series of crimes, and Darla's special square dance knowledge helps figure out the connection between the crimes. In *Load the Boat*, Darla's curiosity gets her in trouble while she works as an entertainer on a Caribbean square dance cruise. Darla left her career as an investigator with the State Attorney's Office in Florida and moved to Texas wanting nothing more to do with law enforcement. She never dreamed that her midlife career change to square dance caller would place her in a position to assist law enforcement officials in solving crimes. With Darla's natural curiosity, she and her close friends from the Clearton Square Dance Club keep ending up in the thick of things.

The Darla King series is cozy mystery set in the context of square dancing. The title of each book in the series ties into the story, but is also a square dance movement. The books give a peek into the world of square dancing, charm readers with a whodunit mystery, and include just a hint of romance. The Darla King series is available in both ebook and paperback on Amazon http://tinyurl.com/kashvf9, Barnes & Noble http://www.barnesandnoble.com/c/rosalee-richland, and Smashwords https://www.smashwords.com/profile/view/RosaleeRichland and can be ordered through retail bookstores.

You can keep up with Darla King through Rosalee Richland's blog:
http://rosaleerichland.blogspot.com

Or find Rosalee Richland on Goodreads and Facebook:
http://www.goodreads.com/author/show/6577514.Rosalee_Richland
https://www.facebook.com/pages/Rosalee-Richland/284946448289065

Recipes
14 Darla's Tortilla Rollups

Cozy Food

Becky Lyn Rickman

Becky Lyn Rickman developed her writing through editorials for local newspapers, the voice of Booker the bookshop at (who did brilliant and articulate book reviews and commentaries), website articles for Family Share (http://www.familyshare.com/authors/Becky%20Lyn%20Rickman), well-crafted notes to her children's teachers, captivating shopping lists, scathingly brilliant letters of accusation followed by the inevitable ensuing and heart-wrenching letters of apology. She has completed several novels: *When Renoir Loved Thomas Jefferson* and *Grimm's Last Fairy Tale,* both of which are undergoing massive editing for re-release and *The Convict, the Rookie Card, and the Redemption of Gertie Thump* http://tinyurl.com/mdunawa, from WiDo Publishing. It is the first in the Ongoing Redemption of Gertie Thump series.

Recipes
119 Seven O'Clock: Gobs

Karen Robbins

Known as the Wandering Writer, Karen Robbins is a travel addict as well as a mom of five grown children, a grandmother of nine, and an author and speaker. She and her husband have set foot on all seven continents and by mid-2015 will have circumnavigated the globe. They are also avid scuba divers. She has published in Sunday school take home papers, local newspapers and magazines and co-authored two non-fiction books (*A Scrapbook of Christmas Firsts* and *A Scrapbook of Motherhood Firsts*) with five other writers she met online. *The Chicken Soup For The Soul* books have also featured her stories. Her first love, however, is writing fiction and besides her Casey Stengel Mystery series (*Murder Among The Orchids* and *Death Among The Deckchairs*), she has written *Divide The Child* and *In A Pickle.* Look for the next two in the Casey Stengel series, *Secrets Among The Shamrocks* and *Killer Among The Kiwis.*

Connect with Karen on her Facebook Author Page (https://www.facebook.com/KarenRobbinsAuthor) or at her blog, Writer's Wanderings (http://karenrobbins.blogspot.com), where you can keep up with her travels around the world, get lots of travel tips, and find news about upcoming books.

Recipes
55 Casey's Chicken Comfort Casserole
21 Deckchair Delight (Also known as Pina Colada)

Carolyn J. Rose

Carolyn J. Rose is the author of the Subbing isn't for Sissies series (*No Substitute for Murder, No Substitute for Money,* and *No Substitute for Maturity*), as well as the Catskill Mountains mysteries, *Hemlock Lake* and *Through a Yellow Wood.* Other works include *An Uncertain Refuge, Sea of Regret, A Place of Forgetting,* and five novels written with her husband, Mike Nettleton: *The Hard Karma Shuffle, The Crushed Velvet Miasma, Drum Warrior, Death at Devil's Harbor* and *Deception at Devil's Harbor.*

She grew up in New York's Catskill Mountains, graduated from the University of Arizona, logged two years in Arkansas with Volunteers in Service to America, and spent 25 years as a television news researcher, writer, producer, and assignment editor in Arkansas, New Mexico, Oregon, and Washington. Her interests are reading, gardening, and NOT cooking. Her characters spend more time in the kitchen than she does. They count calories only when other characters are looking.

http://www.deadlyduomysteries.com/
http://deadlyduoduhblog.blogspot.com/

Recipes
128 Cashew Chocolate Chip Cookies
30 Peanut Butter Soup

Pamela Rose

If there is one term that describes me it is 'curious.' My mother swore that upon my quarrelsome arrival into the world the first word I labored to wrap my baby lips around was 'why?' Apparently I liked it where I was and none too pleased to leave. But why is the question that even today haunts me, as in 'why does that do that?' or, 'why does it work that way?' or more intriguing yet, 'why does that person act that way?' Answering that one dogged question has led to some thought-provoking experiences in all kinds of circumstances. Undeniably, there's not much I'm not willing to learn at least a little something about.

To that dubious end I have had more 'careers' then I care to contemplate, as I continue to sample my way through a smorgasbord of interesting occupational possibilities: college instructor, advertising prevaricator and shopping network writer at the top of my list of favorites. Empirically, I've made good use of my bachelor's degree in Telecommunications and my master's in Information and Communication. Over the years I've morphed into the quintessential jack-of-all-trades master of … some. One notable byproduct of this multi-faceted intake of information is more material for writing books than I can possibly exhaust in one lifetime. Who knew that indulging my insatiable curiosity was just excellent preparation for becoming a mystery writer?

Books by Pamela Rose:
The Eyes of the Jaguar
A Thyme to Harvest
Sherlock's Home: The Adventure of the Contentious Crone
Sherlock's Home: The Adventure of the Indigo Inkster

Links:
http://pamelarosebestsellin.wix.com/pamela-rose
www.amazon.com/author/pamelarose
www.facebook.com/pamelarosemysterywriter
www.facebook.com/finnfanclub

Recipes
106 221b Bakery 'Barbe a queue' BabyCakes (courtesy of the Maney Bros.)

Cozy Food

Cindy Sample

Cindy Sample is a former mortgage banking CEO of a nationwide company who decided plotting murder was more entertaining than plodding through paperwork. She retired to follow her lifelong dream of being a mystery author.

Her experiences with on-line dating sites fueled the concept for *Dying for a Date*, a humorous romantic mystery set in the California gold country. *Dying for a Dance* winner of the 2011 Northern California Publishers & Authors award for fiction is based on her experiences in the glamorous world of competitive ballroom dancing. Who knew dancing could be so deadly?

Dying for a Daiquiri, a 2014 LEFTY Award finalist, moves the action to the Big Island of Hawaii. Never has research been so much fun! Cindy is currently working on *Dying for a Dude* and having a blast.

Cindy is a past president of the Sacramento chapter of Sisters in Crime and has served on the boards of the Sacramento Opera and the YWCA. She has two wonderful adult children who live too far away and a cat that refused to leave her lap.

Visit Cindy on her website at www.cindysamplebooks.com
www.facebook.com/cindysampleauthor
www.twitter.com/cindysample1

Buy link for *Dying for a Daiquiri* on Amazon:
http://tinyurl.com/DyingforaDaiquiribyCindySample

Recipes
20 Tiki Goddess

June Shaw

June Shaw, author of the humorous Cealie series, lives near a lazy bayou in south Louisiana's Cajun country, surrounded by fantastic loved ones and their food. Unlike her mother, grandmother, and most women in her area, June does not love to spend time in the kitchen. But she's glad her squeeze Bob, who's a wonderful Cajun cook, does. She gets him to share some of his best recipes in her novels and gladly shares a couple of them with you.

June writes in a variety of genres and represents her state on the board of Mystery Writers of America's Southwest Chapter. She's also the Published Author Liaison for the South Louisiana chapter of Romance Writers of America.

Learn more about her and her work at http://www.juneshaw.com. She'd love to hear from you!

Recipes
67 Eggplant Supreme à la Bob
66 Bob's Shrimp Etouffe`

Connie Shelton

I love food and I love mysteries so the chance to include some of my favorite New Mexico recipes in a mystery cookbook was irresistible. My husband and I really enjoy travel so I am always finding new locations and foods to include in my stories. I write two mystery series and am thrilled each time one of my books makes it to a bestseller list.

The original series features female sleuth, Charlotte (Charlie) Parker, a partner with her brother in a private investigation agency; she's the financial brains of the business who tends to get pulled into solving crimes against her better judgment. Now fourteen books strong, Charlie has garnered praise as a down-to-earth protagonist that reviewers and readers alike have loved.

My newest series introduces Samantha Sweet. Sam breaks into houses for a living. She's also a baker with a magical touch whose dream is to open her own pastry shop. It's just that she keeps getting sidetracked by other things, including the irresistible Sheriff Beau Cardwell. In the first book, Sam is given an odd wooden box which, she discovers, gives her some uncanny abilities—including seeing things that other people can't see. With elements of the paranormal, a little romance, and a lot of mystery, the eight books in this series are a delight for me to write.

Visit my website http://connieshelton.com to discover more recipes, read an interview, and more. While you are there, be sure to sign up for my email newsletter where each month another lucky subscriber wins a new Kindle, Nook or Kobo e-book reader. I love to hear from my fans and I do my best to answer all emails.

You can follow me on
Facebook https://www.facebook.com/conniesheltonauthorpage/
Twitter https://twitter.com/connieshelton
Pinterest http://www.pinterest.com/conniethewriter/

Recipes
146 Connie Shelton's (semi)Famous Breakfast Burritos
61 Pedro's Green Chile Chicken Enchiladas
88 Samantha Sweet's Mexican Flan

Clea Simon

Clea Simon is the author of 15 mysteries in the Theda Krakow, Dulcie Schwartz, and Pru Marlowe pet noir series, as well as three nonfiction books. The latter two mystery series are ongoing and include her most recent books, *Grey Howl* (Severn House) and *Panthers Play for Keeps* (Poisoned Pen Press). A former journalist and nonfiction author, she lives in Somerville, Mass., with her husband, the writer Jon Garelick, and their cat Musetta. She can be reached at http://www.cleasimon.com and is on Twitter @Clea_Simon

See Clea on Amazon http://tinyurl.com/ktducn3
Or Barnes & Noble http://www.barnesandnoble.com/c/clea-simon

Recipes
64 Pru Marlowe's chicken with mushrooms

Cozy Food

Joanna Campbell Slan

Award-winning and National Bestselling author Joanna Campbell Slan is the creator of three mystery series. Her first mystery in the Kiki Lowenstein Mystery series—*Paper, Scissors, Death*—was shortlisted for the Agatha. Joanna's series featuring Charlotte Brontë's classic heroine Jane Eyre begins with *Death of a Schoolgirl*, which won the 2013 Daphne du Maurier Award for Excellence for historical romantic suspense. Her newest series, featuring Cara Mia Delgatto and beginning with *Tear Down and Die,* has quickly become an Amazon Bestseller.

In her past life, Slan has been a television talk show host, an adjunct professor of public relations at Illinois State University, a sought-after motivational speaker, and a corporate speechwriter. *Sharing Ideas Magazine* named Joanna "one of the top 25 motivational speakers in the world." Joanna lives off the coast of Florida on a nearly deserted island.

Visit Joanna's website at www.JoannaSlan.com. See all her books and short stories on her Amazon Author's Page http://tinyurl.com/JoannaSlan. Share the fun and learn new skills on her blog http://www.JoannaSlan.blogspot.com. Follow her on Pinterest (www.Pinterest.com/JoannaSlan). Receive her tweets at http://www.twitter.com/JoannaSlan. Keep up with her on Facebook at http://tinyurl.com/JCSlan or communicate directly with her at JCSlan@JoannaSlan.com.

Recipes
42 Kiki Lowenstein's Hoosier Daddy Kidney Bean Salad

Karen Rose Smith

Award-winning author Karen Rose Smith was born in Pennsylvania. Although she was an only child, she remembers the bonds of an extended family. Since her father came from a family of ten and her mother, a family of seven, there were always aunts, uncles and cousins visiting on weekends. Family is a strong theme in her books and she suspects her childhood memories are the reason.

In college, Karen began writing poetry and also met her husband to be. They both began married life as teachers, but when their son was born, Karen decided to try her hand at a home-decorating business. She returned to teaching for a while but changes in her life led her to writing romance fiction. Now she writes mysteries and romances full time. She has sold over 85 novels since 1991.

Presently, she is hard at work on the Caprice De Luca home staging mystery series for Kensington Books. When she isn't writing, she cares for three rescue cats, strays and feral cats, gardens, and cooks. Married to her college sweetheart since 1971, believing in the power of love and commitment, she envisions herself writing relationship novels, both mystery and romance, for a long time to come!

To learn more about Karen's books, go to her websites http://www.karenrosesmithmysteries.com and http://www.karenrosesmith.com. and Amazon http://tinyurl.com/l86sxx3

Karen also likes to interact with her readers on
Facebook https://www.facebook.com/KarenRoseSmithBooks
Twitter https://twitter.com/karenrosesmith

Cozy Author Biographies

Gilt by Association is coming in February 2015.

Recipes
125 Caprice's Choco Chunks and Chips Cookies

Lane Stone

Lane Stone writes the Tiara Investigations Mystery series. *Current Affairs* was her debut novel, followed by *Domestic Affairs*. She's the coauthor of *Maltipoos Are Murder* (Entangled Press), the first book of a romantic suspense series, set in a doggie day spa.

Lane is a native Atlantan. She, her husband, Larry Korb, and the real Abby divide their time between Sugar Hill, GA and Alexandria, VA. Sugar Hill is the setting of the Tiara Investigations series.

When not writing she's enjoying characteristic baby boomer pursuits: hiking in various countries and playing golf. Her volunteer work includes raising money for women political candidates and Communications for the Delaware River & Bay Lighthouse Foundation. She is on the Political Science Advisory Board for Georgia State University. Lane serves on Sugar Hill's 75th Anniversary Planning Committee.

Lane's personal website is: http://www.lanestonebooks.com/
She tweets as Abby, The Menopause Dog https://twitter.com/TheMenopauseDog and her Facebook page is LaneStoneBooks http://tinyurl.com/lnqex68

Buy her books on Amazon at http://tinyurl.com/lgfrosv
Buy on Barnes & Noble at http://www.barnesandnoble.com/c/lane-stone

Recipes
18 Dates with Goat Cheese and Basil
18 Quince and Manchego

Maria Grazia Swan

I always wanted to be a writer. When I was a little girl I lived with my grandparents in a 3 story house my grandfather built. One rainy day I went up into the attic. This was before phones, before TVs and certainly before computers. I found a wooden crate full of old books. I was hooked.

In school (in Italy) my best grades were in Literature. My teachers liked my writing, often would read it out loud. I remember swapping stories for chocolate with the daughter of the town grocer.

When my parents moved I had to say goodbye to my grandparents, the attic and the books. In Belgium I learned to speak French. Soon my teachers liked my French essays.

Life has a way of playing tricks on our carefully planned tomorrows. So I met an American boy, fell in love, married and moved to the United States. I had to learn English. Then came the divorce, the kids moved out, the Great Danes went to dogs' heaven, the house felt so quiet.

Cozy Food

It was time to write.

To write is one thing, to get your writing published is a whole different game.
I'm not good at games, but I persevered. Eventually *Love Thy Sister* was published. A second book came around, now we had a series, *Italian Summer* is #3 of the series. That one was hard to write, because I had to revisit my hometown for real and was flooded by memories, the good and the bad.

People started to buy my books and I was stunned. *My stories.*

You see, every time one of you wonderful friends buys one of my books, it feels like a pat on the back saying, "You did it, Maria Grazia, you are writing in English and we like it."
And when you post a review it's as if you put a new log on the fire. In my fireplace. And the fire is invigorated and the flames soar high, they crackle and sparkle and the house isn't so quiet anymore, it's full of happy sounds. Thank you.

Here are my series

Mina's adventures series
#1 *Love Thy Sister*
#2 *Bosom Bodies*
#3 *Italian Summer*

Lella York series
#1 *Murder Under The Italian Moon*
#2 *Murder Under The Venetian Moon*

All books can be found on my website www.mariagraziaswan.com

Recipes
77 Buttermilk Gnocchi

Denise Swanson

Denise Swanson, The New York Times best-selling author of the Scumble River and Devereaux's Dime Store Mystery series, began writing after coming face-to-face with evil. She quickly decided she would rather write about villains than encounter them in her daily life. She was also shocked to discover that getting a book published was nearly as difficult as vanquishing scoundrels.
Dead Between the Lines is the third book in her Devereaux's Dime Store Mystery series featuring Devereaux Sinclair, the owner of the old-fashioned shop in Shadow Bend, a small town near Kansas City, Missouri. Dev is torn between a sizzling hot U.S. Marshal and a handsome doctor, both of whom are on hand to help her figure out whodunit.

Little Shop of Homicide was the first book in the series, followed by *Nickeled-and-Dimed to Death*, and most recently Dead Between the Lines. *Dying for a Cupcake* is due out in March 2015.

Her continuing Scumble River Mystery series is set in Scumble River, a fictional small town in Illinois, and features Skye Denison, a full-figured school psychologist-sleuth. *Murder of a*

Stacked Librarian is the sixteenth and latest book in this series and the next one, *Murder of a Needled Knitter*, is due out in September.

Denise's books are in multiple printings and have been on the Barnes & Noble, IMBA, BookScan, and The New York Times Bestsellers lists. They have also been BookSense 76 Picks and Top Picks for RT Magazine, as well as nominated for the Agatha Award, the Mary Higgins Clark Award, and the Reviewers Choice Award.

Denise lives in Illinois with her handsome husband and cool black cat.

Buy links for my books:
on Mystery Lovers Bookshop: http://tinyurl.com/kmku3n2
on Amazon: http://tinyurl.com/m3yqmvp
on Barnes & Noble: http://www.barnesandnoble.com/c/denise-swanson
on audiobooks:
http://www.audible.com/search/ref=a_search_tseft__galileo?advsearchKeywords=Denise+swanson&x=0&y=0

Recipes
145 Devereaux's Dime Store Valentine Muffins

Marcia Talley

Marcia Talley is the Agatha and Anthony award-winning author of thirteen mysteries featuring Maryland sleuth, Hannah Ives. *Dark Passage*, is set on a cruise ship. *Tomorrow's Vengeance*, to be released in 2014, follows the adventures of a quirky group of characters living in an upscale continuing care retirement community on the shores of the Chesapeake Bay. Marcia's award-winning short stories appear in more than a dozen collections.

She is past President of Sisters in Crime, serves on the board of the Mid-Atlantic Chapter of the Mystery Writers of America and is a member of the Authors' Guild and the Crime Writers Association. She divides her time between Annapolis, Maryland and SeaLeggs, a cottage on Elbow Cay in Hope Town, Bahamas.

Marcia's website: www.marciatalley.com

Recipes
66 Annapolis Fish Stew
49 Turkey (or Chicken) Tetrazzini

Nancy Jill Thames

Nancy Jill Thames was born to write mysteries. From her early days as the neighborhood story-teller to being listed on Amazon Author Watch Bestseller List, she has always had a vivid imagination and loves to solve problems – perfect for plotting whodunnits. In 2010, Nancy Jill published her first mystery, *Murder in Half Moon Bay*, introducing her well-loved protagonist, Jillian Bradley, and whimsical Yorkie, "Teddy." She's written seven books so far in The Jillian Bradley Mystery series and is working on her eighth.

Cozy Food

When she isn't plotting Jillian's next perilous adventure, she travels between Texas and California finding new ways to spoil her grandchildren, playing classical favorites on her baby grand or having afternoon tea with friends.

Member of Leander Writers' Guild, American Christian Fiction Writers (ACFW CenTex Chapter), and Central Texas Authors

To learn more about Nancy Jill, go to her
Website http://www.nancyjillthames.com
Amazon http://www.amazon.com/-/e/B003V55RSG
Barnes & Noble http://www.barnesandnoble.com/c/nancy-jill-thames

Recipes
156 Queen of Afternoon Tea's Raisin Scones with Mock Devonshire Cream

Sharon Burch Toner

Sharon Burch Toner is the author of the Maggie McGill Mysteries series. This series of lighthearted mystery adventures features a mother/daughter team, Maggie and Allie McGill. The two strong, independent, and resourceful women romp through their mysterious and frightening adventures with grace and an enduring *joie de vivre* that serves them and the reader well.

Sharon Burch Toner writes a novel a year. The seventh of the Maggie McGill Mystery series, *Maggie in White* will be out November, 2014. She says, "*Maggie in White* is set in a blinding blizzard and is being written with compassion for my friends and family who've been through a very cold winter east and north of here. Writing is what I do. And I love it!"

Sharon's Irish grandmother gave her a lifelong appreciation for a story well told. She was born and lived much of what she considers a nearly idyllic childhood in the hills of southern Indiana where she learned to love the earth and its creatures. She has cherished memories of long summer afternoons on a farmhouse porch while her Irish grandmother wove fascinating tales of the long ago world of her own childhood. From this Sharon Burch Toner acquired a lifelong appreciation for a story well told.

She pursued a career as a psychotherapist for nearly twenty years before she turned to writing as her ideal occupation. After a life as mother, psychotherapist and spiritual explorer, writing is her retirement occupation. She says that for her writing is as necessary as food and shelter.

The Maggie McGill mysteries, in part, are written as an homage to Amy Toner Jones, who taught and inspired Sharon from the moment of her first breath.

Sharon lives with her two feline roommates in southern California

There are six books in the Maggie McGill Mysteries series:
Maggie's Image
Maggie's Art
Maggie's Brujo
Maggie's Island
Maggie at Sea
Maggie's Ghost

The seventh in the series, *Maggie In White*, will be available November, 2014.

My website http://www.sharonburchtoner.com/

Recipes
83 Dark Chocolate Torte with Grand Marnier
38 Allie's Perfect Salad
63 Thad's Favorite Chicken

Elaine Viets

Elaine Viets is a national bestselling author of 26 mysteries. She's written 13 Dead-End Job mysteries, set in South Florida, for NAL. Her latest hardcover Dead-End Job mystery is *Catnapped!*

Marilyn Stasio suggest one way for a fugitive to hide in plain sight is to work at low-wage jobs, which is what Helen Hawthorne has been doing in Elaine Viets's quick-witted mysteries. Elaine's Josie Marcus, Mystery Shopper series, set in Elaine's hometown of St. Louis, has ten novels. *Fixing to Die* was nominated for a Barry Award this April. The tenth, *A Dog Gone Murder*, is due out in November, 2014.

Elaine also hosts the Dead-End Jobs Radio Show on Radio Ear Network; it is in the network's top four programs worldwide.

She is winner of the Agatha Award, the Anthony Award and the Lefty Award for Best Humorous Mystery. Viets has been nominated for the Macavity Award, Barry Award, Anthony, and Agatha Awards.

Viets is a popular guest on local, national and international TV and radio shows, including the Discovery Channel's MythBusters, and Michael Feldman's Whad'Ya Know? She has also hosted the syndicated Travel-Holiday Radio Show and was a commentator for the National Public Radio station KWMU. She hosted a primetime television program, Viets Beat, for KMOV-TV in St. Louis and won two local Emmys. She was featured on National Public Radio station WLRN with Jeff "Dexter" Lindsay on Literary Florida.

Her darkly humorous short stories have appeared in anthologies. She regularly writes short stories for Alfred Hitchcock Mystery Magazine. Her latest is *The Bride Wore Blood.*

Follow her on Facebook http://www.facebook.com/ElaineVietsMysteryWriter.
Check her Website at www.elaineviets.com.
Buy her books on Amazon http://tinyurl.com/loa6kmr
Or Barnes & Noble http://www.barnesandnoble.com/c/elaine-viets

Recipes
18 Pate du Chateau Blanc

Cozy Food

Lea Wait

Lea Wait lives in a house built in 1774 on the coast of Maine, where she loves to bake as well as write, rows her skiff for exercise, and is married to the love of her life, artist Bob Thomas. Her years as an antique print dealer and the single adoptive parent of four girls gave her the background for her 7-book Shadows Antique Print Mystery series and her love of history helped her write the Mainely Needlepoint Mystery series and five acclaimed historical novels for ages 8 and up set in nineteenth century Maine.

For more information about her and her books, including book group questions, more recipes, and teacher guides for her children's books, see http://www.leawait.com. She blogs with other Maine mystery writers at http://www.mainecrimewriters.com

Shadows series: *Shadows at the Fair, Shadows on the Coast of Maine, Shadows on the Ivy, Shadows at the Spring Show, Shadows of a Down East Summer, Shadows on a Cape Cod Wedding, Shadows on a Maine Christmas*

Haven Harbor Mainely Needlepoint series: *Twisted Threads, Threads of Evidence*

For Ages 8 and Up: *Stopping to Home, Seaward Born, Wintering Well, Finest Kind, Uncertain Glory*

Maggie Summer is the protagonist in the Shadows Antique Print Mystery series. She's an antique print dealer and a community college professor, torn between adopting as a single parent and her beau, Will Brewer, who doesn't want children. In *Shadows at the Spring Show* Maggie volunteers to run an antique show as a benefit for a local adoption agency … and then both the show, and Maggie herself, are threatened. Who could object to adoption … or antiques? Will and Maggie's best friend, Gussie, all arrive to help out, so Maggie makes enough lasagna for the whole crowd.

Recipes
46 Maggie's Lasagna
101 Aunt Nettie's Blueberry Cake with Lemon Sauce
87 Maple Bread Pudding

LynDee Walker

LynDee Walker's award-winning journalistic work has appeared in newspapers and magazines across the nation. After nearly a decade covering crime, courts, and local politics, she left full-time reporting for motherhood with a side of freelancing and fiction writing. LynDee's debut novel, *Front Page Fatality*, was nominated for the Agatha Award for Best First Novel. *Small Town Spin* is the third in her #1 bestselling Headlines in High Heels mystery series. The fourth arrives January 2015.

LynDee adores her family, her readers, and enchiladas. She works out tricky plot points while walking off the enchiladas. She lives in Richmond, Virginia, where she is either playing with her children or working on her next novel—but probably not cleaning her house.

You can find her online at www.lyndeewalker.com
On Amazon http://tinyurl.com/n7gecoz
On Barnes & Noble: http://www.barnesandnoble.com/c/lyndee-walker

Recipes
35 Eunice's Spicy Sweet Southern Summer Salad
69 Nichelle's Pasta Pomodoro

Wendy Lyn Watson (aka Annie Knox)

I started writing when I was in high school, an atrocious medieval fantasy (think Game of Thrones without any of the good writing or plot points). Even though I was convinced at the time that my fantasy would be a break-out world-wide hit, I still never really considered a career in writing until I sat down in my early 30s and started an actual book in earnest. I started in romance, but my hero and heroine kept tripping over dead bodies. Finally, my agent said "You ought to be writing mysteries." Duh. I took her advice and have never looked back.

Now, I teach political science to undergraduates by day and write cozies by night. I've written (am writing) two series at the moment. The Mysteries a la Mode (*I Scream, You Scream*; *Scoop to Kill*; and *A Parfait Murder*) were written under my real name (Wendy Lyn Watson), while the Pet Boutique Mysteries (*Paws for Murder*; *Groomed for Murder*; and *Collared for Murder*) are under my pen name, Annie Knox. Whether you want to call me Wendy or Annie, I live in a small town in North Texas along with my insanely patient husband and our three cats. When I'm not in front of a computer, I'm generally in the kitchen whipping up vegetarian fare and lots of desserts to satisfy my wicked sweet tooth!

You can find both of my alter egos on the web:
Webpage: http://wendylynwatson.com
Facebook: https://www.facebook.com/WendyLynWatsonAuthor
Webpage: http://annieknoxauthor.com
Facebook: https://www.facebook.com/AnnieKnoxAuthor

Recipes
109 Hot Grudge Sundae Cake with Dark Chocolate Fudge Sauce

Christine Wenger

I have worked in the criminal justice field for more years than I care to remember! It seems like I was forever going to school while I was working full time, but in the end, I received a dual master's degree in Probation and Parole Studies and Sociology from Fordham University.

Unfortunately, the knowledge gained from way too many years in night school, didn't prepare me for what I love to do the most – writing cozy mysteries.
Love those cozy mysteries!!

The year 2013 began my series of "comfort food" cozies which are set in a small-town 1950's diner: the Silver Bullet (open 24 hours, air conditioned). The Silver Bullet sits on the shore of Lake Ontario and many colorful characters, including the owner of the diner, Trixie Matkowski, live in Sandy Harbor or are just visiting.

The first book, *Do or Diner*, from Penguin/Obsidian books was released in August, 2013. Another followed, *A Second Helping of Murder*, in April, 2014, and a third, *Diners, Drive-ins and Death*, is scheduled for January, 2015. I'd like to continue with this series for as long as readers keep reading about sleuthing Trixie Matkowski's way.

<u>Just for fun</u>
I enjoy watching professional bull riding and rodeo with my favorite cowboy, my husband Jim. We put on our cowboy regalia (I look horrible in a cowboy hat!) and have traveled to events in Las Vegas, Florida, Connecticut, and other states.

Of course I have to do research for my comfort food diner series. That takes me to diners all over the U.S. and Canada (and maybe Europe and Asia!) for meals. It's a tough job, but I just have to do it!

Best wishes to you, and I hope you smile when you read my books!

Website: www.christinewenger.com
Amazon: http://tinyurl.com/lqqfg3n
Barnes & Noble: http://www.barnesandnoble.com/c/christine-wenger

Recipes
163 Raisin-Cider Sauce
42 Citrus Vinaigrette Salad Dressing or Marinade

Gayle Wigglesworth

Gayle Wigglesworth, after 40 years as a banking executive in the San Francisco Bay Area, retired in Houston to begin a new career, writing clean, cozy-like mystery novels.

Gayle's Claire Gulliver Mystery series now has six published adventures. Claire Gulliver, a single, middle-aged book store owner, has occasion to travel and when she does she somehow becomes involved in mysteries. She is not the kind of person to ignore things that are not right and consequently sometimes she becomes involved in terrifying situations. These books are written to enable the reader to participate in the travel adventure as well as in the mystery.

Gayle has also published a stand-alone mystery, *Mud to Ashes*, the story of a woman caught in the empty nest syndrome who moves to the beach to rebuild a new life. And the first adventure in a new series with a paranormal flare, *Murder Most Mysterious*, a Glenda at Large Mystery.

An accomplished cook, Gayle's books always have food and meals playing a big part in the story but the recipes are never included in the book. However, the first book she published, *Gayle's Legacy*, is a cookbook she wrote for her family when she moved to Texas and could no longer host the big family events that were the tradition. This book contains many of the recipes for dishes found in her books and if they're not in the cookbook just drop her a note and she'll attempt to provide you with a recipe.

Gayle and her husband recently relocated to Kirkland WA to be near her youngest grandchildren where she is currently working on the second book in her Glenda at Large series. Check out Gayle's website at www.gaylewigglesworth.com for further information.

All Gayle's books are available in both soft cover and e-book formats.

Amazon: http://tinyurl.com/mwbakq9
Barnes & Noble: http://www.barnesandnoble.com/c/gayle-wigglesworth
Smashwords: http://www.smashwords.com/profile/view/gaylewigg

Recipes
89 Ricotta Dream Dessert
100 Blueberry Pound Cake

Lois Winston

Award-winning author Lois Winston writes the critically acclaimed Anastasia Pollack Crafting Mystery series featuring magazine crafts editor and reluctant amateur sleuth Anastasia Pollack. *Assault With a Deadly Glue Gun*, the first book in the series, received starred reviews from both *Publishers Weekly* and *Booklist*. *Kirkus Reviews* dubbed it, "North Jersey's more mature answer to Stephanie Plum." Other books in the series includes *Death By Killer Mop Doll, Revenge of the Crafty Corpse, Decoupage Can Be Deadly* and the e-book only mini-mysteries *Crewel Intentions, Mosaic Mayhem,* and the forthcoming *Patchwork Peril*.

When Anastasia Pollack's husband permanently cashes in his chips at a roulette table in Las Vegas, her comfortable middleclass life craps out. She's left with two teenage sons, a mountain of debt, and her hateful Communist mother-in-law as a permanent houseguest—not to mention stunned disbelief over her late husband's secret gambling addiction and the loan shark demanding fifty thousand dollars. And that's before she becomes the prime suspect in the murder of the magazine's fashion editor. As Anastasia works to clear her name and find the real killer, she's aided in her sleuthing by food editor Cloris McWerther. Cloris also provides Anastasia with the baked goods that sustain her throughout the day. Each book in the series finds Anastasia moonlighting at various jobs to pay down her debt. Along the way she stumbles over dead bodies and satisfies her sweet tooth with Cloris confections.

Lois is also published in women's fiction, romance, romantic suspense, and non-fiction under her own name and her Emma Carlyle pen name. In addition, she's an award-winning craft and needlework designer. To learn more about Lois and her books, visit her at www.loiswinston.com, and visit Anastasia at the Killer Crafts & Crafty Killers blog, www.anastasiapollack.blogspot.com. Follow everyone on Twitter: https://twitter.com/Anasleuth.

Recipes
135 White Chocolate and Plum Brownies

Joan H. Young

Joan H. Young has been writing stories about the outdoors since the age of 7, when "The Adventures of Skippy the Field Mouse" made its debut. The work survives, but is best left in the box with crayon drawings of squirrels and pressed leaves.

As an adult, Joan has made a career of proving that she can bumble through life without ever deciding what to be when she grows up. She began with a degree in Communication Arts with an emphasis on theater. Realizing that drama, for her, was like whiskey to an alcoholic, she left a possible career in stage management for a driven man and 10,000 teenagers. (What was she thinking?) A few years later the couple had legally adopted one of the teens, and two younger children, but were still feeding most of the stray 10,000 teenagers as well. No time there for writing anything except grocery lists, and a journal of the wild ride!

Cozy Food

In 1986, still longing for a career in sciences, she went back to school, and did receive a Masters in Environmental Engineering from the University of Michigan! Meanwhile, the writing bug still squirmed, and Joan worked hard at collecting rejection slips from a nice series of reputable magazines and publishers.

Also during this time slot she began hiking the North Country Trail (NCT), the longest foot path in the United States. Essays about her hikes on the NCT demanded to be written, and friends urged her to publish. In 2005, *North Country Cache* made its debut for the 25th Anniversary of the North Country Trail. Since then, more and more of her time has been spent writing.

She has recently produced several cozy mysteries, and there are four stories in the Anastasia Raven series to date. They are News from Dead Mule Swamp, *The Hollow Tree at Dead Mule Swamp*, Paddy Plays in Dead Mule Swamp, and Bury the Hatchet in Dead Mule Swamp.

See all Joan's books and learn more at http://www.booksleavingfootprints.com
See her books on Amazon http://tinyurl.com/ms48m3b
Or Barnes & Noble http://www.barnesandnoble.com/c/joan-h.-young

Recipes
139 Pear Almond Bread

Suzanne Young

Suzanne Young writes cozy mysteries set in Rhode Island and is currently working on number five in her Edna Davies series. The second title *Murder by Proxy* takes place in Colorado to please her local fans, but Suzanne feels that Edna really belongs in New England.

Although she's been a Colorado resident for over 40 years, Suzanne grew up in Rhode Island in a house that was built in 1780 by Jeremiah Greene, uncle to Nathanael Greene. Summers were spent at a farmhouse that had once been a stop for stagecoaches and Pony Express riders. In her youth, she was not only surrounded with history, but with the creaks, thumps and groans of aged houses. Attics and cellars were spooky places where she was sent on occasion to fetch a stored article. The cavernous rooms were dark and smelled of old wood, dust and dirt, conjuring up feelings of someone behind her, about to tap on her shoulder with a boney finger. She ran her errands quickly and never lingered.

Suzanne's family always ate meals together. Most of the fruits, vegetables, herbs and flowers were grown on the farm. A pet cow provided milk, and a dozen hens donated eggs. In the fall, everyone participated in canning, pickling and preserving food for the winter. Among Suzanne's favorite chores was helping to make butter or mayonnaise when there was a surplus of cream or eggs.

These fond memories are food for thought when Suzanne writes her stories. More about this author and her books can be found on her web site at http://suzanneyoungbooks.com or on Amazon at http://tinyurl.com/lxvnm5s (where she is sometimes confused with a young-adult writer with the same name).

Recipes
17 Edna's Easy Herb Spread
71 Jillybean's Tacos

Postscript & Outtakes

Writers, no matter how successful, must still work to ensure their books are read. As a reader, you can help us enormously in several ways.

If you have enjoyed this book and the recipes in it, please help us promote it. There's a wide range of ways you can do so including:

- Recommend the book to your friends.
- Post a review on Amazon, Barnes and Noble, Goodreads, and other book websites.
- Review it on your blog and/or ask for a post about the book.
- Tweet about it and give a link to our website at www.goodreadmysteries.com.
- Suggest the book to your book reading group. *Cozy Food* is a great way for you to meet new-to-you authors.
- Post a comment on your Facebook page.
- Tell your Facebook and Google Plus friends about the book.
- Pin it at Pinterest.
- Anything else you can think of!

Many thanks for your help - it's much appreciated.

-- Good Read Publishers and Editor Nancy Lynn Jarvis

Outtakes

Thanks to Susan Whitfield who put together *Killer Recipes*. She offered advice about how to organize a compilation cookbook and said if I followed her advice, I'd stay sane. I did and I did. Some of the communications I had with fellow authors helped a lot, too, if only because they made me smile.

> "I thought the meatballs might actually go under some sort of vegetable entrée type category???? Maybe not since there aren't any vegetables in them and I doubt that's even a category."

"I forwarded your email to Sharon, but I never heard back from her. I forwarded it to one other author, too, and would you believe, I can't remember who it was?"

> "I would love to participate, but I don't have any recipes to offer. My books don't include recipes and I've never written a recipe before. Sadly, I couldn't make up a recipe if I had to."

"I am, I confess, a picky eater. Some of the family recipes that have been the biggest hits are for things that I don't particularly enjoy, like Mom's famous sweet pickle recipe (I only like sour dill pickle), Mom's legendary potato salad recipe (I hate anything involving mayonnaise, and the secret to the potato salad is the aforementioned sweet pickle), and Mummaw's corn pudding recipe (another dish whose appeal utterly baffles me). Dad was a marine biologist so a lot of the family specialties were for seafood, and I've got allergies to some of it and dislike the rest."

> "Thank you. I just made a book trailer for Awkward Moments, but I need to do a little finalizing before I put it up. I may send a link to it. LOL I've got so many irons in the fire that I meant to send that last email to someone else. Sorry."

"I'm supposed to sign International Bestselling Author. It's all so new I need to get used to it, sorry."

> "I'm testing out one of the recipes on my victims...I mean, family - and should have both all written up and to you by end of Monday."

"I already found a couple of mistakes in one of these! Grrr...Note to self: Meat is not spelled Meet."

> "Thank you for including me! Here's my submission:
> .
> .
> Let me know if you need anything else!"

During a phone call to a participant who insisted she had sent in her recipe:

"Well, I didn't receive it."
"Ok, I'll send it again right now. Did you get it?"
"No, I didn't."
"Let me try again. Anything yet?"
"Nothing."
"This is ridiculous! I'm sending it to JBD…"

"That's not me."

"Who have I been sending this to over and over…oh, no. Gonna have to write another letter of apology."

"Yikes, I found your emails in my spam folder."

"I know I keep promising to send in a recipe, but I'm too busy to do it. Please let me know when the next version of the cookbook comes out. I'm sure my recipe will be ready by then and I'd love to be in it."

"I wasn't even in the room when it (the recipe) happened."

"I haven't done many recipes; I prefer to work in less perishable materials."

"Please change…my grandchildren to six. I forgot…that update on Facebook."